Career Transitions for Librarians

Career Transitions for Librarians

Proven Strategies for Moving to Another Type of Library

Edited by
Davis Erin Anderson
Raymond Pun

ROWMAN & LITTLEFIELD
Lanham • Boulder • New York • London

Published by Rowman & Littlefield
A wholly owned subsidiary of The Rowman & Littlefield Publishing Group, Inc.
4501 Forbes Boulevard, Suite 200, Lanham, Maryland 20706
www.rowman.com

Unit A, Whitacre Mews, 26-34 Stannary Street, London SE11 4AB

British Library Cataloguing in Publication Information Available

Library of Congress Cataloging-in-Publication Data

Names: Anderson, Davis Erin, 1981- editor. | Pun, Raymond, 1985- editor.
Title: Career transitions for librarians : proven strategies for moving to another type of library / edited by Davis Erin Anderson and Raymond Pun.
Description: Lanham : Rowman & Littlefield, [2016] | Includes bibliographical references and index.
Identifiers: LCCN 2016001659 (print) | LCCN 2016016513 (ebook) | ISBN 9781442265578 (cloth : alk. paper) | ISBN 9781442263727 (pbk. : alk. paper) | ISBN 9781442263734 (electronic)
Subjects: LCSH: Library science—Vocational guidance—United States. | Librarians—Employment—United States. | Librarians—United States—Interviews. | Career changes—United States—Case studies.
Classification: LCC Z682.35.V62 C36 2016 (print) | LCC Z682.35.V62 (ebook) | DDC 020.23—dc23 LC record available at https://lccn.loc.gov/2016001659

Printed in the United States of America

Contents

Foreword

Endless Opportunities to Empower People through Information

Mary Lee Kennedy

When looking at career choices, there are endless opportunities for information to unlock the potential in human beings. Whether you are considering librarians, information scientists, content managers, information specialists, data scientists—these roles are and will be critical today and in the future. All of these roles empower people through information.

I've had the privilege of working in many parts of the world and in a variety of institutions. Throughout my career, the most exciting challenge has been—and remains—empowering people through information. By this I mean understanding the institutional and individual needs within a highly dynamic ecosystem and then diagnosing, designing, delivering, and continually iterating in order to bring the most valuable information to light, all in an effort to serve the creation of knowledge.

People's lives improve when they have access to information, are able to make sense of it, use it to create new knowledge, and share their knowledge with others. We all need access to quality information in order to survive and thrive at each and every stage of life. Whole societies depend on human beings' ability to learn, create, innovate, and express themselves. But, alas, our society does not currently offer a level playing field; there remains much to do. Every individual's empowerment depends on a broad commitment to policies and practices that increase information access and fluency. Societal advancement depends on each of us choosing how and where we can make a difference.

In every position I have held, adding value depended on much more than applying my knowledge about information and information use. The institutional context had to become *my* context before I could figure out my initial step. That meant building strong relationships with decision makers and users, understanding political and economic realities, and being able to develop a shared understanding of success. In every instance, success depended on developing shared priorities (including the commitment of resources), a common language, and an agreed-on set of expectations.

Trust and progress depend on consistent communication, agreement on recalibrations as needed, and delivery of the final result. As a leader, delivery meant continually supporting others and committing myself to learning, letting go of what didn't work, reflecting, and determining subsequent action. No matter where you are, creating a visible difference is a must in this day and age—*how* it is done is as important as *what* is done.

The ability to do your best work will depend on whether or not you share the institution's values and how well you are able to work within its organizational culture. When considering a move to another institution, it is critical to review the values and culture of your new position first. This, of course, requires clarity about your own values. If necessary, take a few days (yes, *days*) to make a list of all your values and narrow it down to the top three— the three you cannot live without. This will serve you well. Assess these three values along the full cultural horizon: geopolitical fit, fit within a broader institution, fit within a workgroup, fit with your boss—in that order. You will live in a geographical region every day beyond the workweek, you will go to work every day at an institution with its own reputation and rhythm, you will work with your team, and you will have a boss—these last two can and often do change, the others less so.

Aside from geopolitical values, organizational culture (defined here as how decisions are made, the nature and tone of language, how money is invested, and the types of reward and recognition systems) is the most important consideration. It is the essence of how an organization works, what it privileges, and how it supports its people in delivering on expectations. Some institutions are hierarchical and use formal language, whereas others are mission driven and make decisions through consensus. Some reward teams and others privilege individuals. Some recognize value in every functional unit, while others privilege specific job families. Some believe in large financial rewards for top performers, while others spend money only on core operations. Your ability to empower people through information will depend on your ability to work well within the organizational culture. Culture trumps all.

Once the culture fit is clear, you can assess the types of knowledge creation that do and can benefit from your professional suite of skills. You will always be expected to add value and make a difference.

Being excited and realistic about what you can contribute is essential. If you've identified a gap, you've identified an opportunity. What seems obvious about the variety of institutional approaches to information and its use should be examined, as what that means in everyday practice is usually quite complex. We all know that real-time information needs are very different than archival-research needs; college collections are very different than think tank collections; corporations' investments in market research are very different than nonprofit investments; public libraries focused on neighborhood communities invest in information very differently than public research libraries; and humanists approach and use very different types of information than physicists or trading floors.

The flip side of this is that we often become specialists, and it is often this specialization that keeps us tethered to what we do and challenges us when we step outside our area of expertise. If you are switching jobs, do your homework on target user information practices and information trends and sources, and find experts you can learn from. If you don't know the difference at the everyday level of understanding, acknowledge it. A great set of clarifying questions will demonstrate that you know how to learn. Gaining information fluency is like learning a whole new language. In my experience, many people are open to helping when genuine interest and discipline are evident.

This book focuses on career shifts from one type of institution to another. As you read the experiences in the book, you will immediately identify with those that most resonate with you. Be open to all possibilities. Check in first on alignment with your values and the full cultural horizon—geopolitical, institutional, workgroup, and boss. Transferable skills remain tightly tied to organizational and political savvy, clear all-around communications, and shared definitions of success. Since it is difficult to predict the future, choose a journey that reflects your values and your ability to learn. With passion, thoughtfulness, and discipline, you will thrive, and you will inspire others to make a difference through their own creations.

Acknowledgments

We would like to extend our thanks to all of the contributors to this project, who have given their time to compile best practices and to share their narratives, experiences, and stories about how they made their transition work for them and how others can create their transition successfully. We hope this book can serve as a resource for meaningful conversations in our field and to deconstruct the ongoing stereotypes and typecasts that occur in the profession.

Raymond Pun would like to extend his thanks to Janet H. Clarke for supporting this project in its initial stages and acting as a sounding board. He would also like to thank Maura A. Smale for publishing his blog post on *ACRLog*, which started this whole conversation on library transitions in 2014, and Monnee Tong for referring him to other potential writers. In addition, he would like to thank Elaine Carey for encouraging him to work on edited volumes because "it'll be good for your career!"

Davis Erin Anderson would like to thank her parents, Gerald Anderson and Roberta Goering, who literally raised her and her younger sister Kate in the library. She also sends love and gratitude to Jules Roussel for his unwavering support of her career. This book would not have been possible without the support of Davis's colleagues at METRO as well as the wider NYC library community.

Introduction

Davis Erin Anderson and Raymond Pun

Librarians work in all kinds of institutions and organizations. They are needed for managing information, resources, knowledge, and data in different types of environments. Today more and more librarians are transitioning from one type of library to another as they move further into their careers. For new opportunities and to find better cultural fits, librarians are often seeking different positions while making use of finely tuned skills sets. Many of us have been to library school and have learned about the different "types" of libraries and careers in librarianship: special, public, academic, and school media libraries. While it's easy to believe that once you pick a focus, your career will follow a straightforward path, we all know people who have successfully made transitions between the different sectors of our field.

This volume introduces a variety of library professionals who have made a transition from one type of library to another. In addition to contributors from the United States, in the global context we have contributors who currently work and have worked in China, Canada, United Arab Emirates, Sweden, Argentina, South Korea, and the Philippines.

Our contributors have also worked in many types of institutions, including the New York Public Library, Cable News Network (CNN), Harvard libraries, McKinsey & Company, Microsoft, San Diego Public Library, Brooklyn Public Library, Dow Jones, New York University, various school libraries, vendors, and more. Beyond academic, school, and public librarians, our contributors are and were medical librarians, law librarians, museum librarians, archivists, library consultants, LIS faculty, and the list goes on. Many of our contributors have made notable contributions to our field, from the founder of I Need a Library Job (INALJ) to leaders from major library associations like the American Library Association (ALA), International Federation of Library Associations (IFLA), Special Libraries Association

(SLA), and ethnic caucuses like the Chinese American Librarians Association (CALA) and the Asian Pacific American Librarians Association (APA-LA).

Some chapters will also cover internal transitions in the academic library world. These contributions explore how to move from technical to public services, from medical to engineering librarianship, how to get into the world of digital humanities, and how to move from a paraprofessional to a professional. These case studies demonstrate that moves within the academic world can be challenging but doable.

We decided to create this volume because we noticed that there were gaps missing in the professional literature related to supporting these kinds of career transitions. Many people have done it, but we couldn't find a long-form volume that focuses on these kinds of exciting career paths.

We've seen blog posts testifying that librarians can move from academic to public to school to special (all kinds) in their careers, and we wanted to document these experiences to reveal how people can and should switch to different librarianships. For the purposes of this volume, we define *librarians* very broadly and loosely: to us, a librarian is anyone who has an MLS or MLIS from an ALA-accredited program and has worked in an information services setting as a librarian or who has shared very similar professional responsibilities.

We are honored to share the voices of our colleagues who have braved new areas of the library profession. And we hope this volume inspires you to share your story too.

I

From Specialized to Academic Librarianship

Chapter One

Successfully Making Transitions between Academia and the Corporation

Jia Mi

My career path has been full of challenges and has required adaptability, resilience, and persistence. I feel fortunate that I have had the opportunity, through my work in academia as well as in a corporate setting, to gain exposure to new computer technology; to learn about the integrated library system (ILS), Internet technology, and web technology; to perform both basic and applied research; to deal with customers; and to teach at a college. The knowledge and experiences gained from working in both academia and private industry have provided me with a broad background and a unique perspective on research and services and have been instrumental in shaping me as a librarian and an educator.

TRANSITION FROM ACADEMIA TO PRIVATE INDUSTRY

I finished coursework for my MLS in 1994. Throughout my time in school, I had planned on working for an academic library in order to work with professors and students. I was hoping to focus on cataloging since I am not a native English speaker. Right after my first semester, I was lucky to find a part-time job working as a library assistant at NEC Research Institute, a technologically advanced library, while working toward my degree. Working with NEC librarian Jim Berkise really opened my eyes. I was fascinated by the advanced technologies in the library and quickly learned the UNIX system, vi editor, networking, and library databases. In addition to computer technology, this one-person library enabled me to practice every aspect of the li-

3

brary's functions and has provided me with unique research and educational experiences.

I started my career as an electronic resources/systems librarian at a private college after I received my MLS. When I accepted the position, I knew it would be a challenge that would force me to grow, change, and leave my comfort zone. But I never shy away from a challenge! At the time, the library had just started implementing automated integrated library systems with its modules (online public access catalog [OPAC], cataloging, acquisitions, circulation, and serials). I learned the relationship among these modules, how to manage the modules, and how to troubleshoot and run reports. After the implementation period, I was in charge of the daily operation of the library's automated systems and its local area network (LAN) workstations. As a recent graduate, it was a great challenge for me. Luckily, under the guidance of Library Director Fred Nesta, an expert in computing technology, I was able to get firsthand experience in computer hardware, server management, LAN, web design, and electronic resources. It was exciting to struggle and learn at the same time.

In 1998, I accepted a position at Rutgers University as an electronic resources/serials librarian, which was a tenure-track assistant professor position at Kilmer Library. By that time, I had just completed my MBA/MIS degree, so working in this business library was a great transition for me. Compared to my previous library, Rutgers' library system was extensive—twenty-six libraries with a centralized library system office. I was expected to manage fewer tasks directly related to information technology. My job was focused on providing reference services, conducting library electronic resources training and instruction for both students and librarians, joining library committees, and doing research to fulfill the tenure requirement. My work life was a frenetic series of e-mails, department meetings, conference proposals, committee meetings, reference desk hours, and professional conferences. Even the tenure process was completely new to me. The required publishing output was overwhelming. Then one day in 1999, I received a phone call from a recruiter I had met at the Computer in Libraries conference, and it altered the course of my career. In the end, my decision to leave academia for a position in the financial industry did not restrict my career choices, and after four and half years, I returned to academia as a librarian with tenure-track status.

For me, the most important factor that influenced my decision to move from academia to the financial industry was the learning opportunities. I was a little overwhelmed with joining six university cross-library committees and became puzzled by the long process involved in making final decisions. It was important to me to continue to learn new and exciting information technology and to continue to stay connected to the research community.

At Dow Jones, I initially found a totally different working environment. I started as a research specialist, and I dealt with my own customers at a very fast pace. After one year, I was promoted to a system analyst position, where I was able to learn many new technologies. Not only did I have to familiarize myself with all the products Dow Jones supports, but I also had to quickly resolve the customers' issues. Every case was conducted and solved over the phone. After a customer reported an issue, I had to quickly detect the problem and, when necessary, coordinate with the enterprise department, software department, or network department in order to solve the issues.

Problem solving, a team-oriented approach to complex problems, and communication skills are the keys I obtained in order to be successful in the financial industry. Solving customers' issues was the first priority, and constant learning was a must. Making customers satisfied and retaining customers were the goals.

The initial transition from academia to private industry was relatively easy because I was doing much of the same work in both places. One advantage of working in private industry is being able to immerse yourself in learning and keeping up with the latest technologies. Another advantage: not having to write and publish, so my time could be dedicated to learning new products involving experimental design. In business, publications don't matter. Profits matter. The decision-making process can differ greatly between academia and private industry. One major difference is that in academia a formed committee is normally in charge of any new program's direction and decisions; in private industry, you have a boss who ultimately calls the shots. In academia, you are expected to provide librarianship, join committees, and write and publish papers. Your ultimate success obtaining tenure is based on librarianship, scholarship, and services. In contrast, a project often involves a team approach in private industry, and you as a team member may contribute only a small part of the overall project. I found the team approach to projects to be quite satisfying and educational, allowing me to tackle more complex problems that required multiple areas of expertise while gaining an understanding of new areas of technology. Another difference between academia and private industry is that private industry projects can be dropped for various reasons; thus, you must be willing to change directions and to learn and work on a new project quickly.

TRANSITION FROM PRIVATE INDUSTRY BACK TO ACADEMIA

I made my transition back to a tenure-track academic appointment following four and half years at Dow Jones. Based on my previous experience in a tenure-track position at Rutgers University, I was able to come back as an electronic resources/serials librarian, another tenured-track position, at the

College of New Jersey (TCNJ). A critical factor that allowed me to move back to academic library was the library's important function in students' collegiate learning. Plus, it allowed me to spend more time with my daughter.

Transitioning back to academia was a greater challenge than I originally expected. Had I not been in an academic position previously, the transition would have been even more difficult. I was fortunate that I was able to come back as a librarian. No matter how much experience I had gained at my previous job, I was starting from scratch and building my portfolio from ground zero. I needed to learn TCNJ library culture and working environment, and I found that I was taking on a lot more responsibilities.

A tenure-track faculty rank must excel not only in librarianship but also in scholarship and service. The demands of librarianship itself can be great, and one of the biggest adjustments was getting back into research. Writing and publishing papers is a skill that must be acquired and practiced if you expect to be successful. It requires not only finding good research topics but the ability to transform your idea into a written paper within the time frame of the tenure process. Finding mentors with whom to discuss your topic and paper and setting up a practical research plan are greatly advised.

FINAL THOUGHTS

Careers in both academia and private industry can be very rewarding, each offering unique opportunities and challenges. Furthermore, the environment and culture at each company and university can differ, so assess your own strengths and weaknesses and decide on the best fit. Time-management skills are required for positions in both industry and academia. The need to plan ahead and set aside time for writing papers is a must in academia and is critical for making progress and receiving tenure and promotions. It is essential to balance the demands of both research and librarianship.

In closing, my advice is to embrace change and to keep on learning new skills. The library world is rapidly changing, and technology is progressing every day. To many, this is a frightening phenomenon, as most of us crave stability. However, you and your own individual circumstances will change whether you like it or not, whether you want them to or not. Change can and should be a very positive dynamic in our lives. If you become an active and creative participant in your ever-evolving and changing environment, you can be happy and successful in either academic or corporate settings.

Chapter Two

Getting to Great

Transitioning from a Special to an Academic Library

Linda Miles

Transitioning successfully from one library context to another is about more than getting the job and landing on your feet; it is above all about finding a way to thrive in a new situation.[1] The story of my own transformation begins at the library of Lincoln Center Institute (LCI) for the Arts in Education, now Lincoln Center Education (LCE). The library held more than ten thousand physical items plus a modest electronic library of subscription materials. We collected in the areas of educational theory, arts education, the arts, and juvenile literature, and we served the arts education administrators, teaching artists, K–12 educators, and professors of teacher education associated with the organization.

Like so many other industries, arts education took an economic hit in the years following 9/11 and again after the economic downturn of 2008. In 2011, the LCI library closed as part of an effort to form a leaner organization. I was laid off along with the director of the resource center. I had begun my tenure at LCI as a library assistant in 2000 and worked my way up to assistant director, with day-to-day oversight of the library. With multiple advanced degrees plus eleven years of library experience, I was well positioned to transition to an academic librarian position. After eight months on the market, I began working as a public services librarian at Yeshiva University (YU), a private four-year institution in Manhattan.

I had thrived during my years at LCI. I respected, and was respected by, my colleagues across the organization. I was able to apply intelligence and creativity to diverse new challenges as well as core practices of librarianship. I had opportunities to advance within the organization, and I was privileged to be able to give 110 percent to a mission for which I felt an unwavering commitment. It is a tall order, but this same level of engagement and reward was what I was looking for as I transitioned to the academic library world.

Well, I got my happy ending. I landed the job, transitioned to a new context, and I have come to thrive in that new world. Although I was quite anxious during the jobless months, my transition was relatively easy, particularly because I understood the differences between the two library contexts, received some excellent job-seeking advice specific to academia, and thought strategically about navigating expectations in my new position.

BRAVE NEW WORLD

There are many similarities between my former special library context and the academic world in which I now practice. A significant amount of attention in both arenas is paid to careful negotiation of relationships across the library and across the institution. There are alliances to build and political nuances to negotiate.[2] There is an emphasis on marketing the value of the library to the larger organization. As a key player in cross-departmental initiatives at LCI (teaching artist training, for example) I was "embedded" in the educational processes of the organization.

The most significant change between these two contexts is in the orientation of the librarian toward users' information seeking. Often, the goal of the special librarian is to anticipate user needs so that new resources are acquired, excerpted, curated, and delivered by librarians to address known user needs, even before a request is made.[3] Academic librarians, on the other hand, continually balance a desire to efficiently meet the needs of users with a commitment to teaching others how to effectively navigate the twenty-first-century universe of information for themselves.[4] Some special librarians articulate a need to position themselves as those experts who can do what no one else in the organization can do,[5] while the academic orientation suggests that we teach everyone to be able to do this work—in some cases, to do it even better than we do it ourselves.

The organizational structures within which special libraries are situated are often highly hierarchical. In the collaborative ethos of academia, all perspectives are solicited and debated in service of consensus decision making. This may frustrate librarians used to an environment "where the hierarchical structure identifies those in a position to make a quick decision."[6] The pace of the implementation of new practices in academia can seem glacial. In many academic institutions, librarians are granted faculty status and are directly represented along with classroom faculty on the faculty senate or other education policy–focused bodies. At YU, librarians do not have faculty status and so do not have access to power in the same way, but there is still a marked difference in the philosophy governing how I do my job—and how I practice my profession. This difference is felt most keenly in the discretion I am afforded to address the responsibilities of my position as I see fit. Whereas at LCI initiatives were prioritized on my behalf by my director at the behest of the organization's executive director, at YU I am empowered to develop my own ideas for initiatives that I would like to take on; then I work with my supervisor and the director of libraries to determine whether, when, and how to begin the work. It is a great model for "managing up" or "managing from the middle." Some academic librarians, newly transferred from the corporate sphere, have "reveled" in the sense of increased autonomy in their new situation.[7]

Much has been written about the "silos" of higher education,[8] whereby organizational units of the institution are largely uninvolved in, and even unaware of, the efforts taken on elsewhere on campus. In some cases, the library cuts across these silos. YU's administrative leaders have only recently focused on merging some undergraduate academic departments across two campuses, but the YU Libraries have spanned those campuses historically. The silos around us still impact our work, however. At LCI, communication across the organization was recognized as vital to everyone's productivity. At YU, there is sometimes a sense of working in a vacuum, without an understanding of what others in the institution may be striving to accomplish. Since we share common objectives for our students, there is a danger of duplicating efforts or working at cross-purposes. As twenty-first-century academia evolves, some of these divisions are breaking down,[9] and their impact may vary by institution. It is important to deliberately develop an ever-expanding network of relationships, in my case beginning with curriculum-focused discussions that I scheduled with classroom faculty.

Those working in public services will find themselves providing much more instruction[10] and may end up focusing less time and effort on reference work.[11] Academic librarians not in public service positions may also be expected to take on instructional duties. In most cases, new academic librarians will take on the role of generalist in these public service roles. Susan Klopper talks about feeling like a brand-new reference librarian again as she began to field questions outside of her specialized area of expertise.[12] My own academic background is in the performing arts, and in the LCI library I developed knowledge in education and visual arts as well. YU is a relatively small academic library with subject specialists only in Hebraica-Judaica studies. There I provide resources, teach, and address reference questions in most disciplines.

GETTING YOUR FOOT IN THE DOOR

As a job candidate, you can demonstrate your commitment to making a transition to academic libraries not only by articulating a rationale for why you want to make a change, which you absolutely must do, but also by making it clear that you have "done your research." Familiarize yourself with the state of the academic librarianship profession. For instance, you might locate and review the academic librarianship's official policy documents, standards, guidelines, and related materials.[13] *College & Research Library News* is one of the primary publications for academic librarians. The *Ubiquitous Librarian* blog, penned by Brian Mathews for the *Chronicle of Higher Education*, provides timely information about innovations in academic library practice. It is also vital to develop an understanding of the evolving state of higher education. For news and trends, my go-to sources include the *Academe Today*, *Wired Campus*, *Afternoon Update*, and *Weekly Briefing* e-mail newsletters, also from the *Chronicle*. Inside Higher Ed and EDUCAUSE, the latter a technology-focused, higher education–related non-profit, round out my current awareness routine.

Early in my career I discovered the value of involvement in various associations that support practicing librarians. I ramped up this activity during my eight-month job-seeking period, joining a committee of the local chapter of the Association of College and Research Libraries (ACRL/NY), as well as two committees of the national Theatre Library Association. I have since become more deeply involved in ACRL/NY, having served as vice president and currently as president. I also serve as co-convener of a special interest group of the regional consortial organization Metropolitan New York Library Council (METRO). As a result, I have developed lifelong collegial relationships and a unique public professional persona, which has contributed to my suitability for academic librarian positions.

Another way to demonstrate commitment to your transition is to get some training or other type of orientation to academic libraries.[14] Due to concerns about fair labor practices, many libraries will not take on unpaid interns who are not current students, but I was able to tap into local networks to set up "informational interviews" with several librarians in a variety of academic institutions. These are opportunities to meet face-to-face or virtually with working professionals to discuss the nature of their work and the operational structures of specific academic libraries. You may find that you need to assure these individuals that you are not trying to get them to give you a job in order for them to feel comfortable with this practice, but the insight gained is well worth extra effort in arranging these meetings. I was also able to obtain part-time employment as an evening librarian at a local college, supplementing my experience with at least one academic library credit.

While I had transitioned to part-time adjuncting, I spent the equivalent of a full-time job looking for an academic librarian position. Websites like Hiring Librarians, Library Career People, and Vitae are great places to learn about typical library and academic hiring practices. I perused the job notices every day, making use of online sites like INALJ (I Need a Library Job), LibGig, Inside Higher Ed's career page, the *Chronicle of Higher Education*'s website, and Indeed, as well as local listing services for libraries and for academia. In some cases, these systems allow you to set up e-mail alerts based on specific keywords. In fact, although within days the notice for my eventual YU position appeared in several of these venues, I first noticed it in an e-mail alert that I had set up for "librarian" and "New York" on Indeed. Prospective employers also may recruit at regional or national conferences, either informally or through recruitment centers.[15] Susanne Markgren and Tiffany Allen provide an excellent description of best practices for the librarian's job hunt,[16] and Anna Gold's description of the salary negotiation process is also very helpful.[17]

The concept of transferrable skills will be very important to your efforts to attract potential employers or recruiters.[18] There are many functions that are generically similar in different types of libraries, even if the particulars are very different.[19] For instance, service to users is at the heart of every library mission. You should not expect search committee members to simply *get* how you'll fit into their operations by perusing a simple list of your special library qualifications.[20] "I am often more impressed by someone who can sell how well they fit in a position when, on the surface, they may not have relevant experience," writes Laurie Phillips of Loyola University in New Orleans. "It's all about selling your transferable skills and understanding the environment."[21] Fortunately, by the time I found myself out of work, I had more than eleven years of experience, with increasing levels of responsibility, in a library that shared some key characteristics with academic libraries, particularly in relation to collection development policies and educational mission.

You will also need to develop a curriculum vitae, or CV, the academic equivalent of a résumé.[22] The cover letter you write to apply for a specific job will provide you an opportunity to activate your transferable skills by drawing connections to the qualifications articulated in a specific job description. Anecdotally, I had heard from librarians in my network that search committee members at some institutions begin the screening process by reviewing the cover letter, while others never look at it, focusing only on the experience described in the CV. My strategy was to use the initial section of the CV, as well as the cover letter, to demonstrate how my transferable skills qualified me for a particular position.[23] You should also be ready to address questions about your transferable skills in interviews.[24]

In many academic institutions, particularly those where librarians are considered tenure-track or tenured faculty, there is an expectation that all librarians will have the second master's, meaning a master's degree beyond the ALA-accredited MLS or equivalent. It is common for this requirement to show up in the list of minimum qualifications in the job advertisement, and this can be discouraging for some special librarians looking to make the leap. However, certain hiring institutions are willing to support librarians' efforts to complete this requirement posthiring with tuition remission and/or some release time. This benefit is less available when the ratio of candidates to vacancies is very large, but it may still be worth submitting an application without this qualification. Librarians in this situation should prepare themselves to address this shortcoming in application materials and during the interview. Think about a specific discipline that is of interest to you, perhaps related to your undergraduate degree, perhaps a library and information services (LIS) field, or a field related to the liaison responsibilities of a specific job opening. Do your research and prepare to demonstrate your motivation to address this requirement.

FIRST DAYS, FIRST WEEKS, FIRST MONTHS, FIRST YEARS

Expectations for new academic librarians vary greatly from institution to institution, but research and publication, professional development, and a mindfully crafted professional practice can each play significant roles during the first days, weeks, months, and years in your new position. This initial period will seem like a whirlwind of learning how things work operationally and getting a sense of the working climate and day-to-day relationships with colleagues. "Be a 'sponge' during your first while on the new job."[25] Keeping in mind the stated or apparent mission of the institution and the library can help provide an anchor as you begin to navigate the expectations that surround you.

If you are a newly hired tenure-track faculty member, you may find yourself immediately thrust into a process involving meetings with mentors, support groups, and so forth.[26] Tenure requirements vary significantly by institution, and the process might be a well-marked, well-paved thoroughfare, or you could find yourself without obvious direction. Even those who are not in tenure-track positions may have a personal interest in contributing to LIS scholarship. The areas of librarianship that you choose for your initial research and publication efforts can set an agenda that will serve you well throughout your career, even beyond tenure. Strongly felt interest in a topic that fits into a perceived gap in the literature can help you sustain motivation and secure publication interest.[27] Remember that special librarians also assess their practice and share their experiences. In some ways, it is a simple adaptation of past practice to add peer review and publication to the process.[28]

Academic library professionals are often expected to network with and learn from other academic librarians, formally and informally.[29] Professional development offerings run the gamut from online webinars to intensive, multiday immersive trainings and are typically offered through national, regional, or local professional organizations. Regular professional development can be very satisfying and also increases others' professional estimation of you. I have gained much insight and developed a confident, professional voice through participation in workshops, conferences, and symposia; through organized discussion groups or special interest groups; and via taking on increasing responsibilities in professional associations.

Developing a distinct identity as an academic library professional involves distinguishing yourself in service to library, institution, and profession.[30] You can diversify your network and bridge academic silos by serving on committees and task groups with colleagues from across the library or across the institution. You may be encouraged to contribute to local, regional, or national professional organizations. As Gold points out, "There are always more chances to demonstrate leadership and the ability to work with others than there are librarians to go around."[31] In some cases, you may not be granted the discretion to select among these opportunities; this may be determined by your supervisor or your director. Another of the foundations of my identity as an academic librarian is the ability to determine the direction of my own professional practice and the foci of my research and publication efforts.

GETTING TO GREAT: THRIVING

I am fortunate to have experienced a special library situation with responsibilities that varied greatly, and the areas of work represented in my current position are just as diverse. A forward-thinking orientation layered over a strong sense of the library's mission helps me recognize meaningful opportunities for new and challenging work, from which I am empowered to select. Working toward a level of expertise in each area and experiencing the rewards of success and growth contribute to my sense of professional well-being. Just as I have been mentored during my career—especially during the months of my job search—I enjoy sharing knowledge and expertise, formally and informally. I actively seek ongoing learning and professional development experiences. I maintain current awareness of trends and innovations in academic libraries and higher education, providing a realistic framework for my developing professional practice. A wide network of relationships and collaborations across the library, across campus, and across the profession help sustain my commitment to the work I do.

It is difficult to define exactly what it means to thrive in an academic library since administrative structures and individual strengths and interests are highly dynamic variables. The library director, in particular, often sets the big-picture agenda for the organization, even if individuals are given leeway in carrying out their responsibilities. If you are considering a transition to academic librarianship, I advise you to learn as much as you can about academia, academic libraries, and the specific institution to which you are applying. Once you have landed on your feet, take a step back from the day-to-day to consider what strategies will help foster—for you—a sense of professional well-being.

NOTES

1. I am grateful to two former colleagues, Jennifer Poggiali, currently at Lehman College Library, and Julia Furay of Kingsborough Community College, for sharing insight and helping me frame issues related to this transition.

2. Anna Gold writes of academic libraries that they "are no utopian retreats. . . . They are competitive, uncertain, complicated, political, and constantly under pressure." Anna Gold, "Moving to the Academy in Mid-career—a Field Guide for the Experienced Librarian," in *The Successful Academic Librarian: Winning Strategies from Library Leaders*, ed. Gwen Meyer Gregory (Medford, NJ: Information Today, 2005), 184.

3. Alistair Black, "From Reference Desk to Desk Set: The History of the Corporate Library in the United States and the UK before the Adoption of the Computer," in *Best Practices for Corporate Libraries*, ed. Marjorie J. Porter and Sigrid Kelsey (Santa Barbara, CA: ABC-CLIO, 2011), 16–18. See also Susan Klopper, "The Journey from Corporate to Academic Librarian," *Online* 30, no. 5 (2006): 16; Christopher LeBeau, "Transitions to Academic Libraries for Business Librarians and Librarians' Response to Adjunct Teaching," *Journal of Business & Finance Librarianship* 13, no. 3 (2008): 303–5; and Valerie Tucci, "Crossing the Bridge Connecting the Corporate and Academic Library Worlds," *Against the Grain* 24, no. 2 (2012): 22.

4. Gold, "Moving to the Academy in Mid-career," 196.

5. Amy Affelt, "Best Practices for Aligning the Mission and Marketing the Services of the Corporate Library," in *Best Practices for Corporate Libraries*, ed. Marjorie J. Porter and Sigrid Kelsey (Santa Barbara, CA: ABC-CLIO, 2011), 158.

6. Tucci, "Crossing the Bridge," 22. See also Klopper, "Journey from Corporate to Academic Librarian," 16, and LeBeau, "Transitions to Academic Libraries," 303.

7. LeBeau, "Transitions to Academic Libraries," 303.

8. For example, see Carol Geary Schneider and Robert Shoenberg, "Habits Hard to Break: How Persistent Features of Campus Life Frustrate Curricular Reform," *Change* 31, no. 2 (1999): 30–35, doi:10.1080/00091389909602677, and David Ward, "Catching the Waves of Change in American Higher Education," *EDUCAUSE Review* 35, no. 1 (2000).

9. Sue Roberts and Philippa Levy, "(E)Merging Professional Identities and Practices," in *Developing the New Learning Environment: The Changing Role of the Academic Librarian*, ed. Sue Roberts and Philippa Levy (London: Facet Publishing, 2005), 225.

10. Tucci, "Crossing the Bridge," 22. See also Klopper, "Journey from Corporate to Academic Librarian," 16.

11. LeBeau, "Transitions to Academic Libraries," 305.

12. Klopper, "Journey from Corporate to Academic Librarian," 16.

13. Susanne Markgren and Tiffany Allen, "How Do I Get There from Here? Changing Jobs, Changing Roles, Changing Institutions," *College & Research Libraries News* 65, no. 11 (2004): 654.

14. Sarah Morrison, quoted in Emily Weak, "Further Questions: How Can Candidates Changing Library Types, or Fields, Best Present Their Skills?" *Hiring Librarians* (blog), September 13, 2003, http://hiringlibrarians.com/2013/09/13/further-questions-how-can-candidates-changing-library-types-or-fields-best-present-their-skills/.

15. Gold, "Moving to the Academy in Mid-career," 191.

16. Markgren and Allen, "How Do I Get There from Here?" 653–56.

17. Gold, "Moving to the Academy in Mid-career," 193–94.

18. Sever Bordeianu and Christina M. Desai, "How to Read a Job Ad: Seeing the Obvious, and Reading between the Lines," in *How to Stay Afloat in the Academic Library Job Pool*, ed. Teresa Y. Neely (Chicago: ALA Editions, 2011), 54–55. See also Sarah Morrison, quoted in Emily Weak, "Further Questions: How Easy Is It to Switch between Different Types of Librarianship?" *Hiring Librarians* (blog), March 28, 2014, http://hiringlibrarians.com/2014/03/28/further-questions-how-easy-is-it-to-switch-between-different-types-of-librarianship/.

19. Sarah Morrison, quoted in Weak, "Further Questions."

20. Celia Rabinowtiz, quoted in Weak, "Further Questions."

21. Laurie Phillips, quoted in Weak, "Further Questions."

22. For more on the differences between résumés and CVs, see Julie Miller Vick and Jennifer S. Furlong, "The CV Doctor Returns—2010," *Chronicle of Higher Education*, November 4, 2010, http://chronicle.com/article/The-CV-Doctor-Returns-2010/124492/.

23. For great advice about building your CV and tailoring your application materials, see Karen Kelsky, "Dr. Karen's Rules of the Academic CV," *The Professor Is In* (blog), January 12, 2012, http://theprofessorisin.com/2012/01/12/dr-karens-rules-of-the-academic-cv/.

24. Bordeianu and Desai, "How to Read a Job Ad," 55.

25. Petra Mauerhoff, quoted in Weak, "Further Questions."

26. Colleen Kenefick and Jennifer A. DeVito, "From Treading Water to Smooth Sailing: Mentoring for New Academic Librarians," *College & Undergraduate Libraries* 22, no. 1 (2015): 92.

27. Kenefick and DeVito, "From Treading Water to Smooth Sailing," 93.

28. Tucci, "Crossing the Bridge," 22. See also Klopper, Susan M. "The Journey from Corporate to Academic Librarian." *Online* 30.5 (2006): 14–20.

29. Kenefick and DeVito advocate for immediate focus on both formal and informal relationship building. Kenefick and DeVito, "From Treading Water to Smooth Sailing," 91.

30. Newkirk Barnes provides strategies for academic librarians seeking to "carve out a niche" for themselves in "Doing It All: First Year Challenges for New Academic Reference Librarians," *Reference Librarian* 47, no. 1 (2007): 52–55.

31. Gold, "Moving to the Academy in Mid-career," 196.

REFERENCES

Affelt, Amy. "Best Practices for Aligning the Mission and Marketing the Services of the Corporate Library." In *Best Practices for Corporate Libraries*, edited by Marjorie J. Porter and Sigrid Kelsey, 153–66. Santa Barbara, CA: ABC-CLIO, 2011.

Barnes, Newkirk. "Doing It All: First Year Challenges for New Academic Reference Librarians." *Reference Librarian* 47, no. 1 (2007): 51–61. doi:10.1300/J120v47n97_06.

Black, Alistair. "From Reference Desk to Desk Set: The History of the Corporate Library in the United States and the UK before the Adoption of the Computer." In *Best Practices for Corporate Libraries*, edited by Marjorie J. Porter and Sigrid Kelsey, 3–24. Santa Barbara, CA: ABC-CLIO, 2011.

Bordeianu, Sever, and Christina M. Desai. "How to Read a Job Ad: Seeing the Obvious, and Reading between the Lines." In *How to Stay Afloat in the Academic Library Job Pool*, edited by Teresa Y. Neely, 41–55. Chicago: ALA Editions, 2011.

Gold, Anna. "Moving to the Academy in Mid-career—a Field Guide for the Experienced Librarian." In *The Successful Academic Librarian: Winning Strategies from Library Leaders*, edited by Gwen Meyer Gregory, 183–97. Medford, NJ: Information Today, 2005.

Kelsky, Karen. "Dr. Karen's Rules of the Academic CV." *The Professor Is In* (blog), January 12, 2012. http://theprofessorisin.com/2012/01/12/dr-karens-rules-of-the-academic-cv/.

Kenefick, Colleen, and Jennifer A. DeVito. "From Treading Water to Smooth Sailing: Mentoring for New Academic Librarians." *College & Undergraduate Libraries* 22, no. 1 (January 2015): 90–96. doi:10.1080/10691316.2015.1001245.

Klopper, Susan. "The Journey from Corporate to Academic Librarian." *Online* 30, no. 5 (2006): 14–20. http://search.ebscohost.com/login.aspx?direct=true&db=edsgao&AN=edsgcl.150090817&site=eds-live&scope=site.

LeBeau, Christopher. "Transitions to Academic Libraries for Business Librarians and Librarians' Response to Adjunct Teaching." *Journal of Business & Finance Librarianship* 13, no. 3 (2008): 295–309. doi:10.1080/08963560802183328.

Markgren, Susanne, and Tiffany Allen. "How Do I Get There from Here? Changing Jobs, Changing Roles, Changing Institutions." *College & Research Libraries News* 65, no. 11 (2004): 653–56. http://crln.acrl.org/content/65/11/653.full.pdf+html.

Roberts, Sue, and Philippa Levy. "(E)Merging Professional Identities and Practices." In *Developing the New Learning Environment: The Changing Role of the Academic Librarian*, edited by Sue Roberts and Philippa Levy, 220–30. London: Facet Publishing, 2005.

Schneider, Carol Geary, and Robert Shoenberg. "Habits Hard to Break: How Persistent Features of Campus Life Frustrate Curricular Reform." *Change* 31, no. 2 (1999): 30–35. doi:10.1080/00091389909602677.

Tucci, Valerie. "Crossing the Bridge Connecting the Corporate and Academic Library Worlds." *Against the Grain* 24, no. 2 (2012): 20–22. http://search.ebscohost.com/login.aspx?direct=true&db=lxh&AN=75120944&site=eds-live&scope=site.

Vick, Julie Miller, and Jennifer S. Furlong. "The CV Doctor Returns—2010." *Chronicle of Higher Education*, November 4, 2010. http://chronicle.com/article/The-CV-Doctor-Returns-2010/124492/.

Ward, David. "Catching the Waves of Change in American Higher Education." *EDUCAUSE Review* 35, no. 1 (January 2000): 22–30. www.educause.edu/ero/article/catching-waves-change-american-higher-education.

Weak, Emily. "Further Questions: How Can Candidates Changing Library Types, or Fields, Best Present Their Skills?" *Hiring Librarians* (blog), September 13, 2003. http://hiringlibrarians.com/2013/09/13/further-questions-how-can-candidates-changing-library-types-or-fields-best-present-their-skills/.

———. "Further Questions: How Easy Is It to Switch between Different Types of Librarianship?" *Hiring Librarians* (blog), March 28, 2014. http://hiringlibrarians.com/2014/03/28/further-questions-how-easy-is-it-to-switch-between-different-types-of-librarianship/.

Chapter Three

An Interview with Jan Chindlund, Library Dean, Columbia College Chicago Library

Davis: Thanks for speaking with us, Jan! Your career transition took you from a business setting to academia. What led to this move, if you don't mind us asking, and what skills had you developed that made you a great fit for your current role?

Jan: Yes, I thoroughly enjoyed my eighteen years as a business librarian, first in an investment advisory company and then in a Fortune 500 company, where I started the first corporate information center within their research department. That work was fast paced, invigorating, challenging, with new research questions and projects daily—sometimes hourly. We worked closely with internal clients to answer their business questions about the competition, industry and consumer trends, company information. We unearthed information from disparate sources, compiled it into understandable formats, analyzed and synthesized it for our clients to use to make business decisions. I also had the privilege of leading teams of researchers, librarians, and others who took on the challenging questions and assignments with enthusiasm and smarts, turning on a dime, remaining flexible when assignments changed midstream. In both, I worked closely with IT to codevelop systems and services needed by our internal clients.

Relating to vendors, finding the right product or service for our needs, defining requirements, and negotiating for terms were skills honed in each position. Managing the budget was essential. I developed a way to link expenditures to a business need; this helped justify each request. One year we spent all but $7 of our impressive budget; my boss joked we should have finished it off with a cup of coffee.

Really, managing a library or information center is akin to running a small business. I appreciate the opportunity to develop these varied compe- tencies in the midst of the busyness of business. And I must add that parallel to this work experience were the leadership opportunities afforded in getting involved in a professional association . . . for me that is SLA (Special Librar- ies Association). Cross-pollinating learning between work and volunteer po- sitions benefitted me, my workplace, and my chosen association. So, why the career move? Trying another type of setting seemed like an excellent next step. I would be returning to my first love: education. As librarians and information professionals, we are educators. Becoming a librarian and ad- ministrator in an academic setting wedded all of my education, experience, and passion for education.

Davis: Please share some of your philosophy regarding career trajectories in this day and age. Is it still possible—or even ideal—to move linearly through the field?

Jan: Some of us have heard—and believed—the myth that whatever type of library one works in first will determine one's career path forever. I don't believe that myth. I have met many librarians who have worked in two, three, or four major types of libraries. Of course, there are many variations on each of these types, most vividly in special libraries. I daresay many librarians are generalists; we like all knowledge and want to delve and learn and satisfy our own innate curiosity. This makes occasional switching appealing to us.

I've met the most interesting people with the most interesting library and information positions in my time: a carillon librarian, webmaster for a very popular television show, researchers in consulting firms and other busi- nesses, theological librarians. We've heard the statistic that most people will make several career switches in their work life cycle. I think this will become more prevalent in the future. Librarians' bundle of skills and curiosity will help them invent or create jobs for themselves as independents or as "intra- preneurs" within their organizations. And if one has an idea of where one would like to wind up, going down in salary to go up eventually may be the right move.

Davis: For those of us who are in the position to hire new candidates, please share your thoughts on the job advertisements.

Jan: Ah, the job ad. It is packed with information about what the expecta- tions and environment are. Read and heed. Unpack it to understand all of the moving parts. Address each requirement in the cover letter, even if you don't have the skill—mention it and talk about how you have something similar or are taking a course currently to learn about it or are willing to learn on the job. Make the cover letter professional (of course) and personal (to a degree). Let your personality show in the letter. I recommend developing several success stories from experience about oneself and then choosing a few to weave into the cover letter.

The résumé is so formal; the cover letter is the place where you can reveal more of your philosophy and style. Speaking of the résumé, I have mentored many people in transition over the years and only in the last few have I been recommending the functional or competency-based résumé. I think it is well suited for people making a career switch or for those whose career path has not been linear. Make a spreadsheet of every skill or responsibility linked to every position, paid and volunteer. Then tag them to group similar skills and responsibilities together. You will find that you have several major groups. Then create blocks of competencies that can be selected and put in descending order of importance per the job ad you are answering.

Davis: What was it that attracted you to the job ad for your current position? How can we make job ads more suitable for the ways career paths are shaped these days?

Jan: I was attracted to the job ad for the position I currently hold because it did not ask for a lockstep path and progression of certain titles but rather for skills, competencies, experience, and education. I recommend this approach in developing job ads; past titles are not as important as what the person knows and has done.

Davis: One element that unites the editors and authors in this book is the MLIS degree. In these few chapters alone, we've seen our degree put to use in so many different ways. You touch on this a little bit in your article "The Portable MLS" for *ILA Reporter*. What advice did you give in that piece that still rings true to you today?

Jan: The MLS degree is highly portable. The only limits are your own imagination and creativity in envisioning how it fits and your own ability to convince others with demonstration of skills and competencies learned and earned. Advice: Leverage your strengths; network with colleagues from other settings to learn how they are using their strengths; continuously seek knowledge; find out where there are gaps in your organization's work that your skills and strengths can fill; collaborate generously and broadly; don't get fixated on labels and titles; bravely suggest new ideas everywhere and be willing to work on the idea if accepted; experiment, and if it fails, give it up and try again; credit others; accept criticism graciously; be wise and a beginner at the same time.

Chapter Four

From the Hospital to the Academy and Back Again

Opportunities in Medical Librarianship

Lisa Liang Philpotts

After spending most of my paraprofessional career and all of my professional career as a librarian in academic libraries, I am currently a knowledge specialist in a library for a large hospital. Unlike all of the libraries that I've worked in that have had physical collections and public spaces for users, the hospital library is completely virtual. Our department is made up of four librarians, including myself, and three additional support staff.

I specialize in supporting systematic reviews and performing in-depth literature searches, so a significant portion of most of my workdays consists of searching online databases and guiding researchers through the literature review process. As a naturally curious person who enjoys digging around for information, this suits me quite well. I also teach staff how to make the best use of our electronic resources, represent the library at outreach events, serve on a research- and evidence-based practice committee, and answer reference questions over the phone and through an online chat service.

Each day I get to learn about and contribute to research and initiatives aimed at improving patient care at the hospital. I find my work very rewarding. I am especially happy with the setting in which I work because I started my career working in a hospital, not as a librarian but as a nurse.

WHY (AND HOW) I MADE THE TRANSITION

Working as a hospital librarian was a goal I had for some time, and it was one that I thought would take many years to come to fruition. My first library job as a page in a public library was originally intended to be a temporary job to make some money as I looked for a community health nursing position after resigning from a job as a hospital nurse. However, I found myself really enjoying library work. My curiosity was piqued when my coworkers, after finding out that my background was in nursing, suggested that I would make a great medical librarian. I didn't even know that such a career existed!

Wanting to learn more and get some hands-on experience, I looked up a list of medical libraries, saw that a hospital in a neighboring city had one, and called their volunteer department to see if there were opportunities available. Fortunately for me, they had an opening, and I found myself volunteering one day a week under the supervision of a solo librarian named Deniz Ender. Most of the tasks I was delegated were fairly simple, like filling interlibrary loan requests or updating the library website, but one day Deniz asked me to put my background to good use by helping her brainstorm synonyms for a literature search on some specific nursing interventions. I was thrilled that I could still make a positive impact on patient care, and in that moment I decided that I wanted to be a medical librarian like Deniz.

I applied for a full-time paraprofessional position as an instructional assistant at the University of North Carolina Chapel Hill Health Sciences Library, an academic medical library, and enjoyed working there as I worked on getting my master's degree in library science. As my graduation approached, I started looking for professional jobs.

Although I envisioned myself one day working in a hospital library or a consumer health information center, I thought I would need to gain additional experience since most hospital libraries are run by solo librarians who have to do a little of everything. My experience as one staff member of many was limited to the realm of reference and instruction, and the day-to-day requirements of running a library, especially the resource management side of things, were a bit of a mystery to me. There also were very few open hospital library positions, especially for people like me who had to limit their job search to one city.

I ended up applying to and happily accepting a position as a health sciences librarian at an academic library. It wasn't a clinical position, but it was in the subject area I was most passionate about and involved a lot of teaching, something that I really enjoyed. In addition, as it was based out of the main social sciences and humanities library for the university, there was a large staff of supportive librarians who were happy to answer my questions as I learned the ropes.

Three years into my academic job, I was prompted to make the shift into the clinical setting when I saw an advertisement for an ever-elusive local hospital librarian position where I wouldn't be solo and where I would be working with an experienced librarian I knew and respected. I decided to apply, thinking that if I did not get the position that I would happily stay where I was. To my surprise, I was extended an offer despite the crowded job market. Unfortunately, the organization was unable to finish the hiring process, but as luck would have it, another hospital librarian job in an institution with multiple librarians surfaced. I applied for that position, and I was extended another offer, and that's how I found myself in my current job.

HOW TO MAKE THE TRANSITION: KEEP TABS ON JOB OPENINGS

Many job openings in hospital libraries are advertised on MEDLIB-L, a listserv for medical librarians, and that was where I learned about one of the hospital library positions I applied to before the application period was open. I make it a habit to read job advertisements to keep up to date on desirable skills for medical librarians. Even if you're not actively looking to change positions, keeping an eye on job openings can give you an idea of what employers are looking for, and you can take the time to try and gain knowledge in areas where you may be lacking. The Medical Library Association (MLA) also posts career opportunities on their website, and the library commission in my state of residence maintains an RSS feed of professional and paraprofessional library jobs.

GAIN SUBJECT-AREA EXPERTISE

Having prior education in health sciences or medicine is by no means a requirement in securing a position in a hospital library. Many of the mentors I look up to did not have experience in health sciences settings before they became medical librarians. That said, I have found that my nursing background helps me relate to the users I serve in the hospital setting and has often been seen as an asset by others. Other medical librarians have bachelor's degrees in the sciences or even a second master's degree in fields like public health.

However, if you are already working as a librarian, putting the time and money into earning a second degree may be unrealistic. Fortunately, there are plenty of other ways to gain specialized subject knowledge. When I was working as an academic librarian, I took advantage of the fact that my employer provided tuition reimbursement. I didn't commit to a degree program, but I took a couple of classes in health sciences, including one on biostatistics that helped strengthen my ability to understand medical research.

I also took advantage of multiple continuing-education opportunities, which required a much shorter time commitment compared to semester-long classes. I signed up for both online and in-person workshops offered by the National Network of Libraries of Medicine (NN/LM), MLA, my regional MLA chapter, and my local chapter of the Special Libraries Association (SLA). I attended webinars on searching medical databases like PubMed, Embase, and PsycINFO; obtained a consumer health information specialization from MLA; and took a fantastic online class on evidence-based medicine taught by Connie Schardt and Angela Myatt. A hands-on workshop offered through MLA that walked me through the process of how to support systematic reviews proved especially useful. I strongly believe that I would have been significantly less likely to have been offered my current position if I had not taken that class since so much time in my current job is devoted to advising and working with researchers who want to undertake systematic reviews.

My transition was made easier by the fact that I was a liaison to a health sciences department when I worked in academia, but it still required that I take initiative and create opportunities to broaden my skill set. Although most of my job involved working with undergraduate and graduate students, I emphasized to faculty that I was also there to support them with their research.

As I learned about supporting systematic reviews through my continuing education, I reached out to faculty and let them know I was able to help with that process, a service that had not been offered in the past. Eventually, I received requests from staff, faculty, and doctoral students asking if I could help with their projects. The hospital where I am now employed produces a large amount of research, so having prior experience working with researchers at the doctorate level and above proved very helpful.

What if you want to work in a health-care setting but don't have any prior experience? I mentioned that my introduction to the medical library world was through volunteering in a hospital library. I also volunteered for my local health department, organizing patient education materials and assessing multimedia made for patients. There are lots of volunteer opportunities in hospitals, clinics, and health-related nonprofits that can help you test the waters and figure out whether those settings are places where you want to work.

CONNECT WITH OTHER LIBRARIANS

I cannot emphasize how much I have learned from other medical librarians. Besides the fact that they have taught me practical skills or have lent a hand when I've encountered particularly vexing search problems, connecting with librarians who worked in hospitals while I was still in academia helped me understand the unique challenges of working in a medical setting.

I find the MLA listserv and their "Expert Searching" discussion list very helpful. You can join the listservs at https://www.mlanet.org/discussion/ index.html. There are also scheduled medical librarian Twitter chats that everyone, medical librarian or not, are welcome to participate in. More information about those, including past transcripts, are available at http:// medlibschat.blogspot.com/. For those with no access to a medical library who want some background knowledge before diving into dialogue, I recommend the online HLWIKI (http://hlwiki.slais.ubc.ca/index.php/HLWIKI_ International), an encyclopedia on topics of interest to health sciences librarians by health sciences librarians. If concepts like "evidence-based medicine," "PICO," and "MEDLINE" are new to you, you can read up on the basics and discover links to outside resources if you would like to learn more.

Although I love going to the annual MLA meeting, I've found it easier to make lasting connections with other librarians through smaller statewide or regional meetings. These meetings tend to be lower cost and generally are very welcoming to newcomers or students. They are a wonderful opportunity to network with nearby librarians and learn about the projects they are working on.

I also recommend getting involved with professional organizations. When an MLA conference was being held in the city where I live, I volunteered for the hospitality committee because it seemed like a fun and easy way to help out. It turned out that a librarian I met through that committee would later interview me for a job!

Don't be afraid of reaching out to medical librarians if you are interested in what they do. When I was leaving my academic job, I had multiple people contact me to ask about the position I was leaving. I offered to meet with them virtually or over coffee to tell them more about the job and to encourage them to apply. When I noticed that the person who filled my position had asked for some advice on MEDLIB-L, I sent her some resources that I hoped would be helpful. I have had so many mentors in the library community support and help me out as a young librarian that now I like to pay that forward.

FINAL REFLECTIONS

Some say that clinical librarianship is a shrinking field, so I think it's important to ask yourself why you want to go into it. Are you a proactive person, willing to try new things and adapt to change? Do you believe in the value that you can add in a health-care setting? What exactly do you offer to other health-care professionals, patients, and the organization that you want to work for? Being able to articulate the answer to that last question helped me maintain my confidence and convey the value of my profession to others as I shifted careers. I encourage people who are considering careers in medical libraries to think about their answers to these questions and advocate for themselves—and I hope that you will be my future colleagues!

ACKNOWLEDGMENTS

I wish to acknowledge the nurses and librarians who have supported me as I made career transitions: Dr. Ann Newman, Pam Ball, Deniz Ender, K. T. Vaughan, Julia Shaw-Kokot, Francesca Allegri, and Thomas Casserly.

Chapter Five

Flipping the Pages

Tracing Experiences from Both Sides of the Road

Joseph M. Yap

After completing my bachelor's degree in the LIS program and enjoying two months of vacation after my graduation, I landed a job in the health-care sector. I started my career as a special librarian at the Asian collaborative training network for malaria information resource center. My function was to index journal articles related to malaria and vector-borne diseases.

In the Philippines, a qualified "librarian" is one who passed the national licensure examination given by the Professional Regulation Commission. In short, there is a law in the Philippines that governs this statewide board examination. To know more about the law, you may read Republic Act 9246, otherwise known as the Philippine Librarianship Act of 2003.

Most of the fresh graduates seek to find library-related work where a license is not required. They review for the board examination, take the examination, and hope to pass it. If they pass it, they apply for their license, attend the oath-taking ceremony, and may start to find better opportunities. As it was in my case, nongovernmental organizations with special libraries may not require a license at first, especially if you are a new graduate. But you may need to work on obtaining a license within a year after graduation. Luckily, I had passed the board examination in November 2006 after graduation.

FIRST-DAY HIGH

After six months of indexing medical and health journals, my superior assigned me to take control of the whole resource center. This was a "first" in my young career as a librarian and a step toward building a relationship with the ministries of health.

I was tasked with supervising the online repository and managing com munications with eleven member countries in our organization. This position allowed me to work directly with the most prominent medical and health officials in the Philippines and in Southeast Asia. In my new role, I closely monitored our partner libraries to make sure that they submitted government-published resources on malaria and other vector-borne diseases to our repository. I made sure to follow copyright guidelines; we all know that copyright is an issue, especially if research is not freely distributed.

Being an indexer myself, I contracted with other indexers to work on uploaded papers. I also worked with librarians in my region. This was not an easy task, as I was still a very new librarian during that time. Together with our information technology (IT) personnel, we traveled to Cambodia, Laos, Vietnam, and Thailand to train librarians on how to use our system so that they could upload materials by themselves. (Our Chinese partner had already been established and did not need to be trained.) I had already traveled to Indonesia and Malaysia and planned to return to other Mekong countries just to make sure that they were working on the project continuously. After doing this work for almost four years, my director encouraged me to submit paper presentations to international conferences. One of my papers was published by a refereed journal in the field of medicine.

I enjoyed traveling and meeting new friends along the way, but I felt saturated. I thought that I would not grow as a librarian if I only worked on the daily routine of checking uploaded materials, reviewing indexing, and approving document delivery requests. There were no more challenges. There was no more room for growth. But I am very thankful for my position with my first organization. The experience I had with them was truly worth remembering. They were very flexible. I could attend professional library associations on official time. It was while I was working for them that I was elected as the public relations officer (2008–2009) and secretary (2010) of the Medical and Health Librarians Association of the Philippines (MAH-LAP). It was a fruitful three years with MAHLAP. My office also allowed me to undergo a three-month information management training program in Belgium. Moreover, they permitted me to leave work early to finish my graduate studies.

One may say that this was a very ideal work environment. However, compensation was not competitive. All of the experience I gained during my stay with them gave me the opportunity to transfer to another work atmosphere. Although we treated each other as family, I needed to extend my horizons. I needed to develop more as a professional and as an individual.

THE ACADEMIC SHIFT

I'd been thinking of leaving my first organization for quite some time, but I had no place to go. In December 2009, a colleague from De La Salle University (DLSU) shared a vacant post with me. I eagerly submitted my application and was called for an interview immediately. I thought of preparing answers to questions I might be asked during my interview. What were the possible questions that the library director might ask?

The interview was short, and to my surprise I was hired. The questions revolved around all of the activities that I had been doing in my previous post. My networking background and research skills brought me to DLSU, not to mention the fact that I was about to finish my graduate studies during that time—this is what they were looking for. My graduate studies would not have been complete without the thesis grant from the Philippine Association of Academic and Research Librarians.

After the hiring comes the dilemma: how do I tell my kind and generous superior that I have another job offer? I am contemplating accepting the offer since I need to work for three years at DLSU before I become a permanent employee. In my previous position, I only needed six months to become permanent. This would be another challenge for me. Three long years of renewal and evaluation as required by the university. It was hard for me to leave my first job, yet I wanted to find a new professional space. As I needed to decide before the end of the year, I had to tell my boss about my plans. With no hard feelings, she blessed me and told me that it is my future that I am creating. It was a bittersweet moment for me and for her.

It really was a new year for me in January 2010. I had a new working space and new colleagues to connect with. I entered the premises of the university with high spirits and enthusiasm. My first assignment was to catalog print resources. The task was given to me since my experience was more with bibliographic description and indexing. After six months of harnessing my technical skills, I was transferred to a satellite library, where I needed to manage a graduate school business library. I stayed with the graduate school for more than two years. I was independent, and I needed to deal with a lot of challenges. I had to oversee the whole operations of the library with, of course, support from the main library. I was able to establish an International Labour Organization (ILO) corner at the satellite library as well as the main library. My professional responsibility continued as I became an officer in the Association of Special Libraries of the Philippines (ASLP) in 2011. My first volunteer position with ASLP was as public relations officer. I became the president of the association in 2013. Before my presidency with ASLP, the Special Libraries Association (SLA) bestowed the Early Career Award on me in 2012.

My transfer to DLSU was rewarding for me. DLSU hones its librarians so they become the best they can, and it is regarded as one of the top libraries in the country. In 2003, DLSU received the Outstanding Library of the Year award given by the Philippine Association of Academic and Research Librarians (Awards 2006). At DLSU, librarians may enjoy the following faculty development programs (De La Salle University 2012):

- Support for paper presentations in local and international conferences
- Support for participation in local conferences
- Support for graduate studies
- Support for advanced short-term courses
- Support for local trainings, seminars, and workshops
- Support for membership in professional associations

The Faculty Resource and Development program would also provide us with a lot of leave time: vacation leave, sick leave, emergency leave, and service leave. Moreover, DLSU's Office of the Vice Chancellor for Research and Innovation supports the following:

- Incentive program for ISI- and Scopus-indexed journal publications
- Research incentives
- Support for funding of registration fees in international conferences

DLSU also encourages its librarians to be officers in professional library associations. One should continue to further one's professional education by attending relevant professional trainings. This is what I like most about DLSU. They allow me to be invited as a resource speaker and a participant at the same time. Since 2010, I have been able to participate in international conferences through the faculty development program. I am proud to say that I represent the institution at some of the prestigious international conferences like the Academic Librarian Conference in Hong Kong, the Shanghai International Library Forum in China, and the Congress of Southeast Asian Librarians.

At DLSU, we continue to provide new programs and services. From time to time, we are tasked to chair some projects and events. This trust DLSU gives to its librarians literally does not allow for a boring moment. This is also what I like in an academic library. I can talk to real people rather than just communicating online. Certainly, I do reports and follow-up e-mails in response to massive e-mails, yet I can still attend physical meetings. It may drain you for a while, yet it is still the human touch that makes us all feel alive. On the other side, we also do library orientation, outreach programs, and sometimes you may be tapped to give a visitor a tour of a library.

LIFE AT THIRTY-ONE

At the time of writing, I am already thirty-one. There are a lot of opportunities waiting for me out there. Just like the research process, where you do not know if you'll get published or not, you never know what opportunities will be fruitful. So always take the risk and do what you think will be best for your career. There are offers you need to think about, propositions that you need to balance. If you are content with your professional career and it boosts your confidence and makes your personal life happy, then I advise you to stick with it. Hold on to it, but do not forget to stop dreaming, especially if there is still plenty of space for you to grow.

REFERENCES AND FURTHER READING

ASLPWiki. "Joseph M. Yap." Accessed June 19, 2015. https://aslpwiki.wikispaces.com/Joseph+M.+Yap.

De La Salle University. "Awards." De La Salle University website. Accessed June 19, 2015. www.dlsu.edu.ph/library/paarl/awards_list.asp.

———. *Faculty Development Program 2012–2015*. Manila, Philippines: De La Salle University, 2012.

Cichon, Melchor F. "Joseph Marmol Yap: A Proactive Librarian." *Biography* (blog). Accessed June 19, 2015. http://biographynotmine.blogspot.com/2013/10/joseph-marmol-yap-proactive-librarian_5.html.

Gagatiga, Zarah. "Filipino Librarian: Joseph Marmol Yap." *School Librarian in Action* (blog). Accessed June 19, 2015. http://lovealibrarian.blogspot.com/2013/02/filipino-librarian-joseph-marmol-yap.html.

Philippine Association of Academic and Research Librarians Newsletter, January-March, 2006: http://www.dlsu.edu.ph/library/paarl/pdf/news/January_March_2006.pdf.

Yap, Joseph M. "MAHLAP Annual Planning Workshop and Teambuilding 2008." Medical and Health Librarians Association of the Philippines website. Accessed June 19, 2015. www.mahlap.org/index.php?option=com_content&task=view&id=8&Itemid=2.

Chapter Six

An Interview with Gretel L. Stock-Kupperman, Director of the Library, Instructional Design, and Academic Affairs Initiatives, Viterbo University

Davis: Thanks for chatting with me, Gretel! I've heard wonderful things about your career thus far. As I understand it, you are currently working in an academic setting as director of the library, instructional design, and academic affairs initiatives at Viterbo University. What is your average day like?

Gretel: There is no such thing as an average day, and that's a great thing. In a typical week, my responsibilities fall into a few categories: meetings with university administration, relationship building/maintaining, library management tasks, being a resource for my staff, and providing service.

As director, I represent the library at several meetings and participate in university governance. While it takes a great deal of time, I've found that it is critical to be a part of broader campus life and to be present to hear the "music of the conversation." I've been able to take advantage of campus events and initiatives just by being connected to what's going on. When faced with challenges, I've also had the social capital already built for help in solving issues.

Relationship building has similar outcomes to participating in university governance. If people know me, I can connect them to the library and instructional design services and us to their needs. I'm an ambassador, and I encourage my staff to do the same. People on this campus respond well to an informal approach, so I regularly catch people in person instead of sending an e-mail. Not only do I get to run into colleagues serendipitously walking around campus, I have the opportunity to hold conversations with people in their space, which often garners information I wouldn't have access to otherwise.

Library administration involves the nuts and bolts of keeping the doors open. I'm in charge of our budget, facility development issues, and the strategic direction of library and instructional design. Closely related to these tasks is being a resource for my staff. I stay in contact with them formally and informally about what's going on, initiatives they are responsible for, and the activities of the library. We meet both individually and in teams, where my role is to communicate our shared goals and get barriers out of the way so they can do their best work. Working with my team is one of the most rewarding parts of my job; it's great to see them succeed and craft a workplace where we can work together to meet the goals of the institution and the library.

Did I mention I also work regular reference and circulation shifts? There is never a dull moment.

Davis: Immediately prior to joining Viterbo University, you worked at Metropolitan Library System (MLS). Tell me a bit more about your role there.

Gretel: MLS was a state-funded association that provided services to academic, public, special, and school member libraries in Chicago and the surrounding southwest suburbs. At MLS, I was the director of member services, responsible for leading library consulting services, continuing-education events, resource sharing, and delivery of library items. We were the "librarian's librarian," working to connect members to each other as well as services we could provide. One of the major duties of this position was staying in touch with the needs of the membership. If we weren't responsive to their needs, we wouldn't be successful as an organization. Aside from answering individual questions, I took every opportunity I could to attend networking meetings. I would mostly listen, but I also provided information on where we could help. The membership was very diverse and vocal, so this regular contact helped us keep on top of issues as they emerged instead of having to respond unprepared in our public quarterly meetings.

Davis: What aspects of your previous position at MLS do you draw on in your current work?

Gretel: The work at MLS gave me an appreciation for operating in a complex political environment. There were multiple stakeholders that we dealt with on a regular basis; we were funded through the state library, we reported to our board, each of our member types had unique needs and issues, and many of our libraries were subject to elected boards and officials. Our public librarians in particular were very political and very connected to one another. If groups within the public libraries were unhappy about something, it could make our work very difficult to accomplish.

I did gain some specific skills out of working in this kind of environment. One was the ability to listen to critical feedback without taking it personally and to actively listen to gain understanding of the other person's perspective. I also gained the ability to facilitate discussions to allow for disagreement but commit collectively to a decision. A third was the experience of advocating for a position through multiple channels. Finally, I gained a great appreciation for the maxim that if the process is bad, the end product doesn't matter; you pay the cultural toll for poor processes long after success is forgotten.

Davis: You've done a bunch of advocacy work on behalf of the library where you currently work and with MLS. What tips would you like to share about speaking persuasively to audiences of all kinds?

Gretel: First and foremost, know your audience. Get to know their goals and positions. You can discover that through talking to others or asking directly. Once you know your audience, craft your message to align as closely to their goals as you can or to compellingly answer their concerns. Adopt language that resonates with the person you are speaking to. For example, when I write an e-mail to the president of my university, it is very brief and jargon free, and I make a business case for what I'm asking. In contrast, when I'm talking to faculty on the core curriculum committee, I discuss the library's classroom teaching work and instruction of students and how we meet the outcomes of the core.

Keep your outcome in mind. It's easy to get caught up in wanting to get a certain thing, or things, done a certain way. However, you need to be flexible in order to respond to the goals or needs of those who may support you. Some give-and-take is required to move an organization forward. Advocacy is never over. When you've been successful or a project is done, that's the time to continue building and sustaining relationships. The next challenge, hurdle, or project is right around the corner, so don't lose touch with your allies and detractors.

Davis: What's one piece of career advice that's resonated with you? Why?

Gretel: The best piece of career advice I've ever gotten is from my mom, who said, "Keep your options open." She meant to not prematurely close doors on a path or focus too narrowly until you have to. I've adopted it as a flexibility in mind-set: How can my skills be applied toward the success of my organization? How can working at an organization help me meet my personal and professional goals? How can I keep my library's options open by building a relationship, offering a service, or seizing an opportunity for dialogue? This approach has helped me have an interesting career and opened the door for many fulfilling opportunities that I would have missed had I been more narrowly focused.

Chapter Seven

From Public to Corporate to Academic

Tales and Lessons from an Accidental Business Librarian

Celia Ross

My career path has been a winding one, with side trips as a bookstore clerk, a high school health teacher, a venture capital researcher, and a global consulting firm information specialist. There were a few library jobs thrown in for good measure, too, like my very first job as a teenager in my local public library, my internship at the graduate library reference desk, and my first job out of library school as a social sciences librarian at a regional branch of a large urban public library. I certainly did not set a course for a future in business librarianship, but in many ways all of these positions helped pave the way to my current (and longest-running) stint as an academic business librarian.

THE NONLIBRARY JOBS

I'm not the most decisive person; knowing that I wouldn't have to focus on a single discipline was one of the main drivers that brought me to library school in the first place. It took me a little while to even decide to go to library school, however, so after majoring in humanities (and minoring in biology—did I mention I'm indecisive?) as an undergrad, I found myself working in a bookstore just after college, where I was responsible for the magazine section. This was just before the Internet would soon show the world that there's an interest group out there for everyone, so I was both thrilled and amazed by the sheer variety and specificity of the many titles we carried. Everything from goat farming and woodworking to bike racing and toy collecting was represented on those winding, stacked shelves over by the checkout line. In retrospect, it was this exposure to the world of consumer, trade, and industry publications that introduced me to the concept of asking "who cares?" when doing industry research in order to identify potential sources of information. It was also where I began my lifelong contempt for magazine subscription cards, because I would inevitably pick up ten or twenty or thirty a day after they fell out of the journals people browsed.

I got my first "real" job when I left the bookstore to go work for a private boarding school. Ostensibly, the position was to run the high school's small library. I thought this would be great preparation for library school. In reality, the school needed every employee to do a little bit of everything. Running the library was a very small percentage of what I spent my time doing. First year students need a health teacher? And juniors need an honors history teacher? Okay, I can teach those classes. There's no one to drive the bus on field trips and we need someone to get their class C commercial driver's license? Sure, why not? Volleyball and fencing teams need a faculty coordinator, and the girls' dorm needs a summer live-in parent? I'm on it. Need an extra faculty member to go on backcountry camping trips to the Sierra Nevada, Big Sur, and Death Valley? I thought you'd never ask!

Talk about transitions! I learned every day that flexibility and a willingness to try new things were the only way to go. As long as I focused on the students and was there for them, everything else would fall into place. Luckily, I was in an environment that encouraged, if not required, this kind of approach. I had a good amount of support, as well as positive feedback from the students themselves.

Eventually, library school beckoned, and I ended up at the University of Michigan's newly revamped School of Information (SI) program. This was where I had my first real introduction to technology beyond a word processor attached to a dot matrix printer. Although I knew I wanted to follow the traditional library track, I couldn't escape a near immersive introduction into the world of user interface design, coding, and online searching, whether I liked it or not. Flexibility and willingness to try new things came in handy once again.

During my last year of library school, I found myself needing a job. I had worked at the graduate library reference desk my first year, but all of the positions were filled by the time I got back after the summer. I got a well-timed call from a friend who had recently graduated and had been hired as a researcher for a small venture capital firm. He was now looking to hire an assistant. After a few questions from me (such as, "What's a venture capital firm?"), I agreed to come in for an interview. It turned out that the founder of the firm, who had graduated with an MBA, was interested in hiring SI students, with the logic being that it would be easier to train an SI student about business than it would be to train the business students about research. And even though I expressed some hesitation during the interview about whether

I was cut out for corporate research, they ended up hiring me anyway. I learned the basics of company and industry research there, gained some experience in how to vet the not-so-crazy from the crazy proposals, and realized that I *could* do business research. It wasn't even as dull or nefarious as I had envisioned! The takeaway here for me was that it never hurts to keep an open mind and that an SI background, even with a focus on more traditional areas like libraries and archives, helps to prepare you for a wide array of possible careers.

THE PUBLIC LIBRARY

After graduation, I said good-bye to my venture capital colleagues and, I thought, to business research. I was headed to the big city, where I had a reference librarian position in a large urban public library waiting for me. This was where I thought my true calling lay. Never mind that my only experience working in a public library had been for my hometown, population approximately five thousand, back when I was thirteen years old and where my duties primarily involved wrapping plastic sleeves on the new hardcovers. Suddenly I was on the reference desk of one of the largest public libraries in the country, where gate counts of five thousand on a Sunday afternoon were not unusual. It turned out that many of these patrons had business-related questions, and so I applied my company and industry research right away.

The reference desk shifts were busy, but I was new and had energy and enthusiasm to burn. But because I was a new librarian in a huge system, when I wasn't on the reference desk, I sort of fell through the cracks and was put to work cutting scrap paper. I had to learn to pace myself to keep up with the deluge of requests coming in while I was on the desk and to look for ways to channel my remaining energies and motivation when I wasn't. I quickly realized that larger forces than myself were at work. Politics and bureaucracy were in play. I also felt that all of the technological skills I had acquired during my time in library school were quickly fading, while my student loan bills were not. Even though the standard rule of thumb is never to leave a job less than a year in, when a friend of a friend who worked in human resources (HR) for a consulting firm mentioned that they were looking for a researcher, I decided it was worth applying. I ended up with an offer for the position, and I accepted it with a bit of trepidation and some bittersweet feelings about leaving the colleagues and patrons I had come to know in my short time in the public library. It was the right choice at the time, and I was able to take away what I had learned about navigating as a small fish in a big sea and about triaging the deluge of requests that come in on a busy reference desk.

The bureaucracy I encountered, I would later find, exists in nearly all types of work environments.

THE CORPORATE LIBRARY

I had never heard of McKinsey & Company before interviewing there. I didn't know that it was a globally renowned consulting firm working with major companies and nonprofits all over the world. During my interview for an information specialist position with McKinsey's North American Retail Practice, I stressed that I loved to do research (and was good at it!) but was honest in my limited knowledge of the industry. I still remember the way the senior information specialist, who would become a mentor and friend, calmly pointed out that I did, in fact, already know a lot about retail. I shopped for clothes and groceries, didn't I? I had eaten at restaurants, right? He explained that they weren't looking for someone who wanted to be a consultant but rather for someone who loved to search and who could approach a request with creativity and determination. I tell the business students I work with these days, many of whom respect McKinsey and aspire to work for them, that it was my search skills that got me hired there, because my business background was meager at best.

Working at McKinsey was a catalyst in my progression toward becoming a business librarian. I learned a lot about the retail industry and also how to apply the kind of searching and analysis I was doing there to any industry, retail or otherwise. And because McKinsey was by no means lacking in resources, I quickly learned that money doesn't buy everything. At McKinsey, we had access to almost any data resource under the sun, but that didn't mean the answer would be found there. The "answers" come from piecing together what you *can* find and shaping it into a robust overview and educated forecasts built on data. At McKinsey, I learned to search for pieces of the puzzle rather than the "holy grail" and to break down complicated questions into smaller parts.

I also learned that some of the most valuable resources might be sitting right next to you. I learned so much from my colleagues at McKinsey. They were always there to offer support, but more important, I learned to ask for assistance when I needed it and to reach out even if I didn't need help so that I could brainstorm and get different insights into what I was working on. Communication is so important. It's the key to individual success as well as to rewarding and productive teamwork.

THE ACADEMIC LIBRARIES

Although I loved my time at McKinsey, in my heart I knew that the corporate world wasn't for me. I sought out an academic library position where I would no longer be responsible for billable hours and "deliverables" for faceless corporate entities. I had loved my time on the reference desk during graduate school and at the public library and wanted to return to working with real people. I looked forward to showing students and faculty how to navigate through an increasingly vast sea of information, whether it was business related or not. And because of the business reference experience I had gained with my previous positions, I was able to transition into an academic setting by being willing to take on the role of finance and accounting librarian liaison.

The academic library setting provided a great opportunity to explore information literacy and other aspects of teaching and learning through one-off instruction sessions and by offering teachable moments at the reference desk. Additionally, remembering how at sea I felt when I first had to face business topics, I was inspired to develop a workshop for other librarians on how to do business reference (and how not to fear it). These half-day training sessions morphed into an online course that I still teach for the American Library Association (ALA). This experience eventually became the basis for a book I wrote called *Making Sense of Business Reference*. It was during this time that also I began to get involved with professional organizations like the ALA and the Special Library Association (SLA), among other local and regional groups. I found my ALA home through the Business Reference and Services Section (BRASS), and I like to joke to newcomers to be careful—I was just sitting in on a committee meeting one day and found myself elected chair of the section.

After years of being in academic libraries where business was just one of the subject areas, I now find myself in an all-business, all-the-time library. Luckily for me, business is not a discipline that is predictable or monotonous. All over campus there are initiatives popping up related to entrepreneurship, marketing, careers, and other areas that overlap with or complement traditional business areas like management and strategy and finance. And within the business school, there is a strong focus on action-based learning, positive organizational scholarship, and lots of other interesting topics that help keep me engaged and constantly learning. I'm working on developing a course on competitive intelligence and participating in activities that allow me to focus on some of the core components of what I love to do: connecting people to the information they need and showing them how to develop their own set of research skills.

LESSONS LEARNED ALONG THE WAY

In any job, there will be times when things feel overwhelming—the over-booked calendar, the line at the reference desk, the book review you still haven't submitted, the client presentation you still haven't even started and the meeting is tomorrow, and so on. Perspective and deep breaths are key here, as well as a conscious decision not to succumb to the temptation toward negativity. I learned this early on, whether it was from the frustration I felt at picking up yet another magazine subscription card or dealing with the rude patron at the reference desk or wrestling with a seemingly impossible question that came in after 5 p.m. with an ASAP deadline. When I was at the private high school, I had realized that teenagers can be overwhelming even in small doses. In some colleagues, this stress would manifest itself in the form of a negative attitude and too much complaining, and I learned to steer clear from those faculty lounge conversations. Staying positive and focusing on the students sometimes required more of an effort but in the end was far more beneficial and fulfilling.

Learning to pace yourself is also key. As a new student, I was curious and enthusiastic and wanted to do it all. However, it quickly became clear that the learning process is not a sprint but a marathon. It helps no one, especially yourself, if you are overextended or exhausted. Sometimes, this means saying no to a person or a committee or some other type of opportunity. This is especially true if a big part of your time is spent trying to learn lots of new things. I would find myself remembering this, although I can't say I always acted upon it, any time I started a new position.

Transitioning from a corporate to an academic position was a bit of a challenge, but it helped that I moved to a university that had a large business program. They were looking for someone who would not be intimidated by some of the complicated business reference databases. I can remember a time when I myself was one of the intimidated ones, and I can relate to students and colleagues who were new to the subject.

Empathy is a critical skill for all librarians, I think; even if your past positions don't directly relate to a job you are applying for, identify those softer areas where you have more experience than you realize. For example, maybe you have been a children's librarian in a public library and you're looking to transition to a community college. Your ability to plan programs, your work with children and parents, and your experience with the library's board can be aligned with community college counterparts (or academic or corporate, depending on which direction you shift).

Along those same lines, remember that many of your hard skills are transferable, too, regardless of your professional setting. Again, avoid having tunnel vision or blinders on when it comes to evaluating what you are good at. Great reference librarians are great searchers, whatever the job title may be. While you may end up specializing in a particular discipline, at their core, those search skills are subject agnostic. There are plenty of skills to be gained from nonlibrary-setting jobs as well, from dealing with the public and managing projects to planning programs or figuring out creative solutions to the crisis of the day. You may even find yourself taking your skills to a nonlibrary setting and working with a start-up or a nonprofit or a company in some role that doesn't align with any of your past positions. Be open to anything, and don't limit yourself by defining your skill set too narrowly.

I am grateful that, in all of my professional positions, I have had such great mentors surrounding me. Look for those who can teach you and serve as role models and possible mentors. They will become the foundation of your professional network and can help guide you through the maze of an association or committee protocols. I am also grateful to all of the students and patrons I have worked with along the way. Be open to the learning process working in both directions. And seek out those specialized groups of intrepid, like-minded people, from your coworkers to other colleagues in your company or institution to outside professional groups. Just as there is a periodical (or four) out there for every industry, so, too, are there groups of professionals who can help to educate, invigorate, and inspire you. The power of a group of dedicated and smart specialists is not to be underestimated— you'll know when you've found "your people" when you find yourself energized and motivated simply by associating with them.

Finally, don't overlook yourself in the midst of the career equation or lose sight of what you love to do. It's said that one's dream job exists in that intersection of what you love to do, what you're good at, and what you can get paid to do. I wouldn't say that I love business reference, but, as I mentioned, I do love to connect people to information, and I think I'm usually fairly successful in doing this. I wouldn't say no to a raise, but who would? And speaking of getting paid, remember that money isn't everything. Having a short commute or a flexible schedule or access to free training or a professional development budget are worth consideration as you survey your current situation as well as future options. In the end, the key is to keep things in perspective.

Ultimately, everyone's path will be different, but hopefully some of these ideas will help you navigate as you chart your own course in search of career fulfillment. As you look to either shift careers or shift within your current role toward greater job satisfaction, remember that all jobs will have their ups and downs—on the down days almost any job might seem better than what you're dealing with at that particular moment in time. Don't wait for happiness to come to you, though. If you find that the good days aren't outnumbering the not-so-good days, make the time to step back, appraise, and recalibrate if necessary.

Chapter Eight

Uprooting from Buenos Aires, Argentina, to Los Angeles, California

A Professional Journey

Veronica D'Aquino

I'm originally from Buenos Aires, Argentina. I relocated to Los Angeles, California, after getting married. Although I already had eight years' experience as a reference librarian, this "self-initiated expatriate" (SIE) professional journey resulted in a number of occupational changes and ultimately in my recognition of the need to become accredited by the American Library Association (ALA). These changes included but were not limited to downward and lateral job movements, skill transitions, and other challenges before once again being professionally recognized as a reference librarian.[1]

I was first drawn to the field of library science in my early twenties, probably by an unfulfilled childhood desire for becoming an archeologist. Indeed, while working as a reference librarian, I discovered similarities between the work of archaeologists and that of librarians: both occupations unearth vital remains and display activities that involve their recording, analysis, and interpretation.

While still pursuing my degree in Argentina, I began working as a reference librarian for a library that acts as a hub for coordinating services for the University of Buenos Aires. Within a year, and through the encouragement of the person who later became my mentor, I accepted a reference librarian position at the National Library. Transitioning into such a prestigious institution at a young age made me wonder if I would be able to swiftly grasp my new responsibilities as well as the values and culture of the institution. This process went beyond repackaging knowledge and skills; it involved a slow, transformative reorientation of how I perceived my role as a librarian, very much in line with Donald Hall's conceptualization of the protean careerist.[2]

In the late 1990s, a political decision at the administrative level made the National Library responsive to the economic hardships of the country by diversifying services to accommodate new segments of the population, mostly college and university students. The process of moving to a new service model triggered unexpected barriers at the operational level. Due to the quick turnaround, these obstacles could not be strategically overcome without great strain. For example, the increased number of library users far exceeded the initial expectations; thus, the facilities were at full capacity from open to close. The preservation policies were then in contradiction with the new dissemination policies, thereby quickly causing collections to deteriorate. Longtime research members became reluctant to use the existing services due to the changing user population. Having to face these types of dilemmas forced library leadership to modify priorities and policies in order to ensure that the library's cultural mission continued being honored while incorporating the needs of our evolving community.

These unsettling times, characterized by professional controversies and debates in the public sphere, became further heightened due to a series of unpopular measures during the next political administration. [3] Unlike here in the United States, in Argentina public administration organizations are highly politicized, and libraries are not exempt. National politics are ingrained in the fabric of how we operate, which was especially true during my time at the National Library of Argentina. As a result, I became more aware of the crucial role of our social responsibility toward the needs of our communities.

Looking back, I can see how, from the very beginning, my career was marked by continuous learning and questioning, whether through formal education or a series of informal learning experiences stemming from challenging job assignments, interactions with colleagues and library users, or the innumerable opportunities fostered by the National Library, including lectures by visiting scholars of the caliber of Roger Chartier, the provision of courses in Latin and Latin American literature, among many others. The National Library was then, and still is, a remarkable environment for intellectual stimulation and professional growth.

Seeking ways in which to enrich my career, I went back to study English, another skill I would later use in both my career and life. In addition, my mentor Maria Etchepareborda, who was teaching at the National School of Librarians, suggested I take her place as a teacher assistant, which I did until moving to the United States—an experience that I later transferred to my information literacy sessions. I took advantage of an opportunity that unexpectedly showed itself when the award-wining Argentine writer and journalist Belgrano Rawson hired me to conduct research for his book *Noticias Secretas de América*.[4] My dearest memories associated with this work are related to spending long hours in the archives and various libraries around Buenos Aires, delving into late 1800s Argentine and Latin American history. Unearthing facts and myths about my country's political and social history was a fascinating process that helped sharpen my research skills and deepened my knowledge of our cultural heritage.

THE TRANSITION

After seven years of working at the National Library, in December of 2003 I relocated to Los Angeles. I quickly learned that I had underestimated the time and effort that would be required to transition professionally. It was important to forge connections with other librarians. For example, phone conversations with a Colombian librarian, whom I met through a mutual friend, at the San Francisco Public Library offered valuable professional insights. These included the need to pursue an MLIS degree, the benefits of volunteering, and the exploration of professional organizations for networking purposes.

My first position in a library setting involved moving downward to a paraprofessional role as a library media clerk. I ran a small elementary school library for underserved children in Lawndale, California. I went from working with adults to providing library services for children aged five through twelve (and their teachers). While I was learning about the California public school system and the needs of inner-city children, I realized that if I wanted to grow professionally, I needed to pursue a master's degree in library science from an ALA-accredited school.

Building relationships through rich discussions and informal meetings with the district library media clerks proved a helpful strategy for adjusting to a different work environment. Running a library for over eight hundred students, developing meaningful programming and teaching, and building a safe and fun atmosphere for children unaccustomed to regularly visiting a library gave me a great sense of purpose. This elementary school experience was the beginning of my transformative professional and personal journey in the United States and was accompanied by being accepted into the San Jose State University MLIS program in the fall of 2006.

In 2008, I decided to take a risk and pursue an unpaid archival internship at California State University, Dominguez Hills (CSUDH). The Dominguez Hills archivists Greg Williams and Tom Philo provided me with a nurturing environment for developing my archival skills. Greg and Tom entrusted me with significant projects, some of which later turned into paid grants. Working on projects pertaining to women in trades and the Japanese American internment communities exposed me to the proactive role the archives takes through its collection policies and access services to ensure the representation of voiceless and marginalized communities.

Since the archival experience was an internship, I continued applying for various public library positions, especially those seeking bilingual candidates, to no avail. However, university introductions did lead to work as a research assistant with Dr. Lynne H. Cook, the former dean of the CSUDH College of Education, while she was updating her textbook on effective collaboration and interactions for school professionals. After working for a year outside of the library system, I was encouraged to apply for a staff position in the CSUDH Circulation Department. Even though I was over-qualified, I was hired to coordinate the maintenance of the library collections. Within two years of ensuring the optimal accessibility of these collections, a position opened in the Reference Department, and I was promoted to senior assistant librarian, a tenure-track faculty position and one that I currently hold.

THE OPPORTUNITY

Even though my master's degree provided me with a sound conceptual framework and a new set of competencies, I recognized the importance of cultivating professional relationships. My next mentor, Dr. John C. Calhoun, helped me face the day-to-day challenges of serving as a new faculty member in a complex academic environment. As with my mentor at the National Library, this relationship also happened within the context of informal mentoring by working together on several projects and by having diverse discussions with a senior librarian who was willing to share his experiences and career path.

Dominguez Hills is among the most ethnically diverse campuses in the nation, with over 85 percent of our student population identifying as non-white.[5] I see our library as a place where our community in general, and our students in particular, can pursue their aspirations. My role as a reference and instruction librarian enables this pursuit. I believe in the importance of fostering a culture of learning, developing cross-cultural understanding, and encouraging academic exploration beyond formal encounters. Along with pursuing job-related training dealing with copyright, information literacy, and online privacy, I recently completed a postgraduate degree in education and technology at FLACSO, the Latin American School of Social Sciences. This program offered a venue where I could reconnect with Latin American professionals and scholars from diverse fields facing similar issues in a classroom setting. I realized early on that assimilating did not mean giving up my heritage, and this remarkable program reinforced that awareness.

Proactively seeking initiatives to work with Spanish-speaking populations, whether they are elementary school students and their parents or university scholars from Central America or students from the modern languages department, these interactions continue to be empowering to both the serviced community and to me. I soon discovered it was not only about finding connections through my native language but also about making connections to returning adult learners from various countries and cultures who also face the insecurities of learning, again, in a second or third language. Being sensitive to their needs and open to embracing cultural differences often makes a positive impact for new, lifelong learners as they discover the library as an inviting place where differences are honored.

CONCLUDING REMARKS

Understanding the differences in the working environments, embracing challenges, and being conscious of how to use my strengths has helped me navigate diverse library settings and areas. The ease of integrating myself into diverse library settings here in the United States was partially due to being fluent in English, but more important I attribute this ease to my opportunities in multicultural and diverse environments.

The keys to enriching my career have been to remain flexible, continuously reexamine my professional values, adopt a spirit of lifelong learning, and be willing to take lateral and even downward positions if they ultimately allow me to gain a new set of capabilities in pursuit of my professional aspirations.

I believe there is no one right way to successfully navigate one's professional journey. As long as we continue to pursue the best in what we do, believe in the importance of libraries within society, and find ourselves passionate about our work, then we know the effort is worth it and we are in the right field.

NOTES

1. Lan Cao, Andreas Hirschi, and Jurgen Deller, "The Positive Effects of a Protean Career Attitude for Self-Initiated Expatriates: Cultural Adjustment as Mediator," *Career Development International* 18, no. 1 (2013): 57–58. Self-initiated expatriates are considered those individuals whose decision of relocating abroad for professional purposes is based on their own initiative, independent of any organizational assignment.

2. Donald T. Hall, "Long Live the Career," in *The Career Is Dead—Long Live the Career*, ed. Donald T. Hall et al. (San Francisco: Jossey-Bass, 1996), 1–12, quoted in Sherry E. Sullivan and Yehuda Baruch, "Advances in Career Theory and Research: A Critical Review and Agenda for Future Exploration," *Journal of Management* 35, no. 6 (2009): 1544–49, accessed November 18, 2015, doi:10.1177/0149206309350082. Sullivan and Baruch state that Hall defines *protean careerists* as those individuals whose career orientation is self-directed and values driven rather than organization driven. Moreover, these careerists remain marketable by

repackaging knowledge, skills, and abilities, much like the metaphor Hall refers to regarding the Greek god Proteus's ability to change shape at will.

3. "La Biblioteca Nacional Limita su Utilización: Sin Previo Aviso se Negó la Entrada a los Estudiantes con sus Libros," *La Nación*, February 15, 2000, www.lanacion.com.ar/5518-esta-vez-el-pais-eligio-los-libros; "La Política de Renovación de la Biblioteca Nacional: Qué Buscan los Funcionarios del Área Cultural," *Clarín*, February 15, 2000, http://edant.clarin.com/diario/2000/02/15/e-02906d.htm.

4. Eduardo Belgrano Rawson, *Noticias Secretas de América* (Buenos Aires: Planeta, 1998).

5. California State University, Dominguez Hills, "Campus Profile," California State University, Dominguez Hills, website, accessed November 18, 2015, www4.csudh.edu/ir/campusprofile/index.

REFERENCES

Belgrano Rawson, Eduardo. *Noticias Secretas de América*. Buenos Aires: Planeta, 1998.

Cao, Lan, Andreas Hirschi, and Jurgen Deller. "The Positive Effects of a Protean Career Attitude for Self-Initiated Expatriates: Cultural Adjustment as Mediator." *Career Development International* 18, no. 1 (2013): 57–58.

Clarín. "La Política de Renovación de la Biblioteca Nacional: Qué Buscan los Funcionarios del Área Cultural." February 15, 2000. http://edant.clarin.com/diario/ 2000/ 02/15/ e-02906d. htm.

Hall, Donald T. "Long Live the Career." In *The Career Is Dead—Long Live the Career*, edited by Donald T. Hall et al. San Francisco: Jossey-Bass, 1996.

La Nación. "La Biblioteca Nacional Limita su Utilización: Sin Previo Aviso se Negó la Entrada a los Estudiantes con sus Libros." February 15, 2000. www.lanacion.com.ar/5518-esta-vez-el-pais-eligio-los-libros.

Sullivan, Sherry E., and Yehuda Baruch. "Advances in Career Theory and Research: A Critical Review and Agenda for Future Exploration." *Journal of Management* 35, no. 6 (2009): 1544–49. Accessed November 18, 2015. doi:10.1177/0149206309350082.

II

From Academic to Specialized Librarianship

Chapter Nine

One MLIS Degree,
Many Career Possibilities

Sandra Hirsh

The truth is that I went to library school because I didn't know what else to do with my political science degree. Having grown up as the daughter of a famous librarian, I originally rejected the library profession in order to pursue my own path. But when I graduated with a BA in political science, my mom suggested that I pursue the MLIS degree. As she pointed out, even if I never worked as a librarian, the MLIS skills would be useful to me in any position.

Once I was in library school, I was hooked! The field of library and information science is fascinating. I was especially excited about all of the new developments in information technology. I attended the MLIS program at the University of Michigan, where I had the great fortune to be in their Library Associates program. The program focused on academic librarianship, and I began to consider a career as an academic library director. When I looked at job requirements, I noticed that many of the positions required a PhD. I decided to pursue one. No one was more surprised about this decision than I!

I pursued my doctoral studies at the University of California, Los Angeles (UCLA), where I worked on research projects focused on information-seeking behavior within various user groups. I loved my research work at UCLA, and I quickly got caught up in the scholarly culture of academia. So rather than seeking an academic library position after receiving my PhD, I decided instead to become a library and information science (LIS) assistant professor at the University of Arizona. I loved mentoring the next generation of librarians and would have been happy to continue that way for the long term. However, my husband, who had followed me to Los Angeles to pursue my doctoral degree and again to Tucson to pursue the faculty position, had completed his MBA while we were at the University of Arizona. He was recruited to Silicon Valley in 1998 to work at Hewlett-Packard (HP). It was my turn to follow his career and look for new opportunities in Silicon Valley.

Leveraging my personal network, I reached out to potential employers. My UCLA dissertation advisor, Christine Borgman, introduced me to Eugenie Prime, the director of the HP Labs Research Libraries. Eugenie asked me to write a white paper to describe the possibilities for a new opportunity she wanted to create for the library: a research arm that would work closely with research and development (R&D) scientists and engineers at HP Labs. I took a chance and wrote the white paper even though no position was available yet. Eugenie won buy-in from her management, which led to the creation of a new role. They hired me to run the new Information Research Program. I stayed for six years, one year beyond Eugenie's retirement.

As things changed at HP Labs, I felt I was ready for a change, too. Since my job was one of a kind, I was not sure what to do next. I did know that I wanted to engage in work that would benefit everyday people. I also wanted to find a job with a team-based work environment, a change from the solitary research work I had been doing. I made a list of the types of work I enjoyed and the skills I thought I possessed. I looked at job postings to see where there was overlap. I noticed that user experience researcher job postings matched many of my criteria, but they typically required degrees in human-computer interaction, human factors, or cognitive psychology, never the MLIS. I also noticed that most of the user experience researcher job postings asked for experience in the field, which I was able to demonstrate through work I did on projects like a redesign of HP Labs library's website.

I was thrilled when I was hired by Microsoft to work as a user experience researcher on their MSNTV product team. I was excited that my daily work helped consumers accomplish everyday tasks. Over the next several years, I held several roles in consumer product development, including user experience researcher for MSNTV, user experience manager for Hotmail and Windows Live Web Communications, and global user experience research manager for MSN.com.

After working at Microsoft's satellite campus in Silicon Valley for five and a half years, I was ready to take on new challenges. When I heard that the director of the School of Library and Information Science (iSchool) at San Jose State University (SJSU) was stepping down, I thought it might be the opportunity I was looking for. While I believed my background in industry could be valuable, I worried about how long it had been since I had worked in academia. I wondered if it mattered that I had never held an academic leadership position. As I waited to hear about the position, I was offered a great opportunity to build the user experience research team at LinkedIn. The position at LinkedIn appealed to me because it was a large start-up, it had local headquarters, and I was a strong believer in the LinkedIn product. Since I thought I was a long shot for the SJSU position, I accepted the offer to join LinkedIn.

Imagine my surprise when, shortly after I started working at LinkedIn, I was also offered the position at SJSU! I felt that the SJSU position was a once-in-a-lifetime opportunity, and I was excited about the possibility of helping to mentor the next generation of information professionals. A few months after starting at LinkedIn, I left to accept the SJSU position, which I have held since 2010.

My experience has taught me a great deal about what it is like to move between industries, and I would like to share some of what I have learned.

Establish a strong professional network. I personally have never received a job interview or offer based on submitting my résumé to a job application system. All of my job opportunities have come through networking. For example, when I was looking to move into user experience, I identified a local Bay Area computer-human interaction group (BayCHI) and attended one of their local events. By introducing myself, I ended up with two on-site interviews and ultimately one job offer to work at Microsoft in Silicon Valley as a user experience researcher on the MSNTV product team.

Understand the application process. I find the application process for user experience researcher positions rigorous. Some of the positions require prework, such as reviewing their company website and making recommendations or creating a usability testing plan. Sometimes employers ask that you bring in work examples or a portfolio. On the interview day, you typically meet with different members of the user experience team and product group. Some employers ask you to solve usability problems and/or test your knowledge of statistics during the interview. Sometimes they ask you to give a presentation during the interview. Be prepared to tell your own story. What makes you the strongest candidate? When I interviewed at Microsoft, the hiring manager said they normally hire people with human factors/usability backgrounds for user researcher positions and asked why she should hire someone with an MLIS degree. This is a question that you should be prepared to answer!

Find ways to reuse skills. I find that each position I have held, paid and volunteer, has provided valuable experience. When I was at Microsoft, I managed people who lived in different time zones and countries, and I learned how to work effectively in a virtual environment. I was able to apply this experience when I became the director of the SJSU iSchool. As a 100 percent online graduate program, our students and faculty live around the world in more than a dozen countries. Meanwhile, my volunteer role on the Palo Alto Library Advisory Commission taught me how to influence others and manage situations when people have vastly different ideas and conflicting opinions. These skills are useful for every position!

Leverage your skills. Here are a few examples of knowledge and skills I was able to draw on when I applied to and worked for Microsoft:

- **User-centered focus.** Librarians have a deep understanding about user behavior. We always bring a user-centered perspective to our work. My unique understanding of user behavior enhanced product team perspectives.
- **Knowledge organization.** We know how to organize content, how to make that content findable, and how to build knowledge taxonomies for users. This expertise informed recommendations for product enhancements that better aligned with user expectations and needs.
- **Reference interview.** We know how to listen to user needs and how to understand the underlying question. As a user experience researcher, conducting usability studies, interviews, and other user experience studies, these reference interview techniques came in handy.
- **Research training.** We rely on research skills to accomplish our work. My research training was a required part of working as a user experience researcher.

Share your story. You own your narrative! I learned this lesson early in my career while I was working on my PhD at UCLA. Christine Borgman, a UCLA faculty member and later my dissertation adviser, invited me to work on a research project focused on children's use of an online library catalog. I worried about being typecast as a children's or school librarian. I spoke to her at length about this before agreeing to work on her project, which then became the focus of my dissertation, and she assured me that I could tell my story however I wanted. I really took this lesson to heart and have used this principle throughout my career: always telling my story how I want it to be heard and told.

Identify your skill sets, passions, and interests. A skill set is the compilation of skills you have gained throughout your life—through your work experiences, education, extracurricular activities, and interpersonal relations. It is worth identifying the multitude of skills you possess and how they can be clustered together to create and identify new opportunities. Some of the questions you should ask yourself include: What are you good at? What do you like to do? What don't you like to do? What do you want to get better at? When making this list, specifically consider

- your strengths and weaknesses (emphasizing the strengths),
- skills you can leverage in a new job environment,
- past experiences that demonstrate your effective use of skills,
- other people's perspectives about your strengths and skills.

Develop leadership skills. Carol Sawyer identifies several ways that people can cultivate their leadership skills: by doing, learning from others, mentoring, discussing, reading, and reflecting.[1] Get involved in professional organizations and conferences—locally, regionally, nationally, and globally—to build effective leadership skills. Naomi House of INALJ (I Need a Library Job) has said that "joining associations adds value, not only through volunteer work and networking opportunities, but also through opportunities to build new skills and knowledge and learn about emerging trends in the field."[2]

Learn continuously. Getting an MLIS is only the first step in our learning journey as information professionals. Every day, new technology is introduced, more effective and efficient processes are developed, and new knowledge is created. We need to keep up. Learning continuously by reading professional literature, attending conferences, pursuing advanced certificates/degrees, completing workshops, and experimenting with new technologies is key. I myself am still learning every day. Every new project I take on sets the stage for greater opportunities in the future.

Mark Zuckerberg of Facebook is quoted as saying, "In a world that is changing really quickly, the only strategy guaranteed to fail is not taking risks."[3] Throughout your career, opportunities will arise that will push you to be far greater than you are today. Seek out those opportunities. Take them on. Take the risk of learning something new and trying a new role. The possibilities are endless.

ACKNOWLEDGMENT

I grew up in the field of library and information science, the daughter of a well-known librarian, Dr. Gail Schlachter. Her career path in the field of library and information science was fueled by a lifelong passion for reference services. While her focus was consistently on reference, she held varied roles in the field—as a reference librarian, an academic library manager focused on public services, a library school instructor teaching reference classes, a vice president of a publishing company that published reference materials (ABC-CLIO), a professional leader in the field of reference, an editor of *RQ* (*Reference Quarterly*, now known as *Reference and User Services Quarterly*), and an author of award-winning reference materials (financial aid directories) that she published for decades through her own publishing company, Reference Service Press. She was a great role model for me, and I am grateful for her contributions to the field, for her inspiration and mentoring, and for her demonstration of the varied roles that people with MLIS degrees can hold. Without her, I would never have pursued my career in library and information science. I am forever grateful to her.

58 *Sandra Hirsh*

NOTES

1. Carol Sawyer, "Leadership for Today and Tomorrow," in *Information Services Today: An Introduction*, ed. Sandra Hirsh (Lanham, MD: Rowman & Littlefield, 2015), 385.

2. Naomi House, "Career Management Strategies for Lifelong Success," in *Information Services Today: An Introduction*, ed. Sandra Hirsh (Lanham, MD: Rowman & Littlefield, 2015), 371.

3. Mark Zuckerberg, "Mark Zuckerberg Quotes," Inspiration Boost, accessed August 21, 2015, www.inspirationboost.com/mark-zuckerberg-quotes.

REFERENCES

House, Naomi. "Career Management Strategies for Lifelong Success." In *Information Services Today: An Introduction*, edited by Sandra Hirsh, 367–73. Lanham, MD: Rowman & Littlefield, 2015.

Sawyer, Carol. "Leadership for Today and Tomorrow." In *Information Services Today: An Introduction*, edited by Sandra Hirsh, 381–87. Lanham, MD: Rowman & Littlefield, 2015.

Chapter Ten

Going Govie

An Academic Librarian Joins the Civil Service

Deborah E. B. Keller

I have a confession to make . . . I never planned to be a librarian. I always thought that I would be a scientist. All through school, I loved science, especially chemistry and physics. When I got to college, majoring in chemistry seemed like a natural choice. But then I discovered that I really didn't enjoy working in the lab. Nonetheless, I persisted, knowing that a career as a scientist would be both stable and lucrative.

After college, I went on to graduate school, choosing to study pharmacology. I hoped one day to work in the pharmaceutical industry designing new drugs. I thought to myself if I could only get through graduate school and the first few years of my professional life, when lab work would be required, I could spend the majority of my career as a "desk chemist." I didn't know if this position actually existed, but the idea of it seemed appealing to me.

During the first year of graduate school, it became painfully clear that pharmacology was not a good fit for me. The classes that I was required to take were focused more on biology-related topics than on chemistry topics. Not only did I feel underprepared, I just wasn't as interested in what I was learning. In addition to taking classes, I also had to work in a lab. I was encouraged to try working in several labs before selecting the lab where I would spend the remainder of my graduate years conducting research. Again, among all of the research topics being studied in the labs, I could not find one that interested me enough to make me want to spend the rest of my graduate time—several years—dedicating myself to that topic. To make matters worse, I had difficulty connecting with my fellow graduate students. Many of them seemed to have no interests beyond science or school. I missed talking about politics, history, music, movies. I missed the diversity of my liberal arts undergraduate classmates, and I could not imagine a future without these interests in my friends and my daily life.

So I left pharmacology. At the time, I was a nervous wreck because I didn't have a plan for my life anymore. My mother, a reference librarian, made the following observation one day when I was stressed out: "You were the kid who always loved doing research. Have you considered going to library school?" Of course I hadn't. My mother became a librarian after years as an elementary school teacher, so it never occurred to me that the same career might satisfy two people with very different interests.

I didn't know much about the career opportunities for librarians when I went to library school. I had only seen school librarians, public librarians, and academic librarians. I have a naturally competitive streak, so I chose the path that seemed most challenging and prestigious among the options at my library school. I prepared for a career in academic libraries.

Since I didn't have a preformed plan or career objective, I allowed the library school curriculum requirements to guide my course selection. I tried to learn as broad a range of topics as possible, thinking that this would give me the greatest opportunity to find a job once I completed my degree. I took several cataloging classes, finding the detail, rules, and exactness a good fit for my personality. I took a variety of reference courses, figuring that there were more reference positions in existence than any other type of library job. I took a government documents course, having previously done research using government documents and been completely confused by them. I also took a class on the history of the printed book, indulging my interest in history to learn about typography, printing technology, and how books are assembled physically. Maybe that class wasn't as practical, but it seemed like every librarian should know about the Gutenberg Bible and the operation of a printing press.

My academic jobs were a tremendous learning experience for me. In the course of six years, I held three different positions. While my broad preparation in library school served me well, I also quickly learned that my diverse liberal arts background was attractive to employers, too. The first position that I accepted after finishing library school was part time in reference and part time in cataloging. I could not have imagined a better fit for myself. In reference, I was responsible for liaison relationships to six departments in the social sciences. Shortly after accepting the job, however, I learned that the science librarian was close to retirement and that many of his departments were no longer happy with his teaching. Part of my attraction as a candidate for the science librarian position that I applied for was my degree in chemistry, even though nothing to do with science ever "officially" became part of my job description.

At the same time, I was at a distinct disadvantage being so young. To be competitive as an academic librarian in most hiring actions and to be eligible for tenure at many institutions, librarians must have a second master's degree. Immediately after accepting this position, I started on a second master's degree. This time, I pursued history, my second undergraduate major and one of the larger departments in the social sciences group for which I had liaison responsibility.

As the "junior librarian" on the staff, I was given responsibility for many of the leftover tasks that the senior library faculty did not want. This included cataloging government documents, maps, and music CDs; weeding the main book collection; and website development. At the same time, they took advantage of my foreign-language capabilities to catalog a collection of music and history books. I realized that I was being given responsibilities that the others on the staff did not want. However, I welcomed the opportunity to learn things that were beyond what I had been taught in library school.

In my next position, this trend of leftover tasks continued. I cataloged a variety of nonbook materials—maps, curriculum materials, state and federal government documents, and music scores—as well as foreign-language books. I also took responsibility for updating the library's serials holdings in OCLC WorldCat's interlibrary loan module. As before, my broad preparation enabled me to learn quickly, taking on tasks that other librarians either didn't want to do or didn't have time to do.

I completed my second master's and took a new position, moving back to a reference and instruction role. Again I took on some of the undesirable and long-avoided tasks in the library—integrating the curriculum collection, designing a new website, and weeding the government documents collection and social sciences subjects within the main collection. It was a good, stable job at a liberal arts college whose reputation was on the rise. I was in high demand by the faculty as a guest instructor teaching library research skills. I should have been happy, knowing that positions in academic libraries were competitive. But I quickly realized that I was miserable.

In my first year on the job, everything was new and I was constantly learning. Each research skills class that I taught required planning and preparation on my part. Students came to the reference desk with questions that challenged my creative thinking and knowledge as a reference librarian. However, by the second year, I saw that teachers often assigned the same research paper assignments from one year to the next, making the research skills classes that I taught essentially same as well. The students often tried to check their e-mail during my research classes instead of working on the search examples, believing that they already had the research skills they needed. Rather than coming to the reference desk with questions that challenged me, I now found that many students came to the reference desk the night before their research paper was due. They wanted help from a librarian only because they had already spent hours searching the Internet and hadn't found enough source materials. I introduced them to the library's subscription databases. When full-text online articles were available, their stress would be relieved. However, when interlibrary loan was required, stress turned to panic, and sometimes it was directed at me.

As my second school year wore on, I came to dread going to work. I wanted to leave, but without another job to leave for, I felt financially trapped. I was finally pushed over the edge when I was told by two different students that I had to do their research for them because they paid my salary. I was so shocked by the sense of entitlement these students showed that I didn't know how to respond. After a lot of self-reflection, I decided that I would leave before the start of the next school year. I could not continue to work in a place where the students openly showed such disrespect for those trying to teach them and where faculty and administration would not uphold policies requiring students to follow the rules, thereby teaching the students that disrespect and ignoring the rules were both all right.

Like most people, I voiced my frustrations to my friends. One of them, a career army officer, was a student at the National Defense University, a graduate school for senior military officers and government civilians that focuses on policy issues surrounding defense and national security. He was impressed with the help he had received at the university's library and thought that with my background in history I would enjoy working there. I didn't know anything about working in government libraries but started looking into them.

One of the first things I learned was that most government jobs are advertised through a single website.[1] The site allowed me to search for librarian positions in several different ways, as well as specifying acceptable geographic locations and even agencies that I was interested in working for. I created a profile for myself and set up a recurring search that notified me of open library positions each week. The site also has a résumé template that allowed me to create and save my résumé in their standardized format. When I saw open positions that interested me, applying was often as easy as sending the résumé I had saved and answering a few questions about my experience and qualifications for that specific position.

As I started applying to government libraries, I realized that my opportunities were rather limited. I was married at the time, and my husband was a professor at a liberal arts college. I couldn't relocate in order to accept a new job. I could, realistically, only consider jobs that were near the college where my husband was teaching. Thankfully, there were two federal libraries nearby, and during the time that I was looking to transition, both were hiring librarians.

After several months, I accepted a position as a cataloging librarian at the Army Heritage and Education Center. This library and archive collects materials on the history of the army, its units, and its leaders. With a master's degree in history, years of experience teaching research skills to history students, and somewhat of a specialty cataloging government documents, I could not have asked for a better fit for my skills and experience in my first job as a government librarian.

Looking back, I realize that my transition from academic librarian to government librarian was smooth and very easy. My biggest complaint, if I have any at all, is the time that the application process took. Months went by from the time I submitted my application to the time I was called for an interview and then subsequently hired. For much of that time, I heard absolutely nothing. I didn't know if my application had been accepted, if someone else had been hired, if the vacancy had been canceled, or if I still had a chance at the jobs. As I've applied for other positions within the government, I have come to recognize this as fairly standard. For someone unfamiliar with the government application process, however, the slow process and lack of communication can be both scary and off-putting.

One piece of advice that is often given about getting a government job is "just get your foot in the door. It is easier to move around once you are a federal employee." I have found this to be true myself. Many job advertisements that I see are limited to "current federal employees only." Some are limited even further than that—to employees of a specific agency, career series, or geographic area. Sometimes these limitations seem advantageous. Other times they disqualify me from a job that I would otherwise be interested in applying for.

The federal government also requires that its employees have at least a year of experience at one career level before they can advance to the next level. This system is intended to provide employees with jobs of increasing levels of difficulty and responsibility, corresponding with increasing pay. Despite all attempts to standardize positions of the same difficulty and responsibility at the same career level, differences do exist between agencies and geographic locations. This is also frustrating, both to those new to government work as well as to experienced government employees.

I've had two government jobs since my first one and have spent more than ten years as a government librarian. Just like the positions early in my career, my undergraduate chemistry degree, second master's degree, and the diverse range of professional skills that I've developed have been attractive to my employers. I'm a generalist, but I understand science and have made sure to keep up with the technology affecting our profession. Throughout my career, I've worked on both sides of the public services–technical services divide, and I bring both perspectives into projects that I work on. Most government libraries are small, so my broad educational background and wide range of skills and experience are put to use on a regular basis. There are, of course, government libraries where specialists in medical disciplines or law would be welcomed. However, being a generalist allows me more career flexibility. I can change jobs or even change agencies when I need a new challenge.

I've learned many valuable lessons working as a government librarian. One of the most important ones to me is that my customers—busy professionals—love libraries and librarians. After leaving the academic world because of ungrateful college students, I am thrilled to know how much my customers appreciate and value the work that I do for them. I receive wonderful thank-you notes, pictures of their events, copies of documents in which my research has been incorporated, and even the credit of shared authorship. As one professional to another, my colleagues and customers recognize me as a subject-matter expert on the topic of research and regularly ask me to teach classes on this topic. Marketing the library is still important, however. Many employees simply don't know that the agency has a library, especially since it may be virtual or may not be located in the same building where they work. Once they find us, however, happy customers are often helpful sources of word-of-mouth marketing.

In order for librarians to advance through the ranks in the government, I've learned that it is important for them to understand how their agency functions—its missions, priorities, and methods. It is also helpful to have a broader understanding of the government context in which the agency operates. Many successful employees follow congressional activity, focusing on those issues, hearings, and proposed legislation relevant to the agency where they work. In recent years, congressional appropriations bills, agency budgets, and changing acquisitions processes have affected all aspects of government work. Whether or not federal employees face another government shutdown, as they did in 2013, because appropriations bills are not passed before the end of the fiscal year, agencies and employees as individuals are being asked to take on more responsibility with less funding and fewer personnel to accomplish their mission. Those who are able to see the "big picture" and where they fit into it, and with the skills and experience to adapt, take on new responsibilities, and "step into the white space" are the ones who will be the most successful and most comfortable in the current government environment.

It will come as no surprise that the government is very hierarchical. As a librarian in the government, it is essential to develop the skill of "managing up." Because government libraries are small, it is likely that either your boss or your boss's boss will not be a librarian. This means that they don't understand library jargon and likely do not fully understand the services offered by the library or the contributions that the library can make to the organization. You must learn to explain the activities and value of the library in nonlibrary terms, perhaps learning to speak in the "language" that your boss uses. You also need to be persuasive, convincing your boss why your priorities for the library are also in your boss's best interest. This is because he or she must be the one to advance these priorities for you in meetings that you have not been invited to attend.

Like other areas of the library and information services profession, working in the government sector has some unique challenges: shrinking library footprints, positions remaining unfilled, restrictions on technology, security requirements, being accountable to Congress and the president, and probably others. However, it is also a rewarding environment to work in, where the problems that the library helps to address are often the same as those discussed in the national news, in political speeches, and in congressional debates. Employees also ask for help with practical problems such as locating policies, addressing human resources questions, or looking for information necessary to complete job tasks. I enjoy the variety of responsibilities that I have working as part of a small staff. I also find that the sometimes-restrictive operating environment simply forces me to be more creative in order to accomplish my goals and provide necessary resources and services to my customers. I finally found my place in a government library.

NOTE

1. USA Jobs website, accessed on July 29, 2015, www.usajobs.com.

Chapter Eleven

Ten Simple Tips for Managing Your Career

Reflections on an Evolving Career from a
Restless Librarian

Carrie Netzer Wajda

If I had one message for the newly graduating MLS student or for the midcareer professional, it is that linear career progression is overrated. There are many paths along the winding maze to career satisfaction and success. What satisfies you at one point in your life may change. The skills you learn in school will carry you into the beginning of a career, but it is how you continue to develop and learn over time that will open new doors and windows throughout your career.

Somewhat by accident, my career has zigzagged through different types of libraries and many different roles. Along the way I have learned just as much by doing jobs that bored me to tears as I have from the jobs that I've loved. In my experience, the people you work with are more important than the specific job details. To borrow career advice that Sheryl Sandberg received from her mentor, Larry Summers, "I tell people in their careers, 'look for growth.' Look for the teams that are growing quickly. Look for the companies that are doing well. Look for a place where you feel that you can have a lot of impact."[1] If you work with stimulating, energetic, and thoughtful colleagues, you will be much more likely to weather the ups and downs of any job. This philosophy holds true for nonprofit organizations, public libraries, and academia. No employer has a monopoly on creating a great place to work.

My career has evolved in a series of fits and starts, with several detours down some fascinating side roads. Along the way, I have learned quite a bit about what works and what doesn't in the workplace. I offer my story as context for insights to help others understand and navigate their own career arcs. Each tip is something has become clear in hindsight. Few of these lessons were obvious at the time. I hope that this collection of tips will be inspiring guidance to anyone who is at a turning point in his or her library career, whether you are a recent graduate student searching for that first job, a midcareer professional facing burnout, or a senior librarian facing an unanticipated career change. Take what is helpful and know that you are not alone in facing career challenges.

TIP #1: BE PERSISTENT (BUT NOT OBNOXIOUS) IN GOING AFTER WHAT YOU WANT

A few weeks shy of my nineteenth birthday, I walked into my college library armed with work-study funding and a determination to get a job handling books. The library director was not impressed with my punk-rock aesthetic and tried to turn me down. The rules, however, were that work-study students had priority for campus jobs. I kept calling to inquire—politely—about any openings. I suspect that the library director bumped my name down the list a few times, but eventually I was the last one standing and my persistence won her over. I worked at the campus library for the next four years, including summers. I don't think either of us realized at the time that I was embarking on a career.

Eighteen years and two master's degrees later, I have worked in almost every kind of library there is: academic libraries, museums, law libraries, and corporate libraries. I have worked for vendors, although I have not worked in public or school libraries. (Life is long. There is time yet.) I have been happily employed with Y&R Advertising since 2011.

Had anyone told me back in college that I would end up in advertising, I would have laughed out loud. At the same time, it makes perfect sense. The antiestablishment aesthetics of my youth have given way to a professionalism that thrives in the creative sphere; I have found my tribe, for now, and now I dress to enhance my employment prospects rather than to tank them.

I started off in a part-time knowledge management role with Global New Business. Since then, I have branched into a dual role with the company's competitive intelligence group, providing integrated custom internal and external research services to support Y&R's 189 global offices in pitching new business. The pertinent thing is that getting the Y&R job required a similar degree of perseverance. It's never too late to start practicing going after what you want, even if you're not sure what that might be in the long term.

TIP #2: EMBRACE FLEXIBILITY AND FIRMNESS

I embarked on my library degree with the determination to get a tenure-track job with a university library. I wanted to immerse myself in research. I wanted to publish important articles and papers. Summers off with research leave and the prospect of permanent employment sounded pretty great, too.

I had been working in libraries in a paraprofessional capacity since graduating from college, minus a stint teaching English in France. I had considerably more experience than the average MLS student, and with workplace experience I found much of the academic content easy to grasp. I flew through the program, focusing my interests on coursework that tilted toward the theoretical.

In the interest of gaining that longed-for academic job, I duly obtained a series of part-time, entry-level jobs and unpaid internships. I learned a lot on these jobs, although not what I had expected to be learning. For example, I learned a lot about individual organizational quirks, hierarchies both real and imagined, about the difference between rigorous thinking and letting rigor mortis set in, and about leadership. Most important, I learned what kind of work environments I thrived in and what kinds I didn't.

Upon receiving my MLIS degree, I was unprepared for the number of prospective employers who glanced at the date of my degree and disregarded my experience, which was getting pretty substantive by that point. I went on interview after interview, but I could not land a job. It was totally demoralizing. Part of it was being in a highly competitive environment in New York City. A lot of it was simply ageism. After all, I had landed jobs easily without the degree, including professional-level roles. I began to wonder if I hadn't made a big mistake in going to library school.

Eventually I found a job with a vendor, the kind of role that newly minted librarians typically get to obtain some degree of library experience. It also paid less than I had made as a library paraprofessional. The experience was a real blow to my ego. I accepted the job because I didn't want a gaping hole on my résumé and continued my search. I convinced myself that I wasn't getting jobs because I didn't have a second master's degree. Thus I quickly found myself working full-time and enrolled in a subject master's degree program.

TIP #3: BELIEVE IN YOURSELF

When I finally landed my first full-time professional reference librarian job in an academic library, I thought I had finally made it. It seemed a natural fit, enrolled as I was at Hunter College to earn an MA in British and American literature. The second degree seemed required in order to take the next step in my career arc toward that coveted tenure-track job.

It soon became clear that morale was low in my new job. My enthusiasm was quickly tempered by reality. Within the year, I was miserable in my "dream job" and back on the job market. Then the economy crashed, and job openings dried up faster than you could say "housing bust."

I stuck it out for another year as the work situation deteriorated and finally jumped at the first offer that came along. Bonus tip: this is a perfect example of what *not* to do in a job search. The fit was far from ideal. The work was the librarian equivalent of slinging burgers at a fast-food restaurant, a far cry from the immersive research experience I had longed for. On the upside, I had the full support of the administration to acquire and apply new skills, including creating instructional videos for the web and rigorous assessment criteria.

Even though I was only marginally happier in my new job, it gave me enough space to figure out what I wanted out of my career. It was becoming clear to me that the jobs in academic librarianship typically did not offer the kind of employment experience that I had expected and wanted. I used this time to dig deep and explore career areas that I would never have previously considered. I knew that to be happy in my career, I needed to find that intersection between what interested me, what I was good at, and where prospective employers saw value.

TIP #4: GET INVOLVED AND GIVE BACK

I had joined the Association of College and Research Libraries, Greater Metropolitan New York Chapter (ACRL/NY), which was among one of the best moves I ever made. Through ACRL/NY I networked with many top-notch librarians working at every kind of academic institution throughout the New York metropolitan area.

As we worked together on conference planning, new initiatives, and websites, I was finding that virtually no one in the group had the kind of job I wanted. Even the few who did often complained about the lack of leadership or initiative within their organizations.

By now I was truly floundering in my academic librarianship career. I saw little opportunity for growth within the profession. If I was determined to remain in academia, I saw many years of teaching endless bibliographic instruction courses—and as a card-carrying introvert who is easily bored, this was not my forte. I had nearly completed my subject master's degree program, but while I loved the subject matter, I could no longer see any connection to my career. It was a satisfying outlet for my desire to do research and writing, but that would end with graduation in a few months. While I loved working with ACRL/NY, I was also longing for a different direction in my career.

TIP #5: KEEP LEARNING

As a librarian at a business-focused college, I was also learning that I liked the variety, the fast pace, and the immediacy of the business world. Without having a very good idea of what I was doing, I began taking freelance gigs on the side. I wrote press releases, researched and wrote reports, and conducted secondary market research.

I loved it. Shortly thereafter, I decided to leave my job and work as a freelancer. Within one year I had a roster of regular clients and had nearly equaled my employed salary, with significantly more control over my schedule. ACRL/NY was an invaluable source of support during this transition.

But it wasn't all bliss. There were difficult clients, irregular income, and all of the usual difficulties that accompany being a small business. It gave me appreciation for running a business and the difficulty of succeeding as an entrepreneur. I had a safety net in the form of a husband whose income was sufficient to cover our expenses, so in many respects it was a luxury to be able to do this. Without that fallback, it would have been much harder to take the risk. However, I can attest that it is absolutely possible to make a living as a freelance librarian. Anyone who is interested in the idea should connect with the Association of Independent Information Professionals (AIIP).

TIP #6: EXPECT ROAD BUMPS, U-TURNS, AND POTHOLES IN YOUR CAREER PATH

In 2010, not long after starting my business, I was pregnant. Suddenly, financial stability became paramount. Irregular income wasn't going to cut it anymore.

Three weeks after my daughter was born, I returned to taking on clients. In my network of self-employed colleagues (Brooklyn is a hotbed of women-led entrepreneurs, according to Crunch Base in 2015), I have yet to meet a self-employed mother who has taken more than six weeks after the birth of a child before returning to her work. Two or three weeks is not unusual, and it is not enough time.

Client deadlines and baby deadlines inevitably clashed. I found myself longing for the stability of a job and yet loath to give up my small business. A potential solution came along when I found a posting for a part-time knowledge manager with an advertising agency, Y&R. I still remember the feeling of excitement as I read the job description. The requirements matched my skill set almost exactly, although I had never worked in advertising before.

I applied very thoughtfully and was invited for an interview. The environment was dynamic and fast paced, everything I liked about being self-employed. The people were impressive and capable.

I was not offered the job.

Although I was crushed, I nonetheless leaped at a follow-up chance to do freelance work with the new business team. I doubled down on my small business, determined to find a solution that worked for my family. A few months into the freelance project, I received a phone call.

The selected candidate had not worked out. Was I still interested? I jumped at the opportunity and remain with my employer, Y&R Advertising, four years later.

TIP #7: GATHER NO MOSS

Employers want to hire the people who are doing the work they need done now. Yet sometimes they can overlook the importance of cultural fit. When I was hired for my "dream job" that didn't work out, I looked like a great candidate on paper and they looked like the perfect employer for me. There was no way for me or for my employer to know in advance that it was not going to be a good cultural fit.

The interview process is not designed well enough to do more than identify candidates that meet specified qualifications. Yet the interpersonal skills that make a successful match are critical. Some hiring managers understand that and are skilled at probing to find the right candidates. Others are excellent at working to get the best performance possible out of their teams despite interpersonal differences. Sadly, many managers are promoted without ever acquiring these critically important skills.

I walked into my first knowledge management job at Y&R with very little relevant work experience. This is what had led the team to select the other candidate. While I had related experience and was able to articulate why my transferable skills were relevant to the position, I wasn't already doing that kind of work.

What I did bring to the job, and why I have been there for four years, is an entrepreneurial approach that has proved advantageous to working in a very large global organization.

I also learned everything I could about knowledge management practices and applied those insights as rigorously and as creatively as possible in a fast-changing landscape. Under the guidance of executive stakeholders, I set about learning about our company, its history, its geographic footprint, and key leadership—all of the details that are crucial for understanding the context in which knowledge is produced and disseminated. The ability to get things done in a large organization operating in over ninety countries and my ability to build relationships in a virtual environment proved to be just as valuable to my employer as formal knowledge management capabilities. I was fortunate to work with top-notch leaders who knew how to manage change within an organization that had at times struggled.

TIP #8: APPRECIATE OTHERS, EVEN WHEN THEY SAY THINGS THAT YOU DON'T WANT TO HEAR

Conflict is hard for me. Looking back over my career, there are times when I wish I had read the book *Getting to Yes: Negotiating Agreement without Giving In*, by Roger Fisher and colleagues, years ago. My boss's wise observation that I was conflict-averse prompted me to start addressing the problem.

There are times when you must stand up for your work or ideas. It is really hard to do this without being called inflexible or rude, particularly when you are working in institutions that are struggling or clinging to a certain way of doing things. Learning how to manage conflict in search of the most productive outcome is the most important workplace skill, and one that few programs teach. It is an acquirable skill set—but generally you have to learn it outside of library school. It takes a great deal of practice, and I have by no means mastered the art yet.

On a personal level, it hurts when you have invested a great deal in a project or idea and someone questions its validity, practicality, or efficacy. But those are important questions to raise in any project. Learning to separate personal criticism and evaluate it critically enables you to defend your work against feedback that is negative for the sake of being negative.

I have found that reading up on negotiation and conflict management are worth the invested time and effort. We all have areas to improve. Identifying your "opportunity areas" may be as simple as actively listening to your biggest workplace detractors. You don't have to start liking them. But you have nothing to lose by listening.

TIP #9: STAY CREATIVE AND FRESH

Recently, I moved into a full-time role blended across two departments at Y&R. While I am busier, I am now able to confine work to slightly more traditional hours. This has enabled me to return to my initial passion—research and writing—in a new way.

While I enjoy the research and writing I do for work, I am now able to actively pursue a completely new and different side career: writing fiction. It is, of course, highly unlikely that I will ever be able to replace my day job with a writing career. And I am not even certain that I would want to if the opportunity presented itself, having already been down the path of self-employment.

Taking that time—even if it is fifteen minutes of thumb typing on the subway into work in the morning—to connect with my creativity helps me to focus on my job. You can't bring fresh ideas when you are fresh out of creativity. Nurture the wellspring in the way that is meaningful to you. One of my colleagues became a certified yoga instructor and led a summer series of donation-based yoga classes to raise money for charity. She loved it so much that she is leaving us to teach yoga in Costa Rica. Others teach classes on aromatherapy or do astrological readings. Find your passions and nurture them, even if they lead you to places you thought you would never go.

TIP #10: EMBRACE OPTIMISM (TEMPERED WITH REALISM)

The news media, including the *Harvard Business Review*,[2] the *Atlantic*,[3] and others, report that robots are increasingly replacing human labor, including previously safe white-collar work. Some sources estimate that almost half of U.S. jobs will be replaced within twenty years.[4]

Even without a robot invasion, the Bureau of Labor Statistics (BLS)[5] predicts just 7 percent growth in librarian jobs over ten years (2012–2022). That's not very much growth. The BLS concedes that it can be very difficult for librarians to find work in the first decade of their careers. Optimistically, the BLS also predicts that the need for librarians will grow faster later in the decade. I am not sure I agree with that analysis.

What I do know is how easy it is to feel overwhelmed by dismal predictions when you are in that tough first decade of your career. None of these sources has a crystal ball, and their predictions may or may not come to pass. What will carry you through the troubled times is embracing your unique, creative approach to solving problems. Use the skills that you have acquired in your library school training in new ways and look for problems to solve. We do not know what the libraries of the future will look like, but we cannot take part in shaping them by conceding defeat.

Closer to home, in the past eight months or so, I have observed multiple examples of mid- and late-career women being pushed out of their jobs. While none of them were librarians, collectively they offer an example of what can happen easily in this era of relentless budget cutting, downsizing, and fierce competition. I am inspired by their different responses to similar major career setbacks.

One woman decided she was close enough to retirement to spin out the next year or two on a combination of savings, severance, unemployment income, and eventually a part-time job. She had been through round after round of layoffs and was disillusioned with her entire industry. This woman is thrilled to be semiretired and wants to find just the right part-time role. It's going to be her career capstone, and she intends to enjoy it.

Another woman fought the good fight and is back with the company in a new role more closely aligned with her personal values. The extraordinarily difficult few months she endured eventually allowed her to shed the parts of her job that she didn't enjoy and had little control over; she, too, is happy, for now.

A third woman has taken the long view toward assessing her personal strengths and is navigating her way into a completely new career path. It is hard work, but I have no doubt that she has identified the area where she will provide tremendous value and will be completely successful once she gets there. I am inspired by all of these women's approaches to the mid-to-late stages of their careers. Given their experiences, I am reminded that having backup plans for my backup plans is prudent in order to allow for the greatest maximum flexibility in the future.

On a final, optimistic note, I meet librarians working in nontraditional capacities on a regular basis. The need for people who have the ability to find, organize, and analyze information is not going to blow away in the wind, although we may have to find new venues and ways to employ our skills.

I have no doubt that in ten years I will be doing something very different from what I am doing now. I cannot imagine what that future will look like. But I trust that it will be just as stimulating and interesting as the first ten years have been. If I am in fact replaced by a robot or shown the door at my job, I will refocus on the areas that interest me most, whether that is writing fiction or something I haven't thought of yet. If I have learned one thing from my restless career ramble, it is that the path to career success lies in staying true to my interests, both now and in the future. I hope and trust that you will find your path, too, wherever it may lead.

NOTES

1. Elizabeth Vargas, Elizabeth Stuart, and Susanna Kim, "Best Advice Sheryl Sandberg Received: If Offered a Seat on Rocket Ship, Get On," Yahoo, March 11, 2013, accessed September 9, 2015, http://news.yahoo.com/blogs/newsmakers/best-advice-sheryl-sandberg-received-don-t-idiot-161459450.html?soc_src=copy.

2. William H. Davidow and Michael S. Malone, "What Happens to Society When Robots Replace Workers?" *Harvard Business Review*, December 10, 2014, accessed September 9, 2015, https://hbr.org/2014/12/what-happens-to-society-when-robots-replace-workers.

3. Derek Thompson, "A World without Work," *Atlantic*, July/August 2015, accessed September 9, 2015, www.theatlantic.com/magazine/archive/2015/07/world-without-work/395294.

4. Jeff Ward-Bailey, "If Robots Replace Half of US Workers, What Role Will Humans Play?" *Christian Science Monitor*, May 28, 2015, accessed September 9, 2015, www.

csmonitor.com/Technology/2015/0528/If-robots-replace-half-of-US-workers-what-role-will-humans-play.

    5. Bureau of Labor Statistics, U.S. Department of Labor, "Librarians," in *Occupational Outlook Handbook, 2016–17 Edition*, accessed September 9, 2015, www.bls.gov/ooh/education-training-and-library/librarians.htm.

REFERENCES

Bureau of Labor Statistics, U.S. Department of Labor. "Librarians." In *Occupational Outlook Handbook, 2016–17 Edition*. Accessed September 9, 2015. www.bls.gov/ooh/education-training-and-library/librarians.htm.
Davidow, William H., and Michael S. Malone. "What Happens to Society When Robots Replace Workers?" *Harvard Business Review*, December 10, 2014. Accessed September 9, 2015. https://hbr.org/2014/12/what-happens-to-society-when-robots-replace-workers.
Thompson, Derek. "A World without Work." *Atlantic*, July/August 2015. Accessed September 9, 2015. www.theatlantic.com/magazine/archive/2015/07/world-without-work/395294.
Vargas, Elizabeth, Elizabeth Stuart, and Susanna Kim. "Best Advice Sheryl Sandberg Received: If Offered a Seat on Rocket Ship, Get On." Yahoo, March 11, 2013. Accessed September 9, 2015. http://news.yahoo.com/blogs/newsmakers/best-advice-sheryl-sandberg-received-don-t-idiot-161459450.html?soc_src=copy.
Ward-Bailey, Jeff. "If Robots Replace Half of US Workers, What Role Will Humans Play?" *Christian Science Monitor*, May 28, 2015. Accessed September 9, 2015. www.csmonitor.com/Technology/2015/0528/If-robots-replace-half-of-US-workers-what-role-will-humans-play.

III

From Specialized to Public Librarianship

Chapter Twelve

How Being an Untraditional Librarian Allowed for a Library Career in the Arts

Kara West

Not everyone with a master's in library and information science becomes a librarian—I didn't. At least, not at first. For just shy of two years now— several years outside of earning my degree—I have held the position of library arts and culture exhibition manager at the San Diego Public Library. Prior to that, I spent six and half years as the assistant director for the Balboa Art Conservation Center (BACC), a private nonprofit regional art conservation center. Strictly speaking, it was not a library job; however, it was instrumental in helping me acquire many of the skills necessary for the position I hold today.

My decision to major in art history as an undergraduate was fraught with doubt. So much so that, while at the University of California at Santa Cruz (UC Santa Cruz), I narrowly survived economics, drop/failed a computer science course on C++ programing, and considered taking a year off, all in an effort to embark on a "practical" career path. I eventually came to terms with my failures and assessed the coursework I was enjoying. When I told my father that I was excelling in art history courses, he encouraged me, with the caveat that while an undergraduate in the liberal arts was a useful education, my graduate degree would define my career path. He was right, of course, but that path has not been straightforward.

Years later, while managing a relocation and adapting to a new job as a mother, I started seriously considering graduate school options. Armed with a variety of museum and gallery experience, I began to seek out museum studies programs. My "ever the practical" mentality set in, and eventually my research segued into library and information science. A light bulb went on. I had spent over half of my college years at UC Santa Cruz working at the reserves desk of the McHenry Library. I loved it. I loved having access to information; I loved the job satisfaction of helping people access information; and I loved supporting curricula. It follows that I was good at it, even though I had been so wrapped up in obsessing about the right major that I didn't notice how much I loved my library job. Hindsight is always twenty-twenty. By the time I was in my midtwenties and ready to start graduate school, I had the wisdom that came with a few less-than-inspiring jobs.

Between working part- to full-time and raising a young son, it took me three years to complete my MLIS. I had a wonderfully flexible job as the registrar at BACC for those three years. The job kept me connected to collecting institutions and the arts and helped me develop records and project management skills. While I wasn't working in a library, I was using what I was learning in school in very real applications at the conservation center: database design, controlled vocabularies, responding to technical inquiries, literature searches, and the ever-important customer service. Eager to "start my career," I left the center shortly after obtaining my degree to take an archival internship at pharmaceutical company and then a curatorial/archivist position at a local historical society.

Almost a year later and stuck with only short-term or part-time work, the executive director of BACC asked if I would be interested in returning to the center as the assistant director for operations and field services. In this capacity, I was told, I would be charged with assisting with the day-to-day operations of the nonprofit, managing the Western Region Field Service Program, and supporting preservation efforts at collection-based institutions throughout BACC's four-state region.[1] These responsibilities had previously been held by an art conservator, but the director explained that the preservation management skills I had learned in graduate school would be an asset in the newly developed position.

It didn't take me long to accept the job. No one seemed to be hiring in that first year out of school. I had the degree, but "librarian" wasn't a title that anyone seemed to be looking to fill. I believed in the work that BACC was doing, and I knew that I could continue to apply the skills I had learned in school to the position. My project management skills were used in developing and coordinating workshops on basic preservation theory and practice. I helped support the conservators' produce preservation planning surveys, and I was often the first step and last step in reference and technical inquiry response services. Everything I did was in consultation with the conservators, the true subject specialists and some of the smartest, creative, most dedicated individuals I have ever had the pleasure of working with.

I also learned a great deal of non–MLIS-related skills in those six and a half years, including things like nonprofit governance, grant writing, and grant reporting. I also had opportunities to travel, speak, and teach at state and regional museum conferences, and I contributed to state steering committees and conference program committees.

In late 2012, however, I started thinking about my next step, especially since the position I was in had little room for advancement. As much as I valued my MLIS skill set, I felt further away than ever from the librarian profession, and I worried that the gap would only get wider.

As 2013 began, I made a resolution: I was going to open myself up to new opportunities. In those first months of "being open," I considered pursuing a new career direction in public art administration. I had the project management skills and I understood the stakeholders, but I wasn't keen on moving, and all the opportunities I saw were out of state. When the San Diego Public Library (SDPL) opened an application for librarian I positions, I thought, why not? I am open to new opportunities.

Shortly after I applied, I heard a rumor that SDPL was looking for a new curator, someone who would have the unique responsibly of administering their visual arts program. I was both amazed and anxious when I was asked to interview for the librarian I position but was shocked when many of my questions were arts- and exhibition-related. Once I realized I was a candidate for the curator position, there wasn't much more to do but wait and watch while the city prepared to open the new Central Library. It's worth being perfectly clear: transitions can take a long time. No individual has complete control. From my position, it seemed like the hiring process stood still while this amazing new facility was readied for its debut. While I waited in hopes of a second interview, I filled my time by researching and benchmarking similar library exhibition programs, of which there are not many. I looked to neighboring professions, specifically university and municipal galleries. I combed through the SDPL website for mission- and strategic-planning information, trying my best to understand the values of the library, as well as the history of the visual arts program.

I was hired as the library arts and culture exhibition manager shortly after the new Central Library opened to the public. While the library previously had a curator, my position had been designed as something different. I manage a dedicated two-thousand-square-foot gallery at the Central Library, where I curate a few shows a year, bring in guest curators, and help build the capacity for community gallery spaces within many of our thirty-five branch libraries. I work closely with the Commission for Arts and Culture, another city department that manages our public art program.

Two years later, as I write this, I feel like I am still in transition, learning new things each day. Maybe this is what keeps me in this place between libraries and museums. I have always been fascinated by middle space. In the undergraduate art history degree that I worried so much about, my senior thesis was on the idea of Nepantla and Chicano identity. *Nepantla* is a Nahuatl word for an in-between state, that uncertain terrain in crossing from one place to another. Victor Turner similarly wrote of liminaries—they evade ordinary classification, for they are not this or that, here or there, one thing or the other.[2] These things taught me that transitions allow opportunity for liminal space; while liminality can be disorientating, it is also full of potential.

Being in a career transition, in a between space, is uncomfortable. Pursuing a new job takes courage and patience. The desire for better pay and the potential for career advancement are strong motivators, but opening oneself to new opportunities is not going to happen without the courage to embrace change. It takes courage to put yourself out there, to believe your ambitions can lead to something new, and ultimately to embark on new challenges and responsibilities. Patience is required both to find jobs that match your aspirations and to navigate the often-lengthy application and interview process. Couple that courage with the waiting and you have a combination that makes most job seekers extremely anxious. I found the courage to embrace change when I felt my career projection had stagnated, but finding the patience to sustain me through the search and interview process was much more challenging. I approached the job seeking as a second job in itself. I didn't apply for jobs without doing a lot of research; I spent a lot of time and attention on applications; and if I made it to the interview process, I stepped up my research, expanding it to include benchmarking and studying up on interview techniques. Rather than try and distract myself from the waiting, I immersed myself in being proactive.

Speaking specifically to the hybrid library/museum professional, one of the remarkable characteristics of the professions is the interdisciplinary nature of both. I believe that my resistance to become highly specialized allowed me to gain the skills I needed for my current position. From reference to research, customer service to interpretation, collections management to curation, project management to risk management, I picked up skills from every single internship, job, or professional development opportunity. The term *silo* is a metaphor suggesting a similarity between grain silos, which segregate one type of grain from another, and the segregated parts of an organization. Beyond our organization, I would argue that we have silos in our professions. There is a lot that we can learn from our colleagues, other like-minded professions, and potential allies. Sometimes I feel like I have an algebraic formula running in my head. When I meet someone who is outside my silo, I try to figure out what our common denominator is. What do we have in common, and what can we learn from each other? How can we help each other?

Museums and libraries are part of a shared-learning ecosystem, as we work to integrate information, art, and heritage into a vibrant learning grid. We provide our communities with centers for exploration. This belief has helped with my transition from museum services to public library, as has following my father's advice—he was almost right: my graduate degree defined my path, but what I have discovered is the path is anything but narrow.

NOTES

1. "Balboa Art Conservation Center," Balboa Art Conservation Center, accessed July 30, 2015. http://www.bacc.org/

2. Victor Turner, *Blazing the Trail: Way Marks in the Exploration of Symbols*, ed. Edith Turner (Tucson: University of Arizona Press, 1992), 48.

REFERENCES

Turner, Victor. *Blazing the Trail: Way Marks in the Exploration of Symbols*. Edited by Edith Turner. Tucson: University of Arizona Press, 1992.

Wallace, D. P., ed. *Library and Information Science Education Statistical Report 2012*. Chicago: Association for Library and Information Science Education, 2012.

Chapter Thirteen

Setting Up Shop

From Business to Public with a Little Entrepreneurship in Between, an Interview with Lorene Kennard

Davis: Thank you for sharing your thoughts with me, Lorene! What fascinates me about your career is that you moved from a business setting at a financial firm to, ultimately, a public library. Tell us a bit more about your journey between these two roles.

Lorene: I went to library school so I could work in a public library. Like many librarians, I had wanted to be a librarian since I was little. When I went to college, there were still a few undergraduate library programs around, including at Illinois State University, where I was a student. After my first year at ISU, the school discontinued the program. As I had not taken any classes in the major yet, I had to figure out a new major. I was always a good reader and writer, so communications, specifically public relations, became my major. I minored in English.

After graduation, I worked at MetLife. The job technically had nothing to do with my major, but management knew about my degree and asked me to start a newsletter for the two-hundred-plus people in the department. So I was able to use my PR skills on my first job out of college. I moved around MetLife for seven years and decided to go to graduate school and finally get that library degree.

While working on a project on art libraries, I contacted Carolyn McClendon. Carolyn had graduated a few years ahead of me at the University of South Carolina and was working as the feature animation librarian at Walt Disney World. I interviewed her for my project, and we kept in touch. Carolyn has been a great mentor. Later that same year, she called me about an

internship in the advertising and marketing library at Disney. I was selected
and worked for a semester cataloging and researching videos. I started my
job search while I was working in that corporate library and decided to look
for jobs in corporate and public libraries. I ended up receiving job offers from
both types of libraries and accepted the offer from Morningstar.

Morningstar is very entrepreneurial. I found out that I loved being creative and entrepreneurial in building my library and providing services to my
coworkers. I worked at Morningstar for eight years and decided to be even
more entrepreneurial and start my own freelance research business. While I
was building my business, I took a job as a part-time adult services librarian
in a public library for a steady stream of income. After a few years, the
economy turned south, and so did my business. I started thinking about what
my next step would be and thought I might want to be a public library
director. A golden opportunity came along when my friend Layla Johnston
told me she was leaving her director job to move to another job. She asked
me if I would consider filling the job on a part-time interim basis while the
board worked on filling the job permanently. I jumped at the chance. So for
almost a year, I worked as the co-interim director at the Pontiac Public
Library with children's librarian Michael Harms as the other co-interim director. I loved the work and confirmed for myself that I did, indeed, want to
be a director.

Davis: What advice do you have for peers of ours who find themselves
piecing together multiple positions?

Lorene: Full-time librarian positions are tough to come by in public libraries
these days outside the management level. Public libraries are funded largely
by property tax, and when the economy changed, home values crashed and
tax revenue went down. Entry-level master's degree jobs in public libraries
are almost always going to be part time. Many jobs in special libraries went
away or changed dramatically when the economy turned. Many people in our
profession are cobbling together multiple positions. My advice is take advantage of any opportunity. Be entrepreneurial. If you have your degree but are
not working in libraries yet, volunteer somewhere. Talk to the director of a
nearby library and offer to work the reference desk on the weekend. Ask to
help with projects in the type of library you want to work in. Make it clear
you are trying to get experience and do not constantly ask them to hire you. If
they like your work and something comes up, they will talk with you about it.

Davis: What was it like to start up a consulting business? Where did you turn
for resources as you moved from a corporate setting to building your own
business?

Lorene: Starting my business was the most fun! I was free to be creative in coming up with my business name, designing my logo, website, services, etc. I don't know how you can start an information business without being a member of the Association of Independent Information Professionals (AIIP). AIIP negotiates discounts for resources like proprietary databases that otherwise would not be affordable for an independent info pro. The annual conference is the best conference I ever attended. The whole time people are introducing themselves and asking how they can help.

Davis: Like many librarians, you've transitioned from a task-oriented role to one in administration. How have you applied the skills you've gained as a researcher to your work as a public library director?

Lorene: Half the battle of being a good librarian is knowing your audience and your collection. As an administrator, knowing your staff and community is very similar. Knowing what your staff can do is important so you know what you can ask of them. Knowing your community is twofold. First, one has to know the needs of the community to decide what services and programs to provide. Second, an administrator needs to know who in the community can provide services and information to assist in the operation of the library, whether to help market programs or fund grants.

Davis: What's the best piece of career advice you've received?

Lorene: My technical services professor at the University of South Carolina, Heidi Horrmann, always said, "Library school is a hors d'oeuvre. Your career is the main course." There are so many things we can do with our skills. We do not need to limit ourselves to one type of library or one type of job.

Chapter Fourteen

Make Your Own Luck

The Story of a Recent Transition from Art Librarian to Teen Services Librarian

Holland S. Kessinger

I thrive on change. In the past twenty-five years, I've attended five different colleges, lived in four different states, and moved fifteen times. I've worked as a grocery store bagger, a tennis court monitor, a bookseller, a telemarketer, a receptionist, a project manager, a retail clerk, and finally, an art librarian. I can now add to the list a public librarian as well, having recently transitioned from ten years as a solo librarian in a small art museum to a teen services librarian in a large, urban branch of a very big and diverse public library system.

To say that the transition was difficult would be an understatement. I struggled, confused as to why on earth I had chosen this new path and fearful that I would never, ever be successful at it. I doubted my sanity and choice-making ability, and ultimately, I questioned whether or not I had made the right career move. Ten months later, the waters are calmer, the job itself has become easier, and I have a much better perspective on how and why I made the change. Ultimately, everyone has his or her own career paths, but for me the path has been defined by my willingness to make my own luck and my desire to work extremely hard—and enjoying a bit of serendipity along the way.

STRIKE WHILE THE IRON IS HOT

In talking with other librarians over the years, it seems my own library career started very typically: an undergraduate degree in the humanities (mine is in art history), a general dissatisfaction with the practical career path I had previously chosen (design), a passion for books as objects of power and beauty, and a realization that helping others wade and dig through layers of information and data and research was, to me, pure delight. After a quick application for even more student loans, I was off to library school. Once there, I aimed to start immediately acquiring library experience and began volunteering at the library at the Museum of Photographic Arts in San Diego (MOPA). I had some familiarity with photography. Having done some research as an undergraduate for a photography historian, I thought I might one day like to work for a museum or arts institution. Strangely enough, soon after I started, the library assistant who was currently in charge of the library and its collections resigned to move back east and attend library school herself. All at once, I was offered the incredible opportunity and responsibility of managing a twenty-thousand-volume collection that was not yet cataloged or open to the public.

WHATEVER YOU ARE, BE A GOOD ONE

Panicked, excited, and overwhelmed, I finished library school quickly and jumped into the new position with absolute enthusiasm and total naive optimism. I cataloged to my heart's content (and then some), learned everything I could about photography, developed policies and procedures, joined professional organizations, and talked to anyone and everyone about how best to manage and showcase this newly created library. Being so young and new to the industry, I felt that I had to earn the position I had been hired for, and so I worked very hard to exceed the expectations of my colleagues and supervisors. Over the next few years, I focused on garnering a diverse set of skills, a sort of "little bit of everything rather than an expert at one thing" approach. I took as many webinars and workshops as I could, networked, participated in mentorship programs, attended conferences and events, and did my best to stay current on the state of librarianship and photography. As the years went on, the library progressed to more than 90 percent cataloged. It finally opened to the public, serving hundreds of visitors, researchers, and students every year. I offered instructional programs to museum staff, managed volunteers and interns, and participated in museum exhibitions and activities. I was incredibly proud of the library and remain grateful to all of the dedicated museum staff, volunteers, and interns who over the years helped me turn it into a productive and fully functioning research institution. Like any job, I was more successful at some things than others, but in general the library thrived, and I felt challenged and content with where I had serendipitously landed.

ALL GOOD THINGS MUST COME TO AN END

Fast forward ten years later, and I'm miserable, burnt out, frustrated, and blaming my job for all of it. Turns out, the job hadn't changed but I had, and I found myself desperate for new challenges and goals. Having worked primarily by myself for ten years, I knew that the position wasn't going to change much in the future. There were no plans to expand the library's collections or programs, and while there was always work to be done and systems to improve, I began to feel like I had learned as much as I was going to from managing that particular collection and facility for as long as I had. I started to worry that my skill set had become so specific and limited to my current job that there was never going to be another opportunity for me to work anywhere else. And yet at the same time, I was terrified of leaving the comfort and security that comes with working in one place for so long. Was I really willing to give up everything I had worked so hard to achieve in the past decade? The sad, yet freeing, realization was that yes, yes I was. In order to continue growing and learning in my career, I needed to move on. I was hopeful that my hard-earned skill set would translate to an exciting new position in libraryland, so off I went searching for a job.

ROME WASN'T BUILT IN A DAY

This is the part of the story where I cry. Job searching is intimidating and depressing and makes you feel like all of your hard work has been for naught, as every available position requires a certain specialty or knowledge that you don't have. I remember being told before enrolling in library school that a graduate degree in library and information science could translate into a lucrative career in a variety of industries in everything from information technology to education, business, and the list goes on. What I quickly discovered is that the skill set of an art librarian is quite different from that of a medical librarian or a records manager or an archivist or a metadata analyst. I still had a job and was not in jeopardy of losing it, yet I spent many an hour thinking I should reconsider any grand career ambitions. But somehow I reminded myself that I had ended up where I had not because I was a highly qualified expert but because I was eager to learn, willing to work hard, and committed to the goals and values of the institution I worked for. I was hopeful that I would find an employer who would value those same attributes.

FORTUNE FAVORS THE BOLD

At this juncture, it was time to self-reflect and reevaluate my goals, because the alternative was to do nothing and stay put. I realized that what mattered to me most was having an opportunity to make a true difference in someone's life. As sentimental and shopworn as it sounds, I wanted to make an impact, and so I focused on jobs in public and school librarianship. Realizing that I was wholly unqualified for positions in either sector, I started researching the job descriptions of these positions and began considering ways that my current position aligned with those skill sets. I reached out to public librarians I had previously met in my networking travels and took them out for coffee, asking tons of questions about their jobs and what they viewed as the most necessary and desired attributes of a successful public librarian. Although I already had my MLIS, I enrolled in the Instructional Media Resource Assistant program through the San Diego County Office of Education in order to diversify my experience and learn the new vocabulary being used in school and public librarianship, such as *connected learning*, *makerspaces*, and the *common core*. My goal in the eight-week program was to identify the current hot topics and trends in school and public librarianship.

Once through the program, I assessed the local institutions I was interested in working for and then began applying to whatever was open and available. I submitted applications for anything related to libraries, even school positions that I would never have accepted because of their low salaries. My reason was this: serendipity had played a big part in my career so far. I thought I should encourage it to see if new opportunities would come again. And further, writing cover letters and résumés and going on interviews is always good practice, as every well-meaning person who already has a job always says to the job seeker. But it's true.

A WATCHED POT NEVER BOILS

Unlike colleagues who are willing and able to move cities for job opportunities, I am happily tied to San Diego. While a lovely place to live, staying here limits my job options tremendously. Fortunately, however, the city is home to the San Diego Public Library System, a large city system made up of thirty-five branches spread throughout the city with a large, brand-new Central Library located in downtown San Diego. Also fortunately, the city's budget had recently improved a bit compared to the previous years during the recession, and for the first time in a very long time, the city was accepting applications for all levels of librarians. There was my serendipity once again. So I applied and waited. And waited some more. Six months after submitting my application, I was called for an interview, one of those difficult, tense interviews where the interviewers on the other side ask the questions and furiously write down your answers but don't interact with you at all. And then I waited. And waited some more. Four more months later, I was called for an interview with a specific section of the Central Library. A few weeks later, I was offered a position as a teen services librarian for the city of San Diego, working in the Pauline Foster Teen Center at the new Central Library.

A JOURNEY OF A THOUSAND MILES BEGINS WITH A SINGLE STEP

After working for ten years as a solo librarian in a small research library, the noisy and boisterous environment of the teen center in the Central Library was quite literally overwhelming. I was terrified. Everything was big and complicated; I struggled to remember the names of my colleagues, learn all the seemingly endless policies, memorize login passwords, understand how to use the integrated library system (ILS), figure out where things were located, and decipher who was responsible for what, all the while trying to do a good job and make a good impression. Every single night of those first two weeks, I came home utterly exhausted. My body physically ached since I hadn't been on my feet as much in my previous position. I was worried that I wasn't getting it, that I wouldn't be able to connect with the teens I was supposed to be helping, that my colleagues wondered why on earth they had hired me. I started second guessing my decision to give up my previous job and began reconsidering whether or not this was actually what I wanted to do with my life. I was overwhelmed by all of the noise and information and the self-inflicted pressure to do it all perfectly and immediately.

And then, grudgingly, day by day, it got better. One day, my body ached a little less. The next day I had a good interaction with some teens who actually wanted my help. Days later, I was able to share some knowledge I had gained in my previous position with my coworkers, and they appreciated my contribution. Soon after, I helped a teen fill out her first job application, and I realized very quickly that yes, this is exactly what I wanted to do with my life. Now, ten months later, I've sort of adjusted to big-library life. I've helped plan and implement a few programs and am slowly getting the hang of the system and its ins and outs. The teens have started to warm to me a bit and have begun to seek me out when they need help. I've met amazing colleagues, all of whom share an incredible dedication and commitment to serving the public. I still don't remember everyone's names or all the passwords and logins, and I'm not the quickest draw on the ILS or quoting the rules of conduct, but I'm learning more and growing every day.

ACTIONS SPEAK LOUDER THAN WORDS

What has helped was accepting that this is what I am doing now—this job, this commitment to my community. I have come to a place where I can actually make a difference in people's lives, and while it is sometimes messy work, it can also be incredibly rewarding. Further, I am sharing this adventure, and all of its ups and downs, with like-minded peers who offer the remarkable benefits of guidance and commiseration. And unlike my experience at the museum, where I felt like I needed to earn my position, do the job perfectly, and become an expert quickly, I have realized that in this new position, patience, listening, and true understanding are the skills that I need to focus on in order to be successful and content.

A JOURNEY OF A THOUSAND MILES BEGINS WITH A SINGLE STEP

I am now back in the same gathering and learning mode I was in previously when I first took on the position at the museum library: attending as many webinars and trainings as possible, joining new professional organizations, connecting with mentors, and reading and keeping up with all types of resources and news affecting teen services and public libraries in general. It is slightly overwhelming and uncomfortable still, but maybe overwhelming is what growth feels like to me, and when I reach the point of comfortable, it's time to start looking for that next learning experience. For now, my library journey has made a pleasant stop into the bustling teen center of the beautiful Central Library in the middle of downtown San Diego. Obviously, there is no clear and direct path to the right career, and there is no magical formula that makes changing jobs any less painful or chaotic, but if there's a takeaway at all from my career story, I hope it is this: make your own luck, work extremely hard, and keep your eyes open for serendipity. It might just be around the next corner.

Chapter Fifteen

From Prisons to Public

My Time at Brooklyn Public Library

Brian Hasbrouck

My experience working in prison libraries in New York City was not like the movies. There usually was not a room designated solely for the library or librarians. Typically, the extent of the collection was whatever I brought in my backpack or in bags via the subway and buses.

I have a close relative who is currently incarcerated, which sparked my interest in prison libraries. I shortly found out that the number of books he and his peers had access to was minimal outside the Bible. Any literature they wanted to read was donated, antiquated, or in a great deal of disrepair. Learning should be cultivated and encouraged; if books were indeed kept in that condition, I think that sends a message to the incarcerated persons. That message, to be clear, is that their learning is not important and, by extension, neither are they.

With this information, I reached out to a number of the individuals who run the public libraries' outreach efforts in libraries throughout New York City (including Rikers Island). After meeting with a number of librarians who were working in prisons, I was lucky enough to be hired part time by the Brooklyn Public Library. There is currently a big push in libraries toward outreach and for prisons that have no library, I can think of few places that a librarian and their wares can make a greater impact.

The first barrier to entry with jail libraries is identification and badging. I was required to attend an orientation that went over basic gang affiliations, what to expect in a prison environment, and what we had to be careful about. It is difficult to explain the mix of possible threat and gratitude that was intertwined that morning, but my excitement was strong enough to overpower it. The biggest threat conveyed to us was how incarcerated people might try to manipulate us in order to get us to bring in drugs and other contraband. We were told repeatedly not to share where we live in case "an inmate tells a friend to meet you at a bar and tries to get you to bring stuff in," as it was memorably reported to us. Most of the other professionals at the table were from either Alcoholics or Narcotics Anonymous or from a religious organization of one type or another. Although some of the presentation could be interpreted as hyperbolic, I thought it was helpful since I had never been in a prison before.

Naturally, there are great restrictions to the information and resources that can be brought into a prison. A great deal of people in the general public think that incarcerated persons have access to a reasonably stocked room devoted to literature. In movies and literature, there is usually a room lined with books and a librarian who might reluctantly bring you to the book you're looking for, but the incarcerated person will walk away with what he or she wanted. That's not how it works in New York City facilities, typically.

In my experience, usually a book cart or two is kept somewhere in the prison (or correctional center, as the New York City Department of Correction would call it) with the books we have brought. The prison I worked at weekly had a book cart with three shelves on each side and came up to about five and a half feet. We initially brought a van's load of materials to the jail—a mix of fiction, urban fiction, history, trade manuals, and other genres. After dropping off the materials, we went back to the library and started services the following week.

Arriving at a prison is always a jarring experience, and I think it is meant to be like that. The priority of the prison, as they see it, is security. In order for security to be maintained, everyone must follow the same procedures and is constantly reminded of what he or she should and should not be doing. Often I would think of Philip Zombardo's famous Stanford prison experiment: undergraduates were assigned either the positions of guards or prisoners and both succumbed to their roles a little too readily. After six days, the experiment was cut off due to ethical concerns. This serves to illustrate what I found myself doing and telling colleagues when they would help: be reactive. Being proactive is not in the best interest of someone since it frequently disrupts procedures.

After you get through security, you have to wait for an "escort," or a correction officer who will bring you to the area where the books are and who then escorts you through the facility. This is rarely a quick process since staffing is always an issue. If the prison is on "lockdown" (if there's been a fight, for example, or a situation where a correction officer may be in danger), then we were turned away; typically, that meant all the books we had brought must now be returned to the library.

Most of the time we did get through, and most of the time we did have access to the incarcerated persons. Due to the limited selection of materials, the most constant issue was how to match the needs of the patrons with what books we had in hand. Although I would write down requests, it was rare that I would be able to bring back the book a patron requested. If someone requested Charles Dickens, I would try to find similar authors and once brought back Alexandre Dumas. In terms of training for readers' advisory, I have a hard time thinking of a better start; my experience forced me to get to know the collection quickly, and then I would pitch patrons on similar books. Unfortunately, there were some books that we just could not keep on our shelves—urban fiction, James Patterson, John Grisham, and a few others were practically worth their weight in gold.

I would often refer patrons to the services of the public libraries of New York City, which is harder than it seems. Since New York City's public library systems predate the unification of the city, there are three systems serving the five boroughs: Brooklyn and Queens Public Library cover their respective boroughs, and the more famous New York Public Library, of Patience and Fortitude fame, covers the Bronx, Manhattan, and Staten Island. So directing patrons to their local library was difficult; since I'm much more familiar with Brooklyn and the Brooklyn Public Library, I was able to refer many individuals to them but would come back the following week, if necessary, with more information if they told me the neighborhood they lived in. It was always difficult in these situations because I was required to deflect questions about where I live, which is not a great way to create rapport with someone and show that you see them as more than their current situation. This was hard for me because I am someone who likes to connect with other people and I really enjoy connecting people with resources, and I know a good number of you reading this do, too.

Working in prison libraries also reignited my interest in social justice. Even though I had been active in the anti–Iraq War movement in college, I had stopped attending meetings and events. Being involved in prison libraries deepened my compassion, and I have become active in New York City's professional development nonprofit for librarians, Metropolitan New York Library Council (METRO).

As I finished my coursework in school, my attention shifted toward getting a full-time job as a librarian. During interviews, I would be asked how my transition might go from working in prison libraries to working in the branches. Often I would respond that the same passion that led me to help those behind bars would continue toward serving patrons on the outside.

Moving from serving incarcerated patrons toward public patrons has mostly felt like a natural shift. I do, however, miss the feeling of directly helping people that our culture seems to have given up on to a large extent.

I've found there are a number of advantages to working in public libraries, where the focus is on the public and building community relations. The most obvious difference is how much easier it is to get into work and when it's time to leave, I can just walk out the front door. In addition, I've found that doing readers' advisory is immensely easier. Instead of tracking down books that are similar to what a patron is looking for, I can usually put a hold on the book and it will be at the branch within a few days. I also have confidence that my colleagues will continue to build services for incarcerated persons.

In general, the reasons to shift from prison librarianship to public service were mostly due to the structure of the job market for librarians in New York City, but I was happy to have learned about how prison libraries operate in New York. I'm glad my career in public service started in such a worthy capacity.

IV

From Public to Academic Librarianship

Chapter Sixteen

On the Road Again

From Public to Community College Libraries

Gerald Anderson

Great news! I've been hired for the library acquisitions position at the library of the local community college. After ten years, I am moving on from an innovative, major suburban public library. Leaving my first professional position in the field. The transition begins. What experiences and skills will I bring to the new job that will enable me to make a meaningful contribution to a new and as yet unknown community?

The year was 1991, and I was leaving Oak Lawn Public Library (OLPL). The southwest-suburban Chicago library had experienced tremendous growth, in step with the Village of Oak Lawn itself, in the decade before my arrival. By the time I arrive, it boasted a staff of seventy and was the largest of its kind in the southwest suburbs.

I was originally hired at OLPL to direct the library's Local History Room, a collection of Oak Lawn Village and regional suburban resources. I worked with two support staff members to provide access to this collection. My primary tasks included providing reference and research support to our public. I was essentially a solo librarian in that regard. A big audience for our collections was the students from local schools who participated in the regional Chicago History Fair. My outreach for our local history collection involved serving as a speaker on Oak Lawn history for the community, school classes, and local organizations.

I also served regular hours at the adult reference desk with eight other professionals. The volume of questions we handled was considerable. Over eight thousand per month. In person and on the telephone. A torrent of questions, a mind-bending range of questions. Fortunately, our services and collection resources were rich enough to support the local college community, which was important when applying for my next job.

My time at OLPL was one of great change in library technology. Oak Lawn was a participant in the Suburban Library System–hosted online automated library catalog. We implemented the first use of public-access touch screens. We saw the advent of CD-ROMs, first in music, then databases, and the onset of the microcomputer revolution. OLPL hosted a microcomputer room for the public, replacing our typewriter rooms.

I benefited greatly from working at a well-funded, innovative library. But when I found myself in my tenth year at Oak Lawn, I knew it was time for a move, to try something new. Joliet Junior College (JJC) was looking for a new faculty acquisitions librarian. The position also required each of the four staff librarians to work reference. Very much within my skill set. The lack of college job experience was mitigated, I think, by the fact that I had worked extensively with the community college students. How would I adapt to the new situation? It was a walk into the unknown. I was excited to move on.

My first day at JJC came at the beginning of the new academic year. It kicked off a week of preparation. Speeches and presentations focused on new developments and themes at the general session. Then lunch—oh my, there are hundreds of people working here! Then a weeklong introduction to the college and participation in the new faculty seminar. I was part of a group of seventeen new faculty members. A generational change was occurring at the college. At the time I was hired, there were 175 or so full-time faculty members and 150 adjunct faculty.

After lunch the first day, I was on my way to the library. I was walked back to the place I was to work. Uh-oh . . . it's located in the back of the library . . . in an old storage room with an open ceiling that did nothing to quiet the open-air cooling ducts every time the air-conditioning kicked in. I shared the space with two library faculty members and a clerical support person. (Interestingly, I learned more about the library and the acquisitions process from our support person than anyone else!)

JJC was one example of many of a library that hadn't embraced the sweeping, evolutionary changes embraced by other libraries. Ordering books was a hands-on anachronism, as opposed to the automated online system used at OPLP. The facility had remained physically the same since opening in the early 1970s. The two librarians left on staff had been hired then, too. Budgetary support had been proportionally higher when the library opened due to massive support from the federal government for higher education at the time.

This was not the case on my first day in 1990. Funding and staffing had been on a slide throughout the 1980s. Two administrative positions had been reduced to the responsibility of a faculty librarian with a special pay contract. Media services had been separated from the mix. The Library Resources

Center (LRC) had become insular. Even though the LRC was a member of the local Heritage Library System and the Northern Illinois Library Resource Consortium (NILRC), no one was attending any of the meetings or workshops. Nor had a professional American Library Association or Association of College and Research Libraries conference been attended for I don't know how long.

I was slowly learning the differences between my previous position and my new one. For instance, the public library I had worked for had its own functional units. The library's existence and mission were self-evident. All library, all the time. A singular focus. But at JJC, the LRC was just a small part of a much larger organism. As I grew over the years into greater responsibility at the college, this singular difference proved to be the source of an ongoing set of challenges.

I eventually came to understand that the library faculty were an anomaly within the greater institution. Along with the faculty counselors, we were not considered frontline teaching faculty. Yes, we were tenured. Yes, we enjoyed the same privileges under the union faculty contract. Yet it was always a struggle to be on the same footing professionally. We strived for years to become an academic department. Even though the LRC retained a seat at the table of the Curriculum Committee, we did not gain the right to vote on issues for over a decade. Eventually, we were included in department chair meetings, which helped us learn what the departments needed, what the current issues were, and how the library could shape our services in response.

Through the years, there was to be a sea of change, too, in how we maintained our relevance. With time, access to the Internet meant that a faculty member could do without us. Where once we had provided teaching opportunity with tours of the facilities, in time these sessions fell off in demand. We had to be able to adapt to these ever-changing developments. Having been able to shape the recruitment process over the years, I was able to bring capable people into the program. To move away from the dog-and-pony library tour, we adapted by offering strong information literacy sessions in the classroom space I had been able to develop within the library.

Did I have a systematic plan for working through these challenges? No, not on paper. It was more, "Hey, I think this would work here. It makes sense." Ruminate through the options. Read the literature. Go to workshops. Talk with your peers. My first baby step in technological innovation was to request funds for a new computer and CD-ROM reader from my academic assistant vice president—and to subscribe to a library book ordering database. An easy solution to upgrading and streamlining our acquisition work flow.

I also started reaching out to faculty by first sending out book catalogs that were appropriate to the many disciplines around campus. Later, I would use e-mail to target my audience. A lot of this was based on the conversations

I had with faculty members. Eventually, I asked to be invited to departmental meetings to market what the library could do. The most intensive interaction with a number of departments—nursing, fine arts, and emergency services, for example—came when professional certification reviews required a library component in the department's documentation.

Representing the LRC in professional organizations was essential. I attended NILRC meetings. I volunteered to join in statewide meetings of the Illinois Library Computer Systems Organization (ILCSO). I also went outside of the box of my immediate peer group by attending the Illinois Special Library Association meeting, information technology (IT) conventions, the Illinois Community College Administrators Association, and the League for Innovation in the Community College. Basically, I wanted to participate in anything that provided a different perspective in the profession!

Internally, whenever there was an opportunity to join a committee on campus, I accepted. The Curriculum Committee provided insight into the needs of new and revised courses. The Assessment Committee linked student accomplishment with the educational goals of each academic department and every course on campus. Then there was the Technology Committee, chaired by the vice president of academic services and head of IT. My goal for all of this committee work was to move beyond the spaces where the value of libraries was understood. My role became one of constantly asserting our value.

When the supervisor of the library fell ill, I assumed his duties. This eventually led to my taking charge of the administration of the LRC. Having no budgeting experience skills from my previous job was a bit daunting. No formal training was available then, so I had to reach out and work with new areas and people in the college. And when it came time to step up and lead the library? I had retained a vision of the possibilities for the library, which I had developed during my years at the Syracuse School of Library and Information Science (SU). The key idea: we are in an age of information, and change is inevitable. The ethos there was that Toffler's age of future shock was upon us. The vision inculcated at SU was born out by the transformation and possibilities I saw throughout my career.

I understand now that a key to my transition to academic librarianship, one that would continue uninterrupted, was the desire—and the know-how—to adapt to new technologies and forge new practices. An ability to play in the sandbox and discover new things and ideas. I was always open to new possibilities and eager to explore them. Politically, I retained a willingness to champion a new practice, idea, or technology and then persist. I learned how to win the trust of my direct supervisors (in our case, the assistant academic vice president, later the academic vice president). More often than not, they had never worked with a library under their charge. Each had more on their plate than just the LRC. I also made sure to talk with a wide range of administrators, which helped immensely.

The ability to work with a wide range of people, from library users to professionals, was essential. While a high percentage of students were advancing to other colleges and universities after fulfilling their general education requirements, we also needed to develop services for adults returning to school in order to seek new careers, first-generation students, ethnic minorities, high school students achieving college-level coursework before graduation, and other groups. This was a great chance to experience how the impact of a culture of sharing across libraries—and the greater community college, for that matter—benefits the larger community.

Last day: Looking back at how I transitioned from a large public library to a community college library and now that I've retired after twenty years at JJC, I can see a record of tangible accomplishments. Most important of which was a renovation of the library and then its move to a totally new facility in a major, new college building that was more central to students and had multiple teaching labs and small meeting rooms, media walls, and a technology area. I can say that I've been successful in my push to move the LRC's operations firmly into the center of the culture at JJC.

Chapter Seventeen

A Time to Plant, a Time to Uproot

My Transition from a Large Public Library to a Small Seminary Library

Sachiko Clayton

My first full-time job out of library school was in the Milstein Division of U.S. History, Local History, and Genealogy at the Humanities and Social Sciences Library of the New York Public Library (NYPL). I was hired as an entry-level reference librarian working primarily at the reference desk, and my work also included creating content for our division's social media accounts and website in the form of subject guides and blog posts. In addition, I helped with collection development and created metadata for photograph collections. Looking back on this brief job description, I realize how fortunate I was to have had such diversity in my work from the very beginning.

I also had the privilege of working with two extremely talented and supportive managers: Ruth Carr and Maira Liriano. Both Ruth and Maira instilled a deep respect in me for NYPL as an institution and both gave me the freedom and encouragement to try new things, learn as much as I could, and grow in leadership. Within my seven years of working at NYPL, I had been promoted three times. The final promotion made me the assistant manager, and soon after I was promoted to acting manager of the division.

Reading about my experience at NYPL, one may wonder why I decided to leave such an exciting and supportive environment. It was a challenging decision, but I made the choice to leave for a few key reasons. Primarily, staying at NYPL felt like the safe thing for me to do. I had experienced a degree of success there, and while NYPL offered many opportunities, I had accomplished even more than I had expected to upon being hired. I decided that if I didn't take a risk by leaving, I might find it increasingly challenging to change course later on. Secondly, the opportunity I was offered was very appealing: City Seminary of New York (CSNY), a relatively young institution with an inspiring mission, was developing its library and looking for a librarian to oversee the process. If I were to take on this new role, I would be working with a small group of people, including the director and the dean. This meant I could influence decisions I could never be part of at NYPL, either because they cut across several departments or because of long-established policies. Finally, I felt as though the prospective work at CSNY could be an opportunity to shape an institution in a unique way from its nascence.

A VERY LONG JOB INTERVIEW

Often when we hear that a friend has endured a very long job interview, the response is sympathetic. In my case, the very long job interview was not quite an interview per se but a growing relationship with the institution. This was extremely helpful in my decision-making process. CSNY had started as an extension campus for Westminster Seminary in Pennsylvania, offering an MA in urban missions. Later, they created a certificate program for laypersons and bivocational ministers working in churches in New York City. Active in our congregation, my husband and I had enrolled in the certificate program in 2011.

Learning of my work as a librarian, CSNY sought my opinion in the development of their library. The conversation continued as I worked alongside them as a consultant. During this time, I was able to help them craft their librarian position. In the course of these conversations, there was an understanding that I would be a welcome candidate. Having had the experience of working with this group, I was becoming more and more interested in the possibility of formally joining their team. In time, I was asked to join them and did.

TRANSLATING SKILLS AND LEARNING NEW ONES

It's an interesting experience to be an institution's first librarian. While CSNY's library had a collection, a defined scope and mission, and a scholar in charge of its care, there had not been a degreed librarian overseeing its growth, development, classification, and organization. It was exciting to bring my experience as a trained librarian into the process. I made decisions such as selecting an integrated library system (ILS), joining professional organizations, and reclassifying the collection into Library of Congress Classification. I was also asked to research and write library policies on privacy and donations, standardize our collection development, define our information literacy program, and establish a library budget.

For some of these responsibilities, I was able to draw on my past experience at NYPL. I had been on a working committee to propose changes to the user experience of our library catalog, which was helpful in considering what features to look for in an ILS. Also helpful in selecting an ILS were my years at the NYPL reference desk, assisting researchers in finding relevant materials through the catalog.

For other assignments, such as creating an information literacy program, I relied on experience gained at Hostos Community College and Queens College. At Hostos, I had implemented established, stand-alone workshops focusing on catalog and database use, best practices in searching the web, and avoiding plagiarism. At Queens College, I had developed a single-credit course on college-level research skills. Both experiences helped me consider what elements were essential and what skills ought to be emphasized in an information literacy program.

For other aspects of my new position at CSNY, I researched best practices and instructional material to fill in gaps in my experience. At times this meant looking at primary literature, such as documents created by other colleges and universities. Other times, I looked to secondary literature in library journals. For instance, I had never considered what a library's privacy policy might entail, so I spent time looking at various privacy policies and noted the specific state law frequently cited. I also searched several library journals for articles on privacy policies within colleges and universities.

Acquisitions was another area in which I needed professional development. In library school, I'd spent a short time working in acquisitions in the Queens College Rosenthal Library, but I didn't have an understanding of how my work fit into the larger scope of the department. Since I would be overseeing acquisitions at the CSNY Library, I decided to enroll in an online course offered through the Association for Library Collections & Technical Services.

DIVERSE EXPERIENCE AND PROFESSIONAL RELATIONSHIPS

In library school, I was often advised to hold out for a job within the type of library in which I was most interested, otherwise I might be pigeonholed into work I wouldn't enjoy. I was told if I worked in public libraries, I would never be hired in an academic library. With hindsight as my guide, I don't agree with that advice, nor would I give it. My experience has proven otherwise. I've also observed the career paths of many colleagues who have successfully worked within different kinds of libraries. In fact, I would consider experience within a different context a strength. It's helpful to bring fresh perspective.

What I would recommend to anyone considering a transition from one type of library to another is to review their curriculum vitae with an eye for a range of skills and experiences. Diversity of experience is extremely helpful when looking to branch out. While specialization is valuable, it is important to have an understanding of the different functions within a library. If you don't have much diversity in your work experience, seek out opportunities to broaden your skill set, whether within your current role at work or elsewhere. You may also want to consider how to reframe your experience to draw connections between your past work and the work for which you are applying.

I would also recommend building relationships across the field. I know that the word *networking* can make some (including myself) a little squeamish since it sounds a bit inhuman. It helps me to consider networking opportunities as chances to build professional relationships. Librarianship remains a collegial field, and relationships do matter. In my case, having a good relationship with my future employers was pivotal to the transition from one institution to another.

While my experience may be unusual, I have found a range of experience, openness to change, and cultivation of professional relationships helpful in my transition from NYPL to CSNY. In the current state of our field, I believe movement between different types of libraries will become even more prevalent. I would encourage librarians seeking this kind of change to take advantage of the opportunities this diverse field of work provides.

Chapter Eighteen

An Interview with Professor Nicole A. Cooke, Graduate School of Library and Information Science, University of Illinois at Urbana-Champaign

Ray: You've worked in a number of libraries throughout your career. Please tell us about your career so far!

Nicole: I've made several shifts in my career. I've gone from a public library to a medical school library to an academic library to a tenure-track faculty position. All of these transitions had their own circumstances related to politics and work environment, but they also enabled me to achieve the next steps in my professional trajectory.

My first job out of library school was as a youth services librarian in a public library. I knew within two months that I had to get out of that job. My strengths do not include working with children. While I knew that there were different types of librarians, I did not realize how real these distinctions and personality requirements were until I was in this position. I moved to the medical library after that, and while that job remains my favorite in terms of the subject matter and the scope of the research, I had no opportunities to teach and train, one of my strengths and something I wanted to do professionally.

I then moved to a university academic library, which provided the opportunity to teach. I entered the academy as a faculty member in order to do serious and sustained research at a level I would not have been able to do in the public library. This position provided the opportunity to do a higher level of research *and* engage in the teaching and training that I enjoy.

Ray: That's a lot of environments to cover in a relatively short period of time! Have you encountered any issues in the application process, in terms of meeting the requirements of each position? How were you able to move fluidly between these roles?

Nicole: I've been able to meet the requirements for all of the positions I've held. Perhaps the trickiest transition was from children's librarian to medical librarian. I think in that case, my networking and the connections I had acquired through professional service helped quite a bit. I also had subject knowledge from my undergraduate studies, which allowed the director of the library to see that I could handle the work. Plus, I had already gained skills in reference, programming, and collection development that would benefit the medical library. Subsequent positions required additional graduate degrees, and I was fortunate that I had the time and resources to dedicate to additional schooling.

Ray: The benefit of your wide-ranging experience is that you've likely picked up a lot of transferable skills. What qualities were most helpful to you as you moved around the library field?

Nicole: Ultimately, I think all the skills we acquire as LIS (library and information science) professionals are transferable, inside and outside the profession. I think my research and technology skills, and certainly my teaching skills, have propelled me from position to position. Interpersonal skills are also important across library type and job function, and my overactivity in professional organizations demonstrated a propensity for networking and lifelong learning that are also desirable to potential employers. A lot of things and tasks can be taught on the job, but some things cannot: collegiality, kindness, manners, professionalism, etc. It's my opinion that these things will get us further than an abundance of book knowledge and certificates—don't get me wrong, these help, but they're not enough if you can't balance them with evidence of being a decent human being.

Ray: We've all been told that we must pick a type of library work to do and to stick with it, that a progressive résumé matters. Do you agree with this? Do librarians get typecast based on their specific space within the field?

Nicole: Yes and no. I say no because I've never felt typecast in my own career. However, I have seen colleagues who have been typecast. For these people, I have to say that they were not professionally active and made no efforts to improve themselves through professional development, additional degrees, volunteering, etc.

I think other considerations to this are geography and mobility. Sometimes there isn't as much flexibility and mobility in a particular area. For example, it may be hard to break into an XYZ type of library because there are two LIS grad programs in the area and the competition is stiffer there. For new graduates, especially, if you have the ability to relocate, even temporarily, to get the right job, do it!

Ray: What's your best job advice?

Nicole: Be mobile, and be flexible. Have patience, and be willing to put the time in at one position if it can propel you to the next (desired) position. Get involved professionally, make yourself known as both a person and a professional, and be purposeful and consistent in your professional development activities. Have a mentor—at least one!—who can look at your CV (curriculum vitae) objectively and help you articulate your transferable skills. They may see traits in you that you don't even recognize. Finally, be serious about your elevator pitch. Learn how to sell yourself, your abilities, and your ideas, and be able to modify that pitch to different audiences, in different situations. We are our own best advocates!

Chapter Nineteen

Career Transition

Why I Left Public Library Service for
Academic Librarianship

Zena George

My pursuit of an academic librarianship position began during my first year of library school. I completed my undergraduate degree in mid-2005 and smoothly transitioned from part-time library college student to full-time library information assistant the same year. With five years of library experience under my belt and a fresh copy of my college degree in hand, I was ready to conquer the world of librarianship.

Working for a great organization such as the New York Public Library (NYPL) was considered "cool" to the average person: good health and dental benefits (check), paid vacation and sick days (check), retirement/pension fund (check), and, of course, regular biweekly pay (check). But after thirteen years of service, I was seeking more from my career. I worked for two years as a library information assistant before pursuing a career as a librarian. I began library school in the fall of 2008 and graduated from Long Island University with a master's in library and information science (MLIS) in early summer of 2010.

The year 2010 was a rough one for anyone graduating with any type of degree. The U.S. economy and job market were struggling, mostly because of the recession. Unemployment percentage numbers were in the double digits and jobs, predominantly for librarians, were either part-time or advertised as internships. In simple terms, no one was hiring!

In late 2010, a few months after completing my master's program, I was promoted from librarian trainee to senior librarian at one of the largest circulating public libraries in New York City, the Mid-Manhattan Library. My new position came with additional responsibilities, one of them being the development of the library's reference collection, which included areas in health, business, literature, social science, and art.

I also collaborated on many other library projects, such as book club discussions, English classes for nonnative speakers, database and computer course teachings, and public programming. Another one of my responsibilities was creating and teaching innovative classes based on library user needs. To research these needs, I met with numerous library users, asking them questions about what their wishes were when they came to use the library. The popular responses were usually job searching and résumé writing, but the one response that fascinated me the most was the request to learn how to sell unwanted stuff. I realized that creating classes such as "Introduction to EBay" and "Online Shopping Made Easy" were very important and highly beneficial to library users; based on the high volume of attendance in the classes every month, my assumptions were right. One of the great things about obtaining public library service experience is the opportunity to work with a diverse population of users and gain exposure to a variety of research topics.

The Mid-Manhattan Library opens seven days a week for seventy-eight hours and with a door count population of appropriately 1,046 library users per month. To describe it in one word: busy!

No two days are alike at this library. You met a variety of people with fascinating backgrounds and sometimes-bizarre life stories.

Nevertheless, as exciting as the senior librarian position was, by the fifth year of my role, I felt very robotic and realized it would be many years ahead before I earned another senior managerial role within the organization. Along with being stuck career-wise, I began craving new challenges and opportunities. I knew I had to do something before long, so in late 2013 I decided to join the masses and began job hunting for a new, rewarding position.

My search for academic librarian positions began in large city areas, such as Washington, DC, Massachusetts, Connecticut, and, of course, New York, with my focus on top colleges in the areas (New York University, Harvard, Yale, and Columbia, just to name a few). During my search, I noticed a pattern in many job openings. Having a second master's degree seemed to be a desired qualification and sometimes a standard requirement for consideration for an academic librarian position. In addition, having one to three years of academic librarianship experience was a common request, and most colleges preferred someone who was very knowledgeable in specific subject areas as well as who had published several scholarly articles. Since I had no prior academic librarian experience, I realized I needed a new approach to the academic librarian world. So I decided to network!

Networking is much easier said than done. It requires time, planning, money, and excellent interpersonal skills. To begin my job networking, I joined numerous library groups. I attended events from institutions such as the American Library Association, the Metropolitan New York Library Council, the Special Libraries Association, the Association of College and Research Libraries—a few well-known organizations of the library world. I made most of these events part of my social life, which at times included me tagging along with friends. I enjoyed networking because it gave me the opportunity to explore other interesting areas within the library field. I met individuals with a variety of backgrounds:

- Information analyst/associate
- Database administrator/programmer
- Records manager
- Business intelligence analyst

I truly enjoyed meeting with these folks and hearing about their work experiences. It was great to learn that an MLIS could go beyond the typical library walls. Another thing I learned from my network experience is always to carry professional copies of my résumé and business card to these events. Even if you do not have current employment, there is no reason not to have your job-hunting tools with you.

The final thing I learned from networking at these events is that the library world is much smaller than we might think. For that reason, it is very important to be polite and humble. Always conduct yourself professionally, particularly when seeking employment. I suggest you avoid having those two or three glasses of wine if you are unable to handle your alcohol. I also suggest you avoid that taste for spinach or garlic dip, and never, ever gossip with strangers!

Along with attending professional library events, I regularly communicated with my alumni connections, both at my graduate and undergraduate schools. Some of these folks were references on my résumé, so giving them advance notice about pending job applications and interviews seems like the polite thing to do.

In 2014, the library job market was slowly getting back to normal. Full-time positions were seen regularly in listservs, and the search for employment was not as dire as in previous years. I had a few interviews with potential academic employers.

In late 2014, I interviewed for my present position as library director for Berkeley College, Brooklyn Campus Library. Like most professional academic job interviews, I met with a committee, which consisted of the vice president of library services, the campus operation officer, two other library directors, and the co-coordinators of information literacy.

I was very pleased with the interview. It was conducted very professionally, and the committee was clearly prepared in their research about my work and educational background, which made me comfortable talking to them about my qualifications and why I was a suitable candidate for the position. The position of library director was offered to me three weeks after the interview, and I began my new role in January 2015.

Being an academic library director certainly has its rewards as well as its challenges. The role is very diverse; you could be a librarian one day, a cataloger the next, and an instructor in the classroom the day after. I collaborate constantly with colleagues, faculty, and other departments of the college. Therefore, if you are not an effective communicator who enjoys interacting with people, this will not be the position for you.

As a for-profit organization, Berkeley College expects high productivity from all employees. The library director's role at this college is not the typical nine-to-five job. There are numerous e-mails to respond to, project deadlines to meet, budgets to balance and track, staff time sheets to approve, collection development to maintain, mandatory meetings to attend, professional development to pursue, and monthly reports to complete. The list seems long, but with proper time management and staffing, your day will always be a productive one. And let us not forget about information literacy and instruction reference. All Berkeley College library directors are involved physically and virtually in the classroom. They are assigned quarterly to classes on their campus or, if needed, at another location. They also provide live online chat for students to support their research and other library needs.

I enjoy my new role and regularly explore innovative ways I can enhance the student experience at the library and within Berkeley College as a whole. One of my favorite projects thus far is the creation of the game challenge Are You Smarter than a Berkeley College Librarian. I collaborated the event with the director of the student development department, and together we succeeded in encouraging students to learn outside the classroom. January 2016 will mark my one-year anniversary with Berkeley College, and like most management positions, I look forward to my performance review. I am excited to reflect on my recent switch and determine if academic librarianship is the right career choice for me.

When I look back on my thirteen years with the public libraries, there are things that were simply challenging. Advocating yearly for funding tops my list. Because public libraries usually are funded by city and state taxes, it is a yearly scuffle of finding and keeping public library finance. Dealing with patrons who are homeless or have mental illnesses are also major issues at public libraries. So, you may ask, why pursue a public librarian position at all? I became a public service librarian for the experience. I wanted to continuously learn how to provide quality reference service to a diverse population. I now have mastered that skill, and I incorporate it daily into specific subject areas of academic librarianship. My public library experience taught me how to help young library users to appreciate the art of reading and assist adult users to find their favorite authors and genres of works.

I now get to personally meet one on one with students and broaden their horizon into areas of research they may have never heard of. I truly enjoyed conducting public library programs and classes. The thank-you notes and expressions of gratitude from the library user were always appreciated. Fortunately for me, I get the same feelings helping Berkeley College students with their research needs in the library and in the classroom. I enjoy hearing their thoughts and ideas during our book discussions. While they browse the new book sections, I ask what their plans are after graduation.

As you can tell by now, my transition was neither good nor bad. I needed a new perspective within my career, and this is the path I chose. Whether you work at an academic or a public library, being a librarian is a rewarding career. The environments are clearly different, but the goals are still the same no matter where you end up. Having the ability to deliver quality reference experience to another individual is a gift, so appreciate yours, as I continue to do with mine.

Chapter Twenty

From Public to Academic

Reflections and Tips for Transitions from a Former Overseas Librarian

Raymond Pun

We all know this to be true: public libraries are very different from academic ones. Additionally, public librarians are not required to publish or present, nor do they need to be seriously active in professional organizations such as the American Library Association (ALA) or the Public Library Association (PLA). Public librarians may just need a master of library science (MLS) to start with and get a lot of "on-the-job" training.

Don't get me wrong here: public librarians end up learning a lot and doing more than what is expected. They can wear many hats, and some can have special focuses, from adult programmer to collections specialist to library management. When you're looking to move to a position at an academic library, what you do as a public librarian must translate and fit well into the academic context. So that means you will also need to convert your résumé into a curriculum vitae (also known as a CV), which lists your training, experiences, education, publications, presentations, committee services, awards, and research much more extensively than a résumé. In addition, you need to have the "appropriate experiences." In this chapter, I will share my own experiences transitioning from public to academic libraries and highlight a set of key skills for academic librarians.

After a few years at a public library, I was prepared enough to be given an opportunity to work in an academic library in spite of my relative inexperience in that setting. However, I will note that my background in a research library in the New York Public Library (NYPL) offered a smoother transition into becoming an academic librarian.

At NYPL, I had the opportunity to work with many scholars, students, and writers. This allowed me to teach a variety of users how to conduct research effectively with digital and print tools. I delivered a series of instructional workshops to undergraduate and graduate classes, mainly in the fields of history and social sciences. I also had the chance to support our fellows in the Cullman Center for Scholars and Writers, where selected researchers won a competitive fellowship to conduct research at NYPL. Their research interests varied from the history of American newspapers to the social and cultural implications of the United Nations. This kind of engagement allowed me to support their needs and become their "personal" or "embedded" librarian. I also organized public programs and demonstrated leadership skills in that context.

Because of my growing relationships with faculty and students, I knew that I wanted to continue working as an academic librarian and focus on serving these key groups. I was also active in ALA, the Association of College and Research Libraries (ACRL), and ACRL's Greater Metropolitan New York Chapter (ACRL/NY), and I participated in numerous committees to support these organizations. In addition, I published and presented widely in webinars, poster sessions, and conference papers in different academic disciplines from library science to East Asian studies. One important drive for me to pursue the academic library direction was several of my past supervisors at NYPL, who kept encouraging me to move into academic librarianship since I was building a CV anyway. One way for me to stay on top of this area was to explore the *Chronicle of Higher Education* and *Inside Higher Ed*, which gave me a glimpse of the ongoing issues, trends, and news in higher education. When preparing for my interview, this information was very helpful so that I could discuss the current state of academic librarianship.

After several years working as a student worker, library assistant, and librarian at NYPL, I was ready to explore other opportunities outside of public librarianship. At that time, I had applied to a few jobs and actually received interviews and even two job offers—one from a special library and another from an academic one. I chose the latter because it was a better fit for me in terms of my professional and personal interests at the time, and it allowed me to work abroad. The special library offer was quite interesting because it would have allowed me to engage with the public differently but also would have required me to develop a specific focus in this particular industry, which meant I would have had a harder time transitioning into academic librarianship later on. Nevertheless, one of my hardest career decisions was turning down that job offer. It's never easy to do.

During the interview process for my academic librarian positions, I was asked about my background as a public librarian and how that background fit into the academic position. This kind of question was interesting and could be asked of all candidates coming from a public library background. I explained that I had been giving numerous research consultations and workshops while publishing and presenting in the field. I felt that I was on the "right track" for it all. I think the main challenge for most public librarians is that they do not realize how different the academic job interview/talk is—it's usually one or two days long and typically requires a presentation or an instructional workshop (also known as a "job talk"). Everyone in the university is invited to watch you present. It can be difficult at first, but if you spend some time organizing your thoughts and practicing your presentation over and over, it should come to you naturally. Just make sure you focus on your audience and their questions. That's often the hardest part. They may ask questions that you might not have expected. It's also important to prepare a series of questions for them since you are interviewing them as well.

So how can you actually get an interview? You may want to build on your experiences first. Here are some tips for those public librarians who would like to transition into academic librarianship in the future.

1. *Committee work and networking.* When people say that you should network, you really should. But how can you network your way into the academic world? You may have to participate in associations locally, regionally, and/or nationally. From ACRL to the Reference and User Services Association (RUSA), there are opportunities for you to meet people who are academic librarians. Your public library background should prepare you for this if you are already active in groups such as ALA, PLA, the Young Adult Library Services Association (YALSA), and so on. By attending conferences, if you can afford to, and by volunteering in sections, committees, or groups in ACRL or RUSA, you are already setting yourself up to prepare for academic librarianship.

From what I've experienced, academic librarians tend to collaborate and form committees internally and externally. In public libraries, I had a few opportunities to join a committee within the library, but they are often limited. For outside committees, you can volunteer to lead the newsletter or website or social media. You become part of a team that is interested in supporting its members, who are often affiliated with a university. Your exposure can happen rapidly depending on how committed you are. Most academic libraries will ask you to join a professional committee or a service committee within the university. This is a job expectation, and one you should get used to. By volunteering to serve in different committees in your associations, you already demonstrate that you are capable of this part!

2. *More degrees.* That's right, you've read it somewhere. Not all universities require an additional graduate degree, but it helps to have a specialization so that you can support your faculty/students in that discipline.

Say you are a public librarian with only an MLS degree, you often deliver genealogy workshops to the public, and you have a huge passion for history, you could consider a second master's in history, focusing on family history research, public history, or genealogical study if you can. You are already developing the expertise to support your patrons regardless of whether they are students.

Getting a second graduate degree can be difficult, especially when it comes to cost. Check with your employers or local/national unions to see if they can support your continuing-education interests. In my experience, after getting my MLS, I decided to pursue another master's degree to develop a specialization since I worked in a leading research library. I chose to pursue an MA in East Asian studies since I also served as the collection liaison for that area of studies and since colleagues knew that I had the language and cultural background for it. My employer and union supported it, and so I was going to school full time while working full time. It was unbelievably difficult but paid off in the end—I landed an academic librarian position that made use of my specialization.

Find out what you are passionate about or pursue something that will help advance your career. These days there are so many online programs for you to get a master's degree. From business administration to global affairs, you have an opportunity to learn more about subjects that may interest you in an entirely online setting. One recommendation is to explore the massive open online course, known as an "MOOC," where you can take online classes from reputable universities for free. This may help you decide if you can do online study or not and if you should go back to school. As stated earlier, not all schools require a second master's degree, but it helps if you want to be a subject specialist, such as women's studies, anthropology, comparative literature, history, and so on.

3. *Writing and publishing.* This is probably one of the hardest tasks of an academic librarian. Depending on the job description, such as tenure-track status, you may not need to be active in publishing. I've known some people who were on a tenure-track process and quit their positions later because they were not actively publishing. The great news is that if your position is tenure track, you might be able to apply for a sabbatical or research leave, which could give you more time to pursue your research. Some universities offer this, and others do not. It becomes a time-management issue to find time to research, write, and publish.

As a public librarian, you should be publishing essays, chapters, or articles in your own time. It can be a challenge, but it is doable. Start with your organization's or association's newsletters. You can contribute to any kind book, reference, or program review. By writing for professional newsletters, you can slowly build your writing experiences and then expand to other areas as well.

In my case, I wrote book reviews for the *Library Journal* and exhibition reviews for a local association newsletter. I also published in open-access journals, such as *College and Research Libraries News*, where my work could be read more widely. These essays came from my coursework in library school and my graduate program in East Asian studies. By revising my papers, I had an opportunity to publish even more than before.

Another option is to collaborate with another writer. This is often a great opportunity for two writers to publish an essay on collaboration. For example, I cowrote an article with a history professor about our collaboration in building a library workshop for history students. If you are a public librarian, you can write about a program you ran with another colleague. You can write about virtually anything, from mentorship to conference and database reviews. You'll have to think creatively about how to publish these pieces. Afterward, you can pursue the peer-reviewed journals, which can take a while to be published. Publishing in peer-reviewed journals is tough, but it can tell you if you can make it in academic librarianship or not.

4. *Programs, services, and emerging technologies.* Academic librarianship is constantly growing and finding new trends to support innovative research. If you can develop competency in these areas, then you may have a huge advantage over other candidates. Growing areas in academic librarianship include data services like data management and geographic information system (GIS) services or GIS librarianship, digital scholarship and humanities, instructional design and technology, and business and economics librarianship. It helps if you have a background in these areas, but you'll most likely have to develop specific skills to support researchers who are interested in data research and analysis or creating open-access resources.

For instructional technology, you may want to start creating library video tutorials for your current library in order to demonstrate your experience using emerging technologies for teaching purposes. You may also want to learn how to use Google Fusion Tables or Google Earth to develop a better understanding of GIS. There are plenty of online classes, from the MOOCs to Library Juice Academy, that teach a lot of data management programs and skills. There are also some free data tools, such as R programming language, which can be difficult to use in the beginning but can make you stand out if you want to learn how to create statistical analysis for any kind of research using data.

In business and economics librarianship, many academic libraries are interested in hiring people who can support their MBA or business programs through research. There are so many sophisticated databases in business research that you may need to take a class in business librarianship, in person or online, to learn how to effectively use them. It is a growing area because many are interested in the field. You may want to read articles published in the newsletters of business library associations to get a better idea of what's going on in that field.

Along with data, digital humanities and scholarships are also big topics in academic librarianship right now. Do you know what they are and why they are important? You'll want to read up on them on sites such as the *Chronicle of Higher Education*'s website to understand why they are important. Today there are plenty of free sites, such as WordPress, Omeka, or Zotero, that can get you started on creating your own "digital humanities project" managing or displaying research collections or resources.

I also find that it is important for public librarians to know how to use citation tools, such as Zotero (which is free), EndNote, and RefWorks, because academic librarians often have to show students and faculty how to use these programs to manage their sources and bibliographies. You can get a trial version to learn how to use these tools or search on video sites such as YouTube to get a better understanding of how they work. As a public librarian, you can collaborate with a schoolteacher to discuss academic plagiarism or intellectual property with a class, which will allow you to gain teaching experience as well.

Another area of technology that could make you stand out is social media. Do you know social media tools beyond Facebook, Twitter, and Instagram? These days Snapchat and Periscope are the most popular tools in the social media world. As an academic librarian, if you can discuss how these social media tools can enhance the academic library's presence in the virtual world and engage users differently, it might make you stand out. If you are currently managing your library's social media page, you can promote scholarly works or programs to make that connection much more explicit. Academic libraries are always interested in finding new tools to promote services and enhance user experiences.

5. *Assessment.* Do you have experience assessing or evaluating programs, services, or collections? Depending on what you are interested in, it's important to know how to read, gather, and analyze data qualitatively and quantitatively. Not all academic librarians do this, but if you work in a public library, you can learn how to build an assessment program to gain this experience. You can start off with a focus group or survey, analyze user experiences from there, and then find ways to improve these experiences. Again, academic libraries are always looking for ways to grow and enhance their services and resources. Knowing how to create an assessment program can strengthen your own career portfolio.

6. *Presentation.* In my position, I present a lot. I speak at new student/ faculty orientations, library instructions, meetings, and conferences. There is usually an expectation for academic librarians to be strong public speakers. It also helped that I presented a lot at conferences and workshops prior to my academic librarianship career. If you hate public speaking, you may not like being an instruction librarian in a university, but to build your CV you should have delivered some presentations. You can get those experiences by pre-

senting at conferences, seminars, workshops, and webinars. You can find ways to present at your local conferences if you haven't already. This is often an important aspect in academic librarianship since you may represent your university in conferences locally and internationally.

I have only outlined few of the skills and experiences that a public librarian can learn and build on to become an academic librarian. However, there are still many other important factors to consider besides what I mentioned, such as your networks and interviews.

If you have a connection with someone from the academic library you are applying to, it can help a lot. For interviews, you are most likely going to meet more than ten people in one day, including the library dean or director, faculty from other departments and library staff members. A variety of people will give the search committee and library dean feedback on your interviews, performances, and presentations. It can be a long and difficult process; many people have written about their experiences in blogs and such. I will say that you will be repeating yourself a lot, but make sure you act professional from the moment you arrive at the library to the end of the interview process.

In academic librarianship, there is always something new to learn, and this can be both required and exciting. If you find yourself wanting to become an academic librarian after many years of being a public librarian, you'll need to build your CV and network strategically. This is true for any other job you might want to look into. Any job requires introspection and self-reflection. Just because the position is in an academic library, it may not necessarily fit with your own personal interests and professional goals. Look at the job descriptions carefully, assess your own strengths and weaknesses, and think creatively about how your current skill set can fit in the academic ecosystem. Unfortunately, it is true that most academic library search committees often will weed out candidates from public libraries immediately. Your goal in the cover letter and CV is to address how your public library background fits into an academic library one. It's not going to be easy, but it's always worth trying.

To summarize, here are some of the main points outlined in this chapter:

- Build a CV first. You can create one on the web for free using Academia, LinkedIn, Google Scholar, or ResearchGate.
- Join a library association that many academic librarians are part of, such as ACRL, SLA, or RUSA. There are also local and regional academic library associations that you can join. Actively participate in these committees to learn how a committee works.
- Getting a second graduate degree is sometimes optional but can make you stand out as a subject specialist or expert in your area; some universities

may prefer or require this second graduate degree. Take an MOOC first to see if you enjoy the subject or not.

- Research, write, publish, and present! These may be requirements in your future academic library career, so prove to the search committee that you can contribute to the intellectual landscape of academia.
- Data, digital, and emerging technologies. Learning how to use different programs, software, tools, technologies, and resources for research and teaching purposes can make you stand out from other candidates.
- Read, read, and read! You can read the *Chronicle of Higher Education, Inside Higher Ed, College and Research Libraries News, College and Research Libraries*, or academic librarian blogs to get a sense of the climate of academic librarianship and higher education. If you don't like what you are reading, then you probably should not be considering a career move to academic librarianship!

V

From Academic to Public Librarianship

Chapter Twenty-One

From Big City Academic Library to Big City Public Library

Arieh D. Ress

In May of 2015, my temporary position at New York University (NYU) came to an end, and a few months later I was hired as a senior librarian at the New York Public Library (NYPL). I had been looking for a full-time librarian position, and while I was mostly applying to academic libraries, I really was open to any position that would make use of my varied skill set. To that end, I attended the American Library Association's annual conference in San Francisco in 2015. I approached the NYPL's recruitment booth at just the right time and ended up being interviewed on the spot. The skills I had were the skills they needed, and the schedule I was looking for was the schedule they were looking to fill. The clouds parted, the stars aligned, and a little over a month later I was hired for the position.

The position I had at NYU consisted mostly of business reference, though in the beginning I had been helping create video tutorials as well. I worked my way into any projects I could, eventually recording, editing, and posting videos of the unCommon Salon guest speaker series. However, the skills I use the most in my current work are actually ones I acquired in my prelibrary life. I've worked in various customer service positions, in a supermarket, in a photography studio, in the Health Sciences Library at the University at Buffalo, and I've done a lot of freelance work in which I taught myself computer skills, including graphic design, photo and video editing, and advanced Internet research. I also tutored people in computer and gadget use. Many of these skills were sitting on the shelf for the majority of the years between graduate school and my time at NYPL, and the feeling of finally putting them to use for the betterment of my community is indescribably wonderful.

While academic librarians wear their fair share of hats, nothing can quite compare to the variety of a librarian in a major New York City public library with late hours (I work until 11 p.m. most nights). The moment I started my new job it was evident that I was in the right place. While we all have some sort of designation (I'm a senior librarian—adult services), the positions involve a wide variety of library work. I teach computer classes and host programs ranging from author talks to the highly popular English Conversation Hour. I write blogs, work with social media, provide reference services in five different areas of the library, shoot photos and videos, organize digital media for use in internal and external promotional and informational materials, provide general customer service and tech support, locate materials for patrons, and soon will be processing holds on books, CDs, and DVDs as well. There is the opportunity to do even more, and every year we can propose new types of classes, programming, or innovative projects. All my skills are used, our patrons and the library itself benefit, and I feel really good about my job.

If you are looking to make this particular transition, know that your new position will require a level of flexibility and constant creativity you may not be used to. It is also important to be the type of person who thrives in very malleable and often fast-paced surroundings: we provide many, very different services to a broad swath of humanity, and interactions range from assisting with hard-core research projects to providing information on what homeless shelter someone will be able to sleep in that night. This is, as the name itself says, dealing with the public on a scale far greater and more intense than one encounters in an academic setting, even if your academic library is open to the public. If you are looking for a quiet, orderly place to work where your hands stay clean and you know what to expect every day, a bustling, big city public library may not be the place for you. There are public libraries out there that focus strictly on research and can provide a more serene setting, but those are few and far between.

I really enjoyed my time at NYU, and I loved the people I worked with, but the position I was in had limited reach and abilities, so many of my skills sat on the shelf. For me, the transition was easy because my current duties are what I envisioned doing when I set out to become a librarian in the first place. I thrive on change, variety, and excitement at work; this job, and especially this particular branch, is absolutely the right fit for me. There is one thing that is taking some getting used to in my transition from academia to public librarianship: the amount of annual leave is drastically reduced. Traveling for the holidays is not really possible in my new position, at least until I am here long enough to gain some seniority. I have a good amount of annual leave per year, but obviously no public library can compete with academic libraries, which are closed for weeks at a time and provide annual leave on top of that. It's a small price to pay and rarely crosses my mind, though. It's a cliché for a reason: if you love what you do, it doesn't feel like work.

Chapter Twenty-Two

An Interview with Catharina Isberg, Library Director, Helsingborg Public Library, Sweden

Ray: Thanks for talking to us! When did you get your first job as a librarian?

Catharina: After finishing my studies in library and information science, I got my first job as a librarian in 1991. During my education, I did work as a library assistant at a public library and then made the decision to focus my study on corporate and research libraries.

My first job was as a librarian within the pharmaceutical industry. I started working in Malmö, Sweden, and after eight years the work moved over the sound to Copenhagen, Denmark. My daily commuting between Sweden and Denmark went on for three years. During my time within the company, I went from librarian to library manager, then library and archive manager, and finally, library director. During my last year, I worked as VP corporate communication and information.

In 2003, I had started working at a university library as library manager of one of the libraries within the Swedish University of Agricultural Sciences. After a couple of years, I combined the work with being deputy library director, and my last year I worked as director of scientific information management as well as deputy library director. In 2013, I started as director at the public library of Helsingborg, Sweden.

Ray: Which skills were you able to bring from your past experience that were helpful in your current position?

Catharina: The most important skills for my present job are my leadership skills and my management experience. These are vital parts of my daily job.

I have continuously been developing my leadership skills through different programs offered within my different workplaces or from other training options. I have also had different mentors and coaches to further develop my management skills.

Conferences and networking are important parts of being up to date within the library field as well as the working arena. My experience working with different kinds of libraries is a plus when working within a changing environment where we need to learn more from each other and also increase our collaboration within the library and information field.

Ray: Do you think librarians and archivists get typecast based on their early jobs?

Catharina: Yes, I think we do get typecast, but I also think there is a need for us to move within the different library types. There is a need for an exchange of skills and knowledge. For example, the public libraries now have a need to get the competence that university libraries have within the information literacy field.

University libraries need to get the knowledge of public libraries' skills on addressing many different target groups and their experience within service management. I also think that we believe that there are fewer opportunities to move between the different fields than there is. We need to take the step and try it.

Ray: What advice would you give for someone who is hoping to work in leadership roles at organizations throughout the field?

Catharina: Go for it! There are many more opportunities than one thinks. If you make the wrong move, you just move back. And you then have an experience that you would not have got if you stayed where you were.

Both the individual and the employer gain a lot of knowledge, insights, new ways of addressing the work, energy, and experience when we move between different employers and between different library fields. After some years, you need to get the energy and new perspectives from a new employer and a new position. That will develop both the individual as well as the organization you work for and, in the end, the library field and the community.

VI

From Public to Specialized Librarianship

Chapter Twenty-Three

A Conversation with Lisa Chow and Sandra Sajonas

Starting Your Own Consulting Gig

Interested in starting your own consulting gig? How do you get started? Should you jump right in or test the waters? Lisa Chow and Sandra Sajonas share their experiences, advice, and lessons learned in this conversation with the editors.

Davis: We are interested in hearing about how you started your consulting company, People Interact. How did you go about doing it? Why did you go that route? What lessons did you learn about it, and how has public librarianship helped you in these new and exciting roles?

Lisa: "How did you get started?" is a common question that we get asked. The answer sometimes surprises people. We started by blogging. Okay, so that's really a simple, long-story-short answer. We started People Interact in 2010. Time flies. I feel like we started before the blog though, unofficially anyway. That's the more complicated answer. How do you remember it?

Sandra: I remember the idea to blog coming up during one of our "water cooler" conversations. At the time, blogging was really taking off, and Lisa knew more about blogging and the tools. I felt that we needed to have something to say and blog about. Over many "water cooler" conversations we would refine the theme of our blog.

Lisa: I didn't realize this until I was looking back and came across some old notes. It turned out when I was finishing up library school in 2009, I had been casually exploring the idea of consulting. The seed had been planted unknowingly, so maybe that's why I feel like we started before the blog. Do we count the seed planting as starting?

Sandra: It's difficult to say exactly when we started calling ourselves consultants. It probably happened naturally when we started to see a theme in the types of work we were doing. We were only accepting projects that we felt confident in our knowledge and abilities to complete.

Lisa: Yeah, and I remember we were pretty hesitant in starting the blog and trying to make things perfect and line our ducks in a row before we launched. We were trying to decide on a name, getting feedback from our friends and colleagues, etc. I remember us spending half the day at New York Public Library's Science, Industry, and Business Library doing research. After a ton of back and forth, debating, hemming and hawing, we decided to just take the plunge. We were afraid of making mistakes and played the "what if" game for months. We eventually realized this type of thinking would get us nowhere and decided to go forth with the blog.

Sandra: I'm glad you pushed us to just launch it and tweak as we go. We decided to model start-ups and tech companies and just launch a beta blog. The theme for our blog was a result of a library school class on design thinking and usability we had taken. Library unusability was a big pet peeve of ours. We started blogging in October 2010 to champion libraries improving user experience. A side goal of our blog was to also assist other library professionals in library-career-related manners.

Lisa: Eventually, after about a few years of blogging, our names started circulating in the library world, and people began approaching us to give presentations and work on projects.

Sandra: We were very selective about the topics of our presentations and projects. It's important that we do not fall into the trap of being jacks-of-all-trades and masters of none. We wanted continuity between our blog and what would eventually become our consulting.

Lisa: Speaking of what would become our consulting, remember before we started People Interact, at that event where we put "aspiring consultants" on our nametags? I figured let's try something different instead of the usual.

Sandra: Yeah, that was a good idea. It initiated a lot of interesting conversations at the event.

Lisa: Yeah, I remember someone asking me if I had lost my job and that's why I was getting into consulting. The person was a little surprised to hear that I have a full-time job and I'm aspiring to be a consultant. Consulting gets a bad reputation sometimes . . . like it's something you do when you don't have a full-time job or other options.

Ray: So why consulting?

Sandra: In the beginning, we romanticized the idea of working for yourself. We did tons of informational interviews with other consultants and asked this same question. We found that being self-employed was ranked pretty low on the list of reasons to consult.

Lisa: With consulting, we are able to work on projects of interest beyond our day-to-day work routines.

Sandra: Consulting also opened up the library world beyond the public library where we both were at the time. When you work a nine-to-five, you have a tendency to become pigeonholed into that area.

Lisa: While we enjoyed the public library, we are also interested in other types and areas of the library world. Consulting allows us to explore different areas of the varied information profession. We also like working on projects.

Sandra: In retrospect, working in public librarianship helped us to transition into consulting. Not only did it give us a jump-start in our careers as librarians by helping us develop all the necessary skills and training, it also allowed us to network, which would come in handy once we started to consult. The public library is also unique in that as new librarians, we were given flexibility in choosing the types of trainings and professional development rather than being categorized in a specific area.

Lisa: Many consultants do their consulting full time. For us, it's a juggling and balancing act.

Davis: Tell us more about that.

Lisa: I juggle consulting while working full time. Juggling consulting while working full time is a challenge, mainly with time management. From the very beginning, I understood that a percentage of my vacation time, weekends, and evenings would need to be spent on People Interact. Understanding is one thing, doing is a whole other thing. There have been times where I needed some motivation, especially on an evening after a long day and really nice weekends. Luckily, I've got Sandra to give me the extra push when necessary.

Sandra and I started talking about consulting shortly after I finished library school, possibly starting off with a blog. Sandra talked about the importance of having a business plan and other business aspects. I agreed with her, but part of me just wanted to jump right in. After spending countless hours researching and talking things through, we decided to launch our blog. Perfection is the enemy of progress, and the turtle only makes progress by sticking its neck out. We were going to learn and tweak as we go.

At first, it took a while to get into blogging, but eventually we were coming up with ideas left and right. Coblogging is easier and a lot more fun. Sometimes we cowrite the blog posts, and sometimes we write blog posts individually. We alternate and step in for each other as needed. It really helps to know that Sandra's got my back if I run into writer's block or just have a really hectic and busy week or month. After a few years of blogging, our consulting grew, and it has led to several projects, presentations, and workshops, both regionally and nationally.

Ray: You work with People Interact as a side business for now. How do you keep up the motivation to work on this while also keeping up with a full-time job, Lisa?

Lisa: I really enjoy doing what I do, but there's a finite amount of time and energy, and unfortunately life and schedules don't always mesh with your energy levels. There are times where I don't feel like working on anything library related. Sounds crazy and unprofessional perhaps? But sometimes I just need a break. So my motivation dwindles for a little while, and usually a quick chat with Sandra does the trick. There's just something about us talking and bouncing around ideas that gets me running again, no matter how tired or unmotivated I may be feeling.

While juggling consulting while working full time is a challenge, there are upsides:

- Less financial pressure to find and accept any and all consulting jobs and projects.
- Working full-time allows me to witness many user experience and design-thinking scenarios and situations that occur in a library setting.
- Working full-time helps keep me connected to the library world.

Consulting and working full-time has worked for me so far. It's definitely challenging timewise, but I am comfortable knowing that I have less pressure and more flexibility when it comes to finding and choosing what projects to take on.

Davis: How about you, Sandra? Tell us more about how you juggle consulting while being a stay-at-home parent.

Sandra: I was the most hesitant to start consulting and even blogging. However, Lisa helped me to realize that having a formalized plan kept us from moving forward and that it was okay to make mistakes, and so our blog was born.

At first, it was very time-consuming to write up posts but eventually became fun, especially because I had a partner to help split the load. There were times, months even, when I couldn't find time or energy to work. Lisa took a lot of the load and also helped to keep me motivated. Additionally, having a partner expanded our scope because we could each contribute our strengths, expertise, and experience to the group.

After a few years blogging while continuing to work, our reputation in the library world began to grow. This was done mainly through our individual efforts in the profession, as well as heavily networking and marketing ourselves as People Interact. This eventually led to several presentations and workshops, including

- DIY usability and user experience workshops

  - Public Library Association Conference in March 2010
  - Metropolitan New York Library Council in April 2012
  - Long Island Library Resources Council in October 2012
  - Massachusetts Library System in October 2012
  - Rochester Regional Library Council in February 2013

- Presentations on leadership and career development, e-portfolios, and so on

  - Kentucky Library Association Conference in September 2015
  - Library 2.012 and 2.013 Worldwide Virtual Conferences in 2012 and 2013
  - Special Libraries Association Hudson Valley Annual Meeting in November 2012
  - Special Libraries Association Click University Webinar in November 2012

- New York Chapter of Special Libraries Association at METRO in March 2011
- SLA@Pratt Skill Share Fair every year from 2010 to 2013

When I finally decided to make the transition to full-time consulting, People Interact and our reputations were in a place we were happy with. At this point, we had steady projects and presentations lined up. I felt comfortable that I would have plenty of work.

While consulting doesn't pay the bills, it was nice to pursue only jobs and projects that interested me. Working from home also cuts out hours spent on extraneous items like filling out time sheets and commuting and allows me to use my time efficiently. I am using the extra time in my day to explore other areas of librarianship that I may be interested in transitioning into. Consulting and working from home allows me the flexibility to explore and meet various people for informational interviews about their area of work.

Paid professional development is one major downside to being self-employed. One goal I had was to further my skills, especially tech-related skills. Luckily, there are tons of free/cheap resources as well as library associations offering webinars and distance learning, such as Metropolitan New York Library Council and New Librarians Global Connection. Some associations are also nice about offering membership discounts for various situations. I do have to be more selective about which associations I join since I am paying for them myself.

Staying up to date is also difficult when self-employed and a full-time mom. I no longer had access to professional magazines or trade resources. Again, the Internet is useful for this. I receive RSS feeds from news aggregators and professional sites like LinkedIn group discussions. I also read about conferences online since I cannot afford to attend them. I'll read about the conference themes, program headlines, and other materials online.

Keeping up my skills and work experience is also something I struggle with. When I stopped working, I didn't want to be penalized in future job hunts because I stopped working full-time. I realized that there are just some skills and abilities that cannot be exercised from home with the Internet. I found a historical society where I volunteer one day a week. After visiting area libraries for story times, I also found one that has a great work schedule for parents and asks as little as eight volunteering hours a week.

All in all, consulting and being a stay-at-home mom works for me in my current situation. I took a big leap, but I am also comfortable knowing that I can go back to full-time work when I am ready.

Ray: What if others wanted to do the same, would you recommend it, and if so, how should they prepare themselves?

Lisa: Over the years, we learned many lessons while making the transition into consulting. While it's possible to fly solo when consulting, and many consultants do, it definitely helps to have a partner in crime for a consulting endeavor. We support each other, bounce ideas off each other, step in when necessary, etc. We have worked on various projects together and know we work well together. Questions to ask include: Do your skills complement each other? Do your work styles work well with each other? Additionally, being a duo allows us to spread our influence when we each work independently on various projects.

Sandra: When we first started, we got caught up in the innumerable online tools for project management. Some were helpful (Google products, Dropbox) and some not so (Trello, wikis). We found that it became a chore just to manage all of our management tools. We dropped some. We recommend for whichever tools you do use, make sure to have a master document with all usernames and passwords.

Lisa: One thing we didn't expect was the massive amount of housekeeping we would have to do. At our annual review, we discard things that are not working or we no longer need, like some of the online tools that Sandra mentioned. We try to digitize as many documents as possible so that it keeps filing cabinets clean but also makes things easily accessible for both of us. We also keep a time-tracking spreadsheet to give us a better idea of what we're investing our time in.

Sandra: We have meetings in person, over the phone, or online as needed. Every year, we come together for an annual review to discuss where we are and where we are going. Individually and together we conduct SWOT (strengths, weaknesses, opportunities, threat) analysis. Doing this also helps to set our expectations for the future. It's important to set goals but also to know your exit plan if you are not reaching your goals or expectations. We have an explicit understanding of when, why, and how we would call it quits.

Lisa: We recommend going the consulting route if you enjoy taking the initiative and working on projects. Start by dipping a toe in the water instead of jumping right in. There are other factors (i.e., having other sources of income, especially a steady income, health insurance, etc.) to consider. Also, consulting might not turn out to be what you expected. Of course, if and when you are ready to go all in, then by all means, go for it.

Chapter Twenty-Four

From the New York Public Library to CNN

How I Transitioned from Public to News Librarianship

Christina Podenski

I worked at the New York Public Library (NYPL) when I was in high school and in college. I was a page and computer page at the Todt-Hill Westerleigh branch and a clerk at the St. George branch in Staten Island. I will never forget how excited I was to go to work and how happy I was being in a library. It was then that I thought a career in the library field would be perfect for me! I love to read, so it made sense that working in a library was the place for me and that a possible career could come out of it.

But I then went off to the George Washington University in Washington, DC, for my junior and senior year of college. The school was in a great location and was close to the White House, the Lincoln Memorial, and the Washington Monument, as well as a short walk from Georgetown. While I was there, I was an intern for the House, Senate, and White House and was a member of the College Republicans. Being in that environment made me realize that I had a change of heart about a career in the library field, and I decided to focus my efforts on politics and the media.

Upon my graduation, I was an intern for Fox News' *Hannity & Colmes* at their world headquarters in New York City. I learned so much during my internship, such as how to write the script for a show's opening segment, how to select the best video elements, how an editor puts together a package, why certain guests are on during the show, how to research and pitch segment ideas, and how a control room works.

Being an intern at Fox News made me so happy, and my eyes were opened to the fascinating world of the news and media. Fox television host

Bill O'Reilly always said hello to me, radio host Alan Colmes became a mentor to me, and Sean Hannity would ask how my family was and what my aspirations were. I met a lot of wonderful people who inspired me every day.

After my internship was complete, I was hired to work full-time as a prime-time graphics production assistant. I continued to work with the staff of *Hannity & Colmes* and began to work with Bill O'Reilly's staff and Greta Van Susteren's staff. Even though I was enjoying myself, I felt like something was missing. I still wanted to accomplish more. This was when I decided that I wanted to go to graduate school. I wasn't sure what I wanted to get my degree in yet, but I knew it was the right next step for me.

I had a very tough choice to make. Do I stay with Fox, where I have a full-time job, and maybe never have the chance to go back to school, or do I leave Fox to go to school and maybe never have the opportunity to work for the media again? I ultimately decided that the best decision was to go back to school, and I left my job at Fox.

It was a hard decision, but I felt that once my master's degree was complete, I would somehow get back into the media. I was hired by NYPL as an information assistant and was assigned to the St. George branch, one of the branches I had worked at when I was in college. After working there for a few months, I decided that I wanted to get my master of library and information science (MLIS) and enrolled at Queens College. I thought that an MLIS degree not only could be applied to my current library job but that it could also help me with a future job in the media.

My time at St. George focused mostly on working with the young adult collection. I was responsible for all of the programming, outreach, collection upkeep, and monthly reports. The area that the library was in wasn't the best, and a lot of the young adult patrons didn't have much of a family life. They often came to the library to escape their situation and would come to me for advice or just to have someone to talk to. Some of the young adults were very friendly, liked to read, and were always asking for book recommendations. They were motivated, did well in school, and talked about where they wanted to go to college. They made me feel as though I was doing a great job and that I was actually helping them to succeed in the future.

Others, unfortunately, were not as motivated. They would start trouble, sit on the computer for hours at a time, and cut school. They could be very disrespectful. I realized that I did not have the patience or energy to deal with these teens. I thought that they were ruining the experience for those teens who were trying to better themselves and were trying to use the library for positive reasons. I was a graduate from a top 50 university and a former White House intern, and here I was—a glorified babysitter and referee. While I enjoyed working with the teens who behaved themselves, I realized that you have to take the good ones with the bad ones, and I decided that being a young adult librarian in a public library was not the place for me. I felt that that my heart still belonged to the media, and that was where I wanted to go next.

I decided to try looking into jobs in the media where I could use my master's degree. I was looking at all the major news outlets—ABC, CBS, NBC—and I finally came across an opening for a librarian in CNN's World Headquarters in Atlanta. I decided that I was going to apply for it because I wanted to get out of New York City. I liked the idea of starting over in a new place, especially one where there wasn't snow! I filled out the application, submitted my résumé, and waited. I kept checking my phone and my e-mail to see if anyone had reached out to me. But there wasn't a response yet.

One Friday during the end of May 2010, I was getting ready for book club when I noticed that I had a missed call and a voicemail from a number that I didn't recognize. The area code was 404, so I decided to look it up and see what area that was from. It turned out that 404 is an Atlanta area code. I wasn't sure why someone in Atlanta would be calling me, so I thought it was a wrong number. Then I remembered the job at CNN and thought that maybe it was someone from CNN calling about the librarian job. I crossed my fingers and listened to the message; it was someone from human resources calling me to set up a phone interview for the position! I couldn't believe it. After my phone interview, they flew me down to Atlanta for an in-person interview, and they offered me the job a week later. I was so happy that I was going to be able to have a career that combined my first love of libraries and my later love of the media. I finished school and received my master's degree on August 4, which was also my last day at NYPL. I started my new job at CNN on August 9, five years ago. Time sure does fly!

I felt that the transition from my job at NYPL to the News Library at CNN wasn't as overwhelming as I thought it would be. CNN was a welcoming environment, and I was able to quickly get back into the groove of being in the news. A big part of being able to succeed at CNN has been my news background, but I also brought over some helpful skills that I learned at the public library. One of them in particular was being able to diffuse a situation quickly. Some of the patrons that I had dealt with at St. George could be difficult, so I had learned the proper way to speak to them to try to keep them calm. This skill was very helpful for my job at CNN because we sometimes get a call from a client who is facing a tight deadline to get archival content on air and is having trouble locating it in our video catalog. We handle those situations with professionalism and assist the client with whatever they need. We rely on our expertise in searching the archive and our skills at conducting reference interviews to quickly help the client and hopefully find what they need, or a great substitute, and get that content on air.

One big difference between the two types of libraries is that since we work with video content at CNN, a lot of it comes with licensing and rights issues. I didn't have to worry about that at NYPL since we never worked with video, but it is a big part of my job at CNN. I have to know which videos are OK for air and which ones cannot be used. We have a department that deals with rights issues, and we have a good relationship with them and we help each other out.

I feel that a big part of where I am today is because of my experience at Fox News and at NYPL. Two of the requirements for my current job were a master's degree in library science and news experience. I never thought that I would be able to combine two of my passions into one exciting career.

As an archive librarian, I am at the video reference desk a few days a week and assist CNN employees from all around the world with video research. The video requests that we receive at the desk vary from day-to-day and some examples include finding a specific sound bite from a speech by President Barack Obama, World War II footage, crowded street scenes from New York City, and families eating dinner in a restaurant. I am also part of a project that gathers elements for breaking news. The team works together to provide the most recent and well-known videos of world leaders, politicians, presidents, and celebrities to play in the background during breaking news.

One of the most rewarding things about working at CNN is seeing your work on air. It makes me so happy when I see video that I helped a client find make it on the air. It's also rewarding when a client expresses their thanks and appreciation for the work that you do. To us, we are just doing our job, but to the client, we did the most extraordinary thing. I really enjoy helping clients with video requests, and it makes me happy when they are happy.

If someone were to ask me for advice on how to transition from one type of library to another, I would suggest trying to get some kind of experience in the type of library he or she would like to work in. Whether it's through an internship or volunteering, this is a great way not only to gain experience but also to find out whether or not you actually want to work or be in that type of library. I would also suggest trying to find people who work in the type of library that you are interested in and get to know them. Ask them questions about what kind of work they do, what their responsibilities are, how they got to where they are today, and what advice they have to offer.

When I first started working at NYPL in high school, I never dreamed that I would be where I am today. I am extremely grateful for all of the experiences that I have had and where they have led me. My advice is to never say never, do what makes you happy, and go above and beyond what is asked of you to get the job done. It shows initiative and that you are a team player.

Chapter Twenty-Five

From Libraries to Museums

Successfully Adapting to Working in a Different Type of Cultural Institution

Laura Ruttum Senturia

Sometimes the best career choice you can make is to jump off into the unknown. Most employment advisors will tell you to plan carefully; that your résumé should display a logical, linear progression; and that you should always have a road map in hand when making a decision. For the most part, this is sound advice. In the field of libraries, however, the current dearth of opportunities requires some creative thinking—identifying other disciplines to which our skills are applicable—in addition to flexibility. Librarians today must be brave when it comes to tackling the employment market. My recent career experience moving into museum libraries has provided a valuable lesson: don't be afraid to cross professional barriers into realms of the cultural world that may have previously seemed foreign to you. Your life will be richer for it.

Cultural institutions such as libraries, archives, and museums are incredibly broad and diverse; however, there are also key competencies that are shared across each of them. Boiled down to the simplest ingredients, cultural institutions are in the business of education, entertainment, and information dissemination. Our methods of approach to these key elements differ, sometimes greatly, but at the end of the (often very long) workday, we're all aiming for the same goalposts. It is with this in mind that I share my own experiences with crossing disciplinary lines.

After completing my degrees, I jumped into archives work as a processing archivist on a short-term grant at a historical society. There I learned a lot about processing; however, I had no understanding of the researchers' needs, nor about how they might approach a collection. Following the grant, I moved to the New York Public Library (NYPL) as a combined processing and reference archivist in the Manuscripts and Archives Division. This divided role provided me a dual view of the archives equation: I learned prevalent research topics, researchers' needs and methods, the challenges of public service, and a closer familiarity with the rich array of collections in the division. In my final year at NYPL, I transferred to the U.S. History, Local History, and Genealogy Division. I developed additional skills crucial to a special collections librarian: genealogy research and the art of working with genealogists.

This was when I made my biggest jump into the unknown: in 2010, I decided to move back home to Colorado, without a job on the horizon. At the time, this was a terrible decision: the bottom had recently dropped out of the local library job market. In addition, there is a Denver-based MLS program pumping out graduates regularly. According to Colorado's Library Research Service, in 2010 there were 264 library job postings—from shelving clerk all the way up to library director—across the *entire state* (Colorado is the ninth-largest state in the country, geographically).[1] Even worse, those 264 position postings saw 728,024 page views![2] Clearly, anyone interested in our field had to be creative.

Over the course of the next two years, I volunteered at three different institutions, began my own fledgling archival consultancy, became involved in local professional organizations, took a part-time paraprofessional position at a medical library, and took a temporary position at an academic library in collection development. I learned something from each of these roles, including copy cataloging at my paraprofessional job.

Then in 2012, the golden opportunity presented itself: a position as library director at a small special collections library at the History Colorado museum. The institution was looking for someone with archives, library, research, and genealogy experience who was interested in trying out new things. To them, my previous, seemingly haphazard experience was seen as a positive. Hallelujah! My enthusiasm was soon dampened when I learned I had a bit of a problem: challenges over territory and philosophy with my collections colleagues (curators and collection managers).

I'll begin by stating that, after the dust has settled, I highly value these colleagues for their impressive knowledge about collections and museum work and the opportunity to work with them on various teams. I regularly learn from them still. At the beginning of my time here, however, we were eyeing each other suspiciously over a vast gulf of misunderstanding, mostly based on differences in philosophies between our disciplines. On occasion, flaming arrows were shot over our fortress walls.

This is where my lesson in flexibility began: I needed to learn how to bridge the gulf between librarians and collections staff and to adapt to being a special collections librarian (a field I knew) situated within a museum (a different animal than any of the institutions I had previously experienced). If this arrangement was to be sustainable, I needed to learn how to adopt the viewpoint, lingo, and values of my colleagues while blending them with our own noble profession's set of principles. With apologies for my lengthy bio, the following are the main lessons I have learned over the past several years:

EXAMINE YOUR SACRED COWS, EMBRACE COMPROMISE

Imagine you work in a library where they hire a management-level staffer who holds an MBA, has no library experience, and espouses ideas entirely counter to what you see as best practice. This staffer suggest changes to your unit without taking the time to learn your basic principles or even terminology. Many of you do not need to imagine this scenario, as it has happened in libraries across the country.

If you are making a jump to a new type of institution, don't be that person, and don't assume you know the territory just because it *looks* similar to what you know. It is easy to run into conflict over values. To a librarian and archivist, access to the information contained within documents or books is the most important principle (while archivists do consider the original object, they often make decisions that preference information over item). To a museum curator, however, preservation is primary before access. Gloves are worn when handling most artifacts, in many cases the objects are only seen through glass on exhibit, and the general public is generally not given on-demand, in-person access to artifacts. This primary focus on preservation stood out most starkly for me when I would hear colleagues talking about the needs of the collection and not considering the needs of the researchers.

At History Colorado, however, our administration wanted to turn the Library and Research Center into a reading room for artifacts as well as traditional library materials. Staff hoped to grant access to 3-D objects on demand, storage location and item size permitting. Retrieving larger or fragile items would require advanced notice, as objects needed to be transferred from off-site storage, or patrons would have to be taken to the artifacts (easier than moving a train from off-site!).

Our differences in values complicated this effort, and our new plan was not without its struggles. Library staff weren't permitted to retrieve artifacts ourselves, but collections staff were initially resistant to the immediacy of customer service requests. Some collections staff insisted patron requests were public information, and librarians defended the privacy of those records. Collections staff wanted to man the reference desk, and librarians refused to cede any territory. We were all acting within the practices of our fields without understanding why our stances sent our colleagues into spasms of frustration.

Eventually, we found a common language. Librarians handle most research requests and patron records, while collections staff handle the physical access in a reasonable time frame, which is under their control. For nine months, we experimented with having collection managers sharing some reference desk shifts—an effort that initially met with great concern from the librarians. We quickly learned that our museum colleagues' knowledge of the collection and the collection management database enriched both patrons and library staff alike.

Ultimately, however, the walk-in public demand for artifact access was not sufficient to require collection managers ' physical presence for dedicated hours. Perhaps better marketing of the service would change this, but for the meantime, collections staff is available on call for immediate requests. It has been a nice compromise.

Through the process of expanding collection access, both sides learned from the other, discovered new ways of seeing things, and ceded some sacred ground. For those librarians among you who gasp at the thought of putting non-MLS staff on the reference desk, it turned out our world didn't end. Instead, we saw that our sacred cow was interfering with good customer service. Our colleagues brought a new knowledge base with them, which in the end served our patrons better than we ever could in terms of artifacts.

SEE THE COMMONALITIES, "STEAL" GOOD IDEAS

All cultural institutions are struggling with the changes technology has wrought over the past twenty years, which has democratized searching, entertainment, and access to knowledge. When we're being honest, we admit these changes have made our institutions, as previously defined, less indispensable than they were in the past. Neither libraries nor museums can assume we hold a monopoly on information. Visitation and use patterns have changed, donations have become less frequent, government funding has stagnated, and grants have dried up. When Bill Gates is suggesting donors send their crucial dollars elsewhere, you know we have a problem.[3] We are all faced with the necessity of redrafting our image, redesigning our services and products, and remaining relevant to a broad audience.

For libraries, this has meant becoming a community center, offering goods and services such as craft classes, free music downloads, coding programs, and makerspaces. For museums, this has meant changing their philosophy from a more paternal, authoritative educational voice to an inclusive, discursive one. To quote Stephen Weil, an influential thinker in the museum studies field, museums have changed "from being about something to being for somebody." [4]

But just as there are many worldviews, religions, and child-rearing practices, different professional disciplines have evolved different solutions to common problems. Libraries and museums can—and indeed *should*—borrow from each other. For example, museums do not have a standard descriptive-subject cataloging system like Library of Congress Subject Headings, nor do they have a union catalog such as OCLC's WorldCat. There is no commonly shared practice for how to format proper names and no subdivided terms to add shades of meaning. The Chenhall system, in use for many museums, is a set of descriptive standards that concerns itself, for the most part, with the artifact's physical format and not what the artifact is *about*. But can we really say what a chair is about, anyway? Long descriptions of the "aboutness" of chairs would not be particularly useful to the museum practitioner. This does create difficulty in searching the lexicon across an entire database or finding common artifacts across institutions. While not currently in use, a unified standard could be helpful to museums.

Libraries, meanwhile, are still making fledgling movements toward determining patron needs and interests through direct audience survey and assessment. Librarians are trained to anticipate needs and to be responsive to them when they are shared with us, but we spend so much effort anticipating that we sometimes forget to ask outright. When is the last time you were handed an iPad at a library and asked to fill out a brief survey? Yet this happens often at museums.

In recent years, museums have developed strong statistical logic models to study their visitors. They conduct regular, iterative assessments of exhibits and programs; some have entire departments dedicated to assessment. Museum staff occasionally stalk their visitors. Yes, stalk them, holding clipboards and stopwatches. They study traffic flows and "sticky" parts of the exhibit that best hold visitors' interest. They analyze which elements of the exhibit generate the most engagement, such as "call outs" to friends and family ("Mom, come look at this!").

History Colorado is particularly committed to these efforts, studying each exhibit's reception at opening and then again months later. Before undertaking new exhibits, we create prototypes that are placed in prominent areas of the museum, complete with paper and pens, asking visitors for their opinions and points of curiosity on the topic. Staff attends public events, such as local fairs and conferences to conduct man-on-the-street audience surveys. Many of our exhibits even include engagement elements of voting for your favorite topic or "talk back" opportunities where visitors can write comments for others to read.

Libraries could stand to double down on this sort of commitment to patron study and experience. Borrowing the brilliant ideas of our colleagues, unusual or strange as they might seem at first, can only stand to improve our own practice. In my own shop, I plan to begin conducting regular patron surveys. While we may guess at researcher needs, without their feedback, we'll never know how we did.

SAY YES TO VOLUNTEERING

As a professional new to a related field, ignore the pop-culture advice that tells you to learn to "say no" to excessive requests in order to remain sane. Say yes as often as you can, at least for the first few years. You'll be overwhelmed for a while, but it will be worth it.

Museums, just like libraries, often have more ideas and projects than people to realize them. If you are asked for help, say yes. If calls go out for volunteers or you see an arena where someone might need help, offer your services. I did this and strongly encouraged my (very amenable) staff to do the same. Some of the projects we've gotten involved in have had very little to do with our daily responsibilities, but they strengthen the museum as an institution. We have begun collaborating with many of our colleagues who know we'll sign up to run trivia at the late-night event, design special classes for the K–8 school groups, and serve on marketing, editorial, exhibit, and even party-planning committees.

Perhaps cynically, this sort of volunteerism not only helps your colleagues, but it also furthers your own agenda. It fills the well of good intentions, smooths ruffled feathers, and pleases the bosses. More important, it affords you a seat at the table for the larger discussions, putting you in the right place to learn about and jump on new opportunities. And perhaps most important, you learn things. You've heard the advice that a good employee would never tell the boss "that's not in my job description." Be the good employee, and expand your job description.

FIND ALLIES; IF NONE ARE APPARENT, MAKE THEM

In my current position, the library had previously held itself apart from the rest of the museum. Former staff did not appear to consider colleagues part of their researcher audience and did not necessarily become involved in museum-wide projects. Some former staff had been openly hostile to our collections colleagues. Thus, I began as a new director in a brand-new building, in a recently rebranded institution where tradition was being thrown to the wind. It was an exciting place to be but also one of much jostling for position. In my role, allies and bridge building were crucial, but the library had few allies, as those bridges had been burned before I arrived. Our initial conflicts and my lack of museum-specific knowledge did not help matters.

Sometimes you will find you have natural allies, and sometimes you need to help fate along by creating them. For my own part, alliance building meant being humble and asking lots of questions, which made peace with some individuals. Marketing our research and free digital photo services to co-workers museum-wide made us friends in other departments. The aforementioned spirit of volunteerism built our reputation, as did suggesting small projects we could add to the general cause.

Perhaps most difficult for me personally was building bridges to people who had consistently challenged me. One colleague happened to be most conversant with a collection that fit well with a new craft program I was launching. I hesitantly asked her to colead the series with me. She has wonderful ideas, knows the collection in and out, and enjoys being involved. Working together allowed us to find each other 's strengths and to work out a more comfortable professional relationship.

These efforts took time and patience but have turned a stressful work environment into a pleasant one where it feels like we're all rowing together. We respect each other's professional priorities. I can't take credit for most of the change, but I do believe altering my attitude and approach was the only direction toward progress.

FINALLY, KEEP LEARNING

This seems obvious to most in the cultural fields but cannot be repeated often enough. We have all occasionally worked with a colleague who has not updated their skill set or knowledge in decades. The drastic changes in our field no longer allow room for this.

Learning should include both self-directed reading and enrolling in additional formal education programs. I can hear the groans from here, especially since so many librarians already have two master's degrees. Self-directed education is great, as are workshops and conferences, but there's no substitute for the ways a professor and fellow students can challenge us. Prior to the museum studies master's certificate program in which I'm currently enrolled, I'm not sure if I would have known where to start in order to educate myself about the full prism of the field. How do you approach the unknown unknowns, to paraphrase a former politician? [5]

Additional formal education might just spark a new enthusiasm in you, as well as sending a crucial message to your colleagues that you respect their discipline. It's common sense: if you plan to have a career in an institution a little different from your training or previous norm, you had certainly better educate yourself on its operations and philosophies! You might learn how to approach even traditional library work from a different angle and thus better serve your audience.

CONCLUSION

For those library professionals considering making the jump to a related field, know that it can be done. As I feel my example indicates, it can be done repeatedly, provided you are the type of person who likes tackling new skills. Be assured that you will learn something useful at each juncture, some of which won't be immediately apparent as such. As your career takes new twists, some of these skills will reemerge and make you a stronger librarian or archivist or museum professional or whatever you have become.

The path will not be effortless and is littered with crumpled tissues and headache medication. You must undergo a metamorphosis in order to learn to magically fit into the new environment in which you have placed yourself. To this end, researching the new discipline—including pursuing some formal education—will always help. Formal study will help you not only land a job but will make you more qualified when you get there, thereby earning the respect of your future colleagues.

Being flexible and willing to reexamine your library assumptions will serve you well. Finding or creating allies and making the institution look good to the outside world will help you succeed. Take a page from the business world and borrow the brilliant strategies of your colleagues: directly survey your audience about what they want, experiment with new ideas, and adapt repeatedly. None of us knows what direction our entire profession, let alone our own professional careers, will take, and I wish you excitement and success wherever your path takes you.

NOTES

1. WorldAtlas, "U.S. States by Size," accessed August 7, 2015, www.worldatlas.com/aatlas/infopage/usabysiz.htm.

2. Library Research Service, "Clearer Skies Ahead? Using Statistics from LibraryJobline.org to Gauge Changes in Colorado's Library Job Climate," accessed August 7, 2015, www.lrs.org/fast-facts-reports/clearer-skies-ahead-using-statistics-from-libraryjobline-org-to-gauge-changes-in-colorados-library-job-climate/.

3. Richard Waters, "An Exclusive Interview with Bill Gates," *Financial Times* magazine, November 1, 2013, www.ft.com/cms/s/2/dacd1f84-41bf-11e3-b064-00144feabdc0.html.

4. Stephen Weil, "From Being about Something to Being for Somebody: The Ongoing Transformation of the American Museum," *Daedalus* 128, no. 3 (Summer 1999): 229.

5. U.S. Department of Defense, "DoD News Briefing: Secretary Rumsfeld and Gen. Myers," news transcript, February 12, 2002, accessed August 12, 2015, http://archive.defense.gov/transcripts.aspx?transcriptid=2636

Chapter Twenty-Six

Nine Qualities to Cultivate across Your Entire Career

Sarah T. Jewell

I have over a decade of experience in science and medical librarianship, having started in public librarianship, moving to hospital librarianship, and eventually transitioning to academic librarianship. Although I enjoyed my experiences in both public and hospital librarianship, my dream to work as a university librarian was formed while I attended library school from 2003 to 2005, and I'm happy to report that I achieved that dream about ten years after graduation by returning to the same institution where I started my pursuit of librarianship: Rutgers University. I developed many helpful qualities along my journey, and I hope that by sharing them with you, you will find some useful insights.

HUMILITY

I was lucky to start my career in librarianship at the New York Public Library (NYPL). Specifically, the Science, Industry, and Business Library (SIBL) on Madison Avenue and Thirty-Fourth Street in Manhattan. The first quality I cultivated at NYPL, which ultimately helped me succeed where other new librarians have struggled, was humility. I was the valedictorian at my high school, earned good grades in my bachelor's in biology in college, and then truly excelled in my master's in library science program at Rutgers University, earning scholarships and awards. So when I started working for SIBL fresh out of library school at the young age of twenty-three, I thought I knew *everything*. I was quickly (but gently) taught that this was not the case. Before I was allowed to take the reins, I had a full month where I observed at the reference desk. I was in awe of the complexity of the research questions the librarians handled. I took full advantage of the observation time I was allowed and took good notes, learning about the most frequently used resources and how they worked. Humility in the face of the breadth of knowledge that we deal with is a good strategy, even if you are not a beginner. Keeping a beginner's mind and not being afraid to ask good questions can advance your career.

CONFIDENCE

When I started working at NYPL, I frequently received questions like "May I speak to a librarian?" or "Where's the *real* librarian?" Part of it may have been because of my youth, but part of it was my lack of confidence. Once I started tackling more reference questions and became more comfortable with my own knowledge and expertise, the questions about my qualifications died down. People seemed to be able to sense that I was the expert who could help them.

I knew I would make it at SIBL the day my colleague received a request for information on gap junctions. He looked over at me, understanding enough to know that it was out of his realm and at the same time trusting that I could handle the science question. Once I confirmed that the patron wanted a basic explanation about what gap junctions were (and not the latest research regarding them), I simply walked the patron to the bookshelf where Bruce Alberts's *Molecular Biology of the Cell* was resting

After a few years at NYPL, I felt confident enough with my abilities that I communicated with my boss about my desire to work in a library with a narrower focus on science or medicine. Fortunately, he supported me in this endeavor. I started applying for other jobs, and I would eventually land a position as a medical reference librarian at the Memorial Sloan Kettering Cancer Center.

PREPAREDNESS

When preparing for an interview with a potential employer, do your homework. Research the culture of the library or company you plan to work for. What is the mission of the library or organization? When writing your cover letter, make sure to use as much terminology from the job description or advertisement as possible, as human resources personnel often keep a running tally of how many pertinent qualifications you seem to meet.

In addition, when you are writing your résumé, make sure you are prepared to back up every bullet point on the list, and beware of embellishing anything too much. Your résumé should accurately reflect your experience and skill levels.

When I was interviewing for my future position at Sloan Kettering, the library's programmer zoomed in on my bulleted list of technical skills. "I see you are familiar with HTML," he said, passing me a piece of paper. "Write me a few lines of valid HTML code." It was a nerve-wracking moment for me, as it wasn't a skill I used every day at work, but I took a deep breath and wrote some simple code for a link to the NYPL website. He was sufficiently satisfied. It can be common for simple tests of skill such as this to occur during job interviews, so brushing up on the basics beforehand can help prepare you for potential questions.

CLARITY

Once I started working at Sloan Kettering, there was a shift in the primary modes of communication I used on the job. At NYPL, we had mostly dealt with in-person reference questions, but at Sloan Kettering the majority came in via e-mail. Thus, at NYPL we had visual cues and body language to inform our reference interviews, but at Sloan Kettering an adjustment had to be made in my dealing with individuals. Early on in my career at Sloan Kettering, I sent out a particularly lengthy e-mail, attempting to describe a process step by step to my client. My boss, included on the e-mail, pulled me aside and explained the value of brevity. She also encouraged me to try picking up the phone from time to time to reach out to our clients. I was responsive to the feedback, and in particular, picking up the phone worked wonders.

Observing and mirroring the way others, particularly successful colleagues, respond to clients can help you develop your own skills. If you are struggling with particular aspects of communication, solicit feedback from colleagues or take a human resources course in business communication. Remember that communication in the business world has different norms than communication in everyday life, and even particular industries and workplaces can vary on the preferred means of communication, so above all be sure to observe the preferred modes of communication when undergoing a major change such as a new job. When in doubt, err on the side of caution and formality, as it is generally harder to apologize for an inappropriate casual remark than it is to merely adjust your level of formality based on a person's response.

PROFESSIONAL ACTIVITY

One of the clearest ways to demonstrate your dedication to your profession is by being active in professional organizations outside of work. There are many choices out there, so it is a good idea to check in with your boss or with colleagues to get a sense of which association would be best for you and worth your time and money. Yet don't be content with just attending events as a member—volunteer to help out when you can. Often professional organizations are struggling to recruit new members who are willing to donate their time.

Donating time outside of work may seem like a burden at times, but it can boost your career, help you gain experiences you would not get on the job, and help you develop rewarding relationships. Going beyond your basic networking and actually carrying out projects with colleagues outside your usual work sphere can lead to a positive reputation and reliable references when it comes to job seeking. Having mentors outside of your workplace can give you a bigger perspective, and they may be a good place to turn to for knowledge about open positions, especially if you don't feel comfortable revealing your job-seeking status at your current job.

GOAL ORIENTATION

One quality that is helpful across the board, no matter what type of library employs you, is being goal oriented. In particular, make sure to align your own goals with the goals of the greater organization, whether it be the library itself or the larger organization. By focusing your efforts on goals related to the larger organization, you increase the likelihood of your personal contributions being recognized as valuable.

Listening carefully to leaders in your organization is a great strategy for learning how to sell your services. What language do they use when describing their goals? For example, I noticed that my boss at Sloan Kettering used the word *share* frequently, and this helped tune me in to what qualities she found valuable in an employee, namely a team mind-set where sharing knowledge and responsibility is crucial.

STORYTELLING

Storytelling is one of the most powerful ways to demonstrate your worth, especially in a limited amount of time, such as meeting someone at a networking event or participating in a job interview. The best storytelling engages the emotions of your audience and has a common structure, which consists of rising action, a climax, and a denouement. When you tell a particularly compelling story about a lesson you've learned during your employment or some excellent customer service that you provided, your listeners actually have neurotransmitters released into their brains, hormones like oxytocin that cause them to bond with you.

It's a good idea to develop an elevator speech, a quick story you can tell about what roles you play at work and how you contribute to your company or client base. Write it to be concise and use accessible language to make it understandable to nonlibrarians, as you want to be prepared for how to explain what you do to stakeholders who are not in your field. For example, you might use the words *teaching* or *training* instead of *bibliographic instruction.*

One of the ways I improved my storytelling skills was by taking fun creative writing and acting classes in my own time. However, if you spin it the right way, sometimes you can convince your employer to reimburse you for classes that could potentially help you improve your presentation or writing skills. While at Sloan Kettering, my boss, upon learning that I was taking comedy classes for fun, was very supportive and offered to argue the case for reimbursement of one introductory course, as she felt it would help improve my presentation skills.

Another way to improve your storytelling skills is by keeping a work diary, a collection of short narratives about different experiences you've had at work. Then you have a document you can consult in times of change, such as when you are applying for a new position or a promotion, and you can scan the diary for tales that will help make your case.

POSITIVITY

No matter what the situation is with your current job, keep a positive attitude while looking for a new position, and reflect on all that you've learned at your current workplace. Try not to burn bridges, and refrain from gossiping or speaking badly about someone you've worked for or with, especially during an interview. Instead, try using illustrative examples of challenges that you've faced in your current job, and highlight your creativity or resilience in dealing with those struggles.

Be prepared to answer questions with a negative slant, such as what is a weakness of yours or what you like least about your job. When selecting a weakness to describe, make sure it is something that is not entirely crucial to the job description, and make sure to explain what steps you've taken to strengthen your weak area. When describing something you dislike about your job, it is best to focus on something that, again, will not be an essential part of your potential new job. Then turn the question around using a positive tone, and explain that while you dislike having to cut through bureaucratic hurdles to get your job done, you learned some excellent techniques for working in a bureaucratic environment.

For example, while I interviewed for my current position at Rutgers University, I resisted the temptation to vent about my frustrations at my previous job at Sloan Kettering and instead focused my conversation on what skills I had developed during my time there, such as my expertise in systematic reviews, which I knew was something they planned to pursue at Rutgers. I also described what new opportunities I might have at Rutgers, such as teaching as an integrated part of a medical school curriculum or having the opportunity to apply for tenure, so they understood my interest and values.

READINESS FOR CHANGE

Rainer Maria Rilke wrote, "Want the change. Be inspired by the flame where everything shines as it disappears." Librarianship is a career that is no stranger to change. Technology is one aspect that requires us to keep up constantly, and librarianship is a field that is based around lifelong learning and constant professional development. The key to keeping up is to catch the wind like a kite and get swept up in the excitement that comes along with change. You need to be willing to try new things, be willing to fail and learn from the failure, and to let go when a service or resource is rendered obsolete. When you transition to a new type of librarianship, from public to special, from special to academic, or even just from one job to another, hesitate when you catch yourself falling into old habits, and hesitate when you find yourself saying, "But we did it *this* way at New York Public Library" or some similar statement. When you learn to love the growth that comes with transitioning to a new job, you will find yourself succeeding, and you may even be able to help others over that hurdle.

VII

From School Media to Academic Librarianship and Vendor Services

Chapter Twenty-Seven

From School Librarian to Technical Support

An Exercise in Reflection

Allison M. Cloyd

When I started library school, I assumed that I would one day be working in a "library" (not any specific one or type, just a general "library"), helping people find books, researching some to-be-determined topic of interest, writing book reviews, and, of course, reading.

I'm not entirely sure what reality this vision had its basis in, but at no point have I ever had a job like that.

My career path has been very brief but winding thus far. It has gone something like this: I started graduate school with two internships and a graduate teaching assistant, worked part time as an access services department assistant (with a six-week stint as a temporary law librarian stuck in there), earned a part-time position as a school librarian, and then went on to my current full-time position in an education technology start-up. While I moved positions quite a bit in the two years after graduate school, the biggest and most surprising shift came when I moved from any kind of library job to the tech start-up world.

I have always loved technology—so many new and shiny things to see and do! When an educational technology company posted a job for customer success, I realized this was access services, my favorite kind of library job— just on the Internet. The application and interview process was intense but fast. I had a phone interview, an in-person interview, a project involving the company's website, and a follow-up phone interview, all within the space of a week and a half. The interview and hiring process was startling, to say the least. I'd never interviewed for a job that got back to me that fast after the

167

initial interview, much less offered a position in that amount of time. I can say now, with hiring experience under my belt at the same company, that this is not a unique experience. In tech, good people aren't necessarily hard to find, but they can be hard to keep. Hiring often moves quickly, with the feeling that if you don't offer a position to someone you like, another company will. This isn't to say that this can't happen in a library, but in my personal experience, library hiring does seem to move more slowly. I've seen good and bad hires made both ways. As the job seeker, I always prefer to move fast, but as the hiring manager, I know there's value in taking time to offer someone a position. Either way, at my current job I went from submitting an application to starting in about a month!

STARTING A NEW POSITION

I was hired to do customer and technical support for a website that supports over forty-seven million users a year—by myself. In this position I have

- handled billing questions and issues for our individual users;
- provided technical support and training for our school subscribers;
- helped the sales team with any product questions they may have;
- worked with the development team to report, fix, and test bugs on the website;
- trained new hires into the sales and support department on our products;
- went from supporting one product by myself to supporting six separate apps and managing a small team;
- offered input and feedback into the development of a new product and the retooling of a second;
- built an entirely new support process for my company while still managing the day-to-day operations of our customer success team.

The first two points were in the job description, the rest I figured out as I went along. In making the transition from school library to edtech start-up, I had a mini-existential crisis. Was I still a librarian? Why did my head hurt so much and my back ache all the time? How can I feel like I'm making a positive contribution to the world if I'm now working in "vendorland," that place all librarians know to be the land of lost corporate souls?

PHYSICAL DIFFERENCES BETWEEN THE LIBRARY AND
BUSINESS WORLDS

The differences between working in a library and working in a business are, to say the least, noticeable. To start with, I no longer had a library to roam. I have a desk with a phone I have to pay attention to (no one ever called the school library, and even if they did, it was never for me), and all of my work is now on a computer. For the first month, I ended every day with a headache until it occurred to me that my body wasn't used to this. I used to shelve, read, clean, process new books, weed the old ones, and shelve what's left. . . . I was on my feet a lot! Now I spend the majority of my day in front of a computer. If I had known what I do now, I would have set a desktop alarm to remind me to get up and walk around from the start or look away from my screen every couple of minutes to give my eyes a break. These are things I've picked up as habit over time instead, learning the hard way after days of headaches.

Now I know that if I need a break, instead of using our office messaging system to ask a question, perhaps I'll get up and take a stroll over to that person's desk. Instead of taking a meeting in the same place every week, I change the conference room, make it a walk-and-talk meeting to get coffee, or just go work in a different part of the office to get a new view. These small things can have a huge impact on workplace happiness.

ADJUSTING TO A NEW PATRON BASE

A second piece of my transition was coming to terms with who my "patrons" are and how I communicate with them. While there are always phones to be answered and e-mail and chat reference questions waiting (the classic conundrum "three patrons are at your desk, the phone is ringing, and chat reference is blinking at you—whom do you answer first?" comes to mind), patron interactions tend to be face-to-face. All of a sudden, in my new role the only people I see in person are my coworkers. All the time.

Eighty percent of my interactions with users are via e-mail, and the rest is on the phone. I don't talk to my users face-to-face except for the very, very rare video-chat meeting. And on top of that, a lot of these interactions can be negative; when dealing with a frustrated user or someone who hasn't realized they've been charged $5 a month for the last two years, e-mail is a brutal method of communication.

While my communication skills were good when I started, I learned to be thrifty with my words and still give as much helpful information as possible. I had a few communication-related "learning experiences": how many e-mails to exchange with a user before it's easier to make a phone call, the best way to explain a certain feature, how many times to explain a feature before going to the product team to ask for a user experience review.

All of this e-mail interaction led me to the realization that this was just a different kind of reference interview. Librarians ask questions to help their patrons find their own answers. Face-to-face you can read body language and tone or ask questions sequentially. In e-mail, you learn to anticipate so your user doesn't get frustrated; you look at their word choices to understand where they are coming from.

My background in access services was, and still is, of the utmost importance here. The angry patron who doesn't want to pay the late fine or the user whose paper is due at midnight and its 11:30 p.m. and the website isn't working—either way, a hard conversation. Customer service is a really difficult job, and it isn't for everyone. Empathy, clear communication, and flexibility are key to working with patrons in a library setting or working with users on the Internet.

RELYING ON THE MLIS DEGREE

As I relaxed into my job, my existential crisis lessened. I still work with librarians, both in my company and outside of it, on a regular basis. In fact, I was one of six librarians on staff when I started. We all worked in different capacities, but those little insider librarian jokes made me feel more at home. When I e-mail librarians in response to technical issues, I refer to myself as a "support librarian" or "technical librarian." This has two advantages: one, it's easier to explain who I am, thus cutting down on confusion, and two, my librarian users know that I speak their language. I use my insider knowledge to help my users and my team, a win-win situation. My research skills have become more important as I navigate the divide between the sales and product teams, and I became the go-to person for database questions. But no matter how many times I tell my coworkers that I didn't memorize the citation style manuals in grad school, they always think I know the answer to every citation question without looking it up!

WORKING IN A TECHNOLOGY START-UP

Some other fun things about working in edtech? The people. I'm lucky to be with a group of talented and brilliant individuals who work hard toward a goal we believe in. And we have a good time doing it.

I'm the first person in my position, so there aren't any rules and there aren't any traditions. If something doesn't work, we change it. I'm learning how to be a manager (hopefully a good one), and that's something that translates to any job. Managing a team while tending to my own projects is a challenge, but the leadership team at my company has shown that they are willing to take on the risk of developing my own management skills, and that's no small commitment.

Start-up life isn't all fun and games (but it's close). Everyone has to be willing to step outside of their job descriptions and pitch in when necessary.

Working for a bootstrapped company has its ups and downs. Resources are limited at times, but I take huge pride knowing that our team's efforts have gotten us where we are. The work is *hard*. I may love that I'm the first in my job, but I also hate it at times. There's no one to look to but myself if things go sideways.

The most important thing I have learned in my transition out of the library space is that I excel the most at my job when I am happy with it. I am challenged, not frustrated. I have the space and opportunity to stretch myself and learn new skills while offering my past experience and knowledge. Innovation is exercise for the brain, and a feeling of contributing, of knowing that I help my team get stuff done, is encouragement of the best sort. Helping students, teachers, and librarians achieve their own goals through what my company does isn't corporate speak, it's genuinely what we want to do.

TRUST YOUR OWN EXPERIENCE

Changing jobs is hard enough; moving from a traditional library setting to a start-up business can make your head spin. My advice: take time to adjust and know that it won't happen in a day. Lean on your professional learning network—so many people have made a similar transition, so don't be afraid to ask for help! Remember that you were hired for the experience and talent you bring, and feel free to use that experience to the best of your ability. And finally, don't feel that a career transition is permanent or binding. Take the big chances, and if it doesn't work out the way you want, you'll have learned something valuable about yourself. If anything, that's been the best part of my own transition.

ACKNOWLEDGMENTS

To my Liberrians—thank you for making me feel so welcome and for demonstrating professional grace and agility. Without your example, I wouldn't have made it this far! Many thanks for my sales and support team—for all of the silly questions you've had to answer and for the even sillier ones you've sent my way.

Chapter Twenty-Eight

An Interview with Yujin Hong, E-resources Librarian, Kyung Hee University Central Library, Seoul, Korea

Ray: Thanks for talking with us! Tell us a bit about your career so far, especially the transition you made from your work at a high school library to a university library.

Yujin: As a graduate of the Korea University College of Education, I've always wanted to be a school librarian, where I can have the opportunity to teach classes and interact with students directly. For my first librarian job, I worked at a very competitive high school. I was the first school librarian that they had ever hired, so the principal didn't have any knowledge or experience on how to manage the library or the school librarian. The principal thought that the school's librarian didn't have many tasks compared to other subject teachers. Thus, I was assigned to teach ethics, be a homeroom teacher for freshmen, and manage the school library.

It was a lot to handle at the same time, and it was especially difficult without having any mentors who could give me advice. I truly enjoyed teaching and being with students, but I realized that the school administrator didn't have any interest in improving the library. Instead, she would rather focus her attention on sending students to top-notch universities in Seoul. Also, most of the teachers and staff did not have knowledge of a librarian's role, library budgets, and facilities in general. All of those things combined made me desire to a move to another job.

I decided not to renew the contract and to look for another librarian job. I never thought I could work at an academic library due to the fact that I didn't have a master's degree in LIS. In Korea, acquiring an MLIS isn't mandatory to become an academic librarian, but it's always better to have it if you want to work at an academic library. I happened to apply to a university library and obtain a temporary librarian position because of another librarian's maternity leave. That university was looking for somebody who had teaching experience, so even though I didn't have any experience in an academic library, I got the job. Working at a university as a librarian inspired me to apply as an academic librarian, and finally, I got to work at my current job as an electronic resources librarian at the university.

Ray: What was it like to transition from a school library to an academic library?

Yujin: Landing an academic librarian job was extremely difficult and tiring because of the competition in Korea. In the beginning, I failed numerous application-screening processes, so I tried to get many certificates and work experiences elsewhere. Sometimes a certificate doesn't guarantee that you are an expert, but it does show how much effort you put into improving yourself. Even though I'm not a tech-savvy person at all, I got the Oracle Certified Professional 10g since most jobs require someone who has good knowledge of databases. In addition, language skill is quite important, so I tried hard to get a good score on OPIc, which is an English-speaking test. After I obtained all of those certificates, I met most of the listed requirements in the job ads and got many interview opportunities.

Ray: Which skills were you able to bring from your past experience that were helpful in your new position?

Yujin: My biggest strength was my teaching experience. Most of the other applicants had a lot of experiences related to cataloging or managing serials, but none of them had ever been in front of students. I often taught tenth and eleventh graders in seventy-five-minute sessions and made all of the class supplements. Therefore, I didn't have any problems with instructing a large class. When I was applying for academic librarian jobs, most universities tried to have mandatory library instruction classes for freshmen. Therefore, they needed somebody who could design library instruction classes and wouldn't have any hesitation in terms of teaching many classes. Human resources liked the fact that I majored in education because I could be a more approachable librarian with a service-oriented attitude in terms of helping users research and study.

In addition, I've hosted many library events with students at the school library, and that experience was helpful when I was marketing library events. For example, making event flyers, organizing expositions, or using social media networks like Kakao, Twitter, or Facebook to promote the events.

Ray: Do you think it's difficult to change tracks once you've got your start in a certain type of position?

Yujin: No, I do not agree with that. It is a new era for librarians and archivists. Librarianship is definitely evolving in so many ways, and I'm very excited to see where the field is headed. When I was studying LIS at the university, I never thought that being a librarian was such an active job. Of course, there are many negative opinions about libraries and books—many believe they will be gone soon, but I don't think so. The materials will most likely change formats, but libraries will never go away. Instead, they will evolve by cooperating with museums, archives, or local communities.

Today you can see lots of university libraries that have learning commons areas so students can meet and work together. Libraries can provide places where users can share new ideas and get inspired. With these changes, librarians need to educate themselves constantly and be open-minded about new technologies. Currently, I'm working as an electronic resources librarian, so every working day is different for me. I'm always learning new databases and technologies, so sometimes it's challenging, but I always love catching up with new learning trends and thinking about how to provide better services to users.

Ray: Making the leap from a school library to a university library is definitely a big career move! Do you have any advice for others who would like to make a similar transition in their career?

Yujin: Obviously, there is a huge difference between working as a school librarian and an academic librarian. However, you can bridge that gap with a passionate and curious mind-set. Some librarians were suspicious about my abilities when I got hired as an academic librarian because they thought that a school librarian job is nonacademic compared to theirs. I do understand these kinds of preconceived notions or "stereotypes," but school librarians can use their teaching experience as a strength.

Even though academic libraries provide scholarly journals or databases, which you may not have managed at a school library, school librarians are fully capable of learning how they work. I sometimes miss being around younger students and giving advice to them about their studies and school life, but working at a university offers a very vibrant and creative environment. If someone is always willing to learn new things, being an academic librarian is the perfect position for them!

VIII

Transitions within the Academic Library World

Chapter Twenty-Nine

Getting Started with Digital Humanities in Libraries

Zach Coble

Providing digital humanities services offers several opportunities for libraries seeking to adapt to ever-changing patron needs. The digital shift has significantly changed many core library services, and the digital humanities field represents one area where a basic foundation of digital skills can be applied to support a growing field. Being an effective practitioner of the digital humanities in libraries requires a breadth of basic computational skills. Librarians already have some of these skills, but it is surprisingly uncommon to possess all of them. The best way to acquire these skills is by gaining experiences.

One challenge for getting started in digital humanities (DH) is trying to define the field and identify which tools and methods comprise the core DH toolkit. In general, most people who identify themselves as digital humanists view the field as a "big tent," meaning DH tends to be more inclusive than exclusive. I take a "big tent" approach and will not bother to put stakes in the ground as to what is and is not DH.[1] It is, however, useful to have some sense of the breadth and depth of activity in the field, so I will briefly sketch out five general areas, borrowed from Brian Croxall,[2] that give a sense of what we talk about when we talk about DH.

1. Examining digital objects from a humanities perspective
   Summary: The fields of media studies and software studies
   Examples: *10 Print*, *Software Studies: A Lexicon*[3]
2. Digital pedagogy
   Summary: Using technology in the classroom

179

Examples: Course blogs, *Journal of Interactive Technology and Pedagogy*[4]

3. Digital scholarly communication

    Summary: Using technology to explore new forms of scholarly interactions

    Examples: *dh+lib Review*,[5] scholarly blogs

4. Digital collections and archives creation

    Summary: Digitizing and providing access to physical and born-digital collections

    Examples: "Chinese Englishmen," Digital Library of the Caribbean[6]

5. Humanities computing

    Summary: Using computers to identify patterns in data (e.g., texts, images) and then interpreting those patterns

    Examples: Text analysis, GIS, topic modeling, network analysis

ACQUIRING SKILLS

Acquiring a broad set of skills will prepare you to be a more effective digital humanist. The DH toolkit is made up of skills that have long existed in libraries but rarely in one person or department. Below I've outlined six areas where I believe DH librarians should be competent. None of them are especially advanced, but taken together they create a foundation that will enable you to effectively contribute to the variety of digital projects that come through the library.

The Research Process. Understanding the research process is important when building relationships with faculty and researchers because it demonstrates that you understand their needs and perspective. It is as important to understand the process at the conceptual level—to be able to articulate how the digital component of a project will strengthen the overall scholarly argument—as it is to understand it at a practical level, to know why making an adjustment to a tool will produce x data, which means you can't make y argument because of z limitation.

Project Management. Project management is a common role for librarians in DH projects and involves planning and organizing people, time, and resources in an effort to accomplish predefined goals. In larger DH projects that involve librarians, faculty, and the information technology (IT) department, it is not uncommon for a librarian to serve as project manager in order to keep the project moving and to ensure the different groups are working together efficiently.

Computational Thinking. Turning now to more technical skills, I can't overemphasize how important it is to have a solid foundation of basic computer skills. You don't need to learn how to build a computer from parts or become a senior programmer, but you do need to be comfortable with computers, have a curiosity about how technology works, and have a willingness to troubleshoot the technical problems that will inevitably arise. Some of these skills are discussed in more depth below, and the following are a couple other areas to explore:

- Digitizing material: learn how to turn analog media into digital using programs designed for different types of files (e.g., video, audio, texts, and images)
- Editing files: become familiar with the tools for editing and producing media. For example, learn how to create video or audio clips, combine multiple files into one, and crop an image and do color correction.

Metadata. Another common role for librarians is providing metadata expertise. It is worthwhile to learn how to import, export, and edit large amounts of data (e.g., using Open Refine or Omeka's CSV Import plugin) and also to become familiar with the intellectual issues around particular metadata schemas and metadata in general. For instance, when would you recommend using Dublin Core, and when would you recommend using VRA Core?

Online Publishing. Putting content online and sharing it with a larger audience is an integral part of most DH projects. It is useful to learn the basics of HTML and CSS, which are relatively straightforward languages and are essential to understanding web design. Similarly, I would also recommend becoming comfortable with a text editor (e.g., Sublime Text) and using an FTP (file transfer protocol) client. If you are responsible for putting content online, these two tools will make your life easier. Also, there are many great content management systems, such as WordPress and Omeka,[7] that simplify the publishing process. Create free accounts and play with these systems to learn the strengths and weaknesses of each. Also, examine other projects using these platforms to understand how your colleagues are using them to organize and deliver content.

Programming. Computer programming skills are not required to be a digital humanist, but they are very helpful. There is no universal language used by DH scholars; it all depends on the type of work you're doing. With that said, if you would like to learn a language but are unsure where to start, I would recommend R or Python because they are more commonly used than other languages in DH, can be applied to different types of DH work (e.g., text analysis or GIS), and each has an introductory book specifically for humanists.[8]

EXPERIENCES AND TRAINING

The best way to develop these skills is to get involved in a project. There are many ways to get started, and it's worth remembering that all of the skills outlined above can be picked up from non-DH projects, so keep your options open.

An excellent place to begin is to find a project your library is already working on. Is anyone in your special collections department digitizing collections? Who in technical services is importing, exporting, and editing large batches of metadata? Can you participate in this process or shadow them? Similarly, praxis-based learning has become a popular model for learning DH skills. For example, the Developing Librarian project at Columbia University Libraries features a group of self-organized librarians committed to teaching themselves DH skills and methods by creating a DH project.[9] Perhaps you could start a Developing Librarian project at your own institution if there are a handful of curious minds and a project idea that interests the group.

Are there faculty or students on campus interested in digital projects? Talk to the humanities subject specialists to learn more about the current landscape and who would be the right faculty to approach.[10] Incorporating a digital project into a course is a great way to start building partnerships between faculty and the library on digital projects and can be done in a way that doesn't require especially strong technical knowledge. For example, I once worked with a history professor (who wasn't especially tech savvy but understood the importance of having students develop these skills) to create a project for a course where groups of students used HistoryPin to create "tours" of soldiers' lives after the American Civil War. The project was a success because we used a hosted platform (i.e., no servers or programming required) and the technology was not difficult for the students to learn, yet they gained experience building online exhibits and in the process learned the nuances of telling stories online.

There are several institutes and conferences that provide valuable DH training opportunities. The Humanities Intensive Learning & Teaching (HILT) and Digital Humanities Summer Institute (DHSI) are two well-regarded institutes for those in North America.[11] Both offer weeklong courses allowing participants to quickly develop a strong working knowledge in a particular subject area. While not as ubiquitous as they once were, THAT-Camps are "unconferences" that provide an informal yet productive way to learn new skills, meet people, and explore different ideas.[12] Additionally, the Digital Library Federation Forum and Code4Lib are more specialized library conferences that are well suited for librarians interested in DH.[13]

Finally, I would recommend reading and keeping up with conversations in DH. There are several quality books on DH that can provide a foundational overview of methods, trends, and issues in the field.[14] A lot of the current conversation takes place over Twitter, and the *Humanist* and the Association of College and Research Libraries' Digital Humanities Interest Group are two listservs where useful information is frequently distributed.[15] The dh+lib website—"where the digital humanities and librarianship meet"—is another resource for keeping up.[16] Additionally, the *dh+lib Review* is a volunteer-driven weekly newsletter that highlights five to eight timely and relevant jobs, resources, calls for participation, and so on. I would recommend volunteering (it's for one week and requires one to two hours of reading) because it provides an easy way to get involved in the community through becoming familiar with the broader conversation.

There is no clearly defined path for getting started doing DH in the library. It is, however, important to be aware of how much time, energy, and resources you and your institution can commit before getting involved in a new project. Similarly, it is critical to remind yourself (and others) that "the digital" is not a panacea for whatever issues your library or institution are facing. With that said, DH projects can and do make meaningful scholarly contributions, and they are often a great way to form partnerships across your institution. Equipped with the right skill set and experiences, you can achieve success—even with modest resources—and in the process help your library adapt its services to better support scholars' needs.

NOTES

1. For a fruitful discussion, see Matthew Kirschenbaum's three-part series on "What Is Digital Humanities." Matthew Kirschenbaum, "What Is Digital Humanities and What's It Doing in English Departments?" *ADE Bulletin* 150 (2010), http://mkirschenbaum.files. wordpress.com/2011/03/ade-final.pdf. Kirschenbaum, "Digital Humanities as/Is a Tactical Term," in *Debates in the Digital Humanities*, ed. Matthew Gold (Minneapolis: University of Minnesota Press, 2012), 415–28, http://dhdebates.gc.cuny.edu/debates/text/48. Kirschenbaum, "What Is 'Digital Humanities,' and Why Are They Saying Such Terrible Things about It?" *differences* 25, no. 1 (2014), https://mkirschenbaum.files.wordpress.com/2014/04/ dhterriblethingskirschenbaum.pdf.
2. Brian Croxall, "Help, I Want to Do DH!" *Brian Croxall* (blog), September 25, 2014, www.briancroxall.net/2014/09/25/help-i-want-to-do-dh/.
3. Nick Montfort et al., *10 Print Chr$(205.5+Rnd(1)); : Goto 10* (Boston: MIT Press, 2013). Matthew Fuller, ed., *Software Studies: A Lexicon* (Boston: MIT Press, 2013).
4. *Journal of Interactive Technology and Pedagogy*, accessed August 12, 2015, http://jitp. commons.gc.cuny.edu/.
5. dh+lib: Where the Digital Humanities and Librarianship Meet, accessed August 12, 2015, http://acrl.ala.org/dh/.
6. Adeline Koh, "Digitizing 'Chinese Englishmen,'" Adeline Koh's website, accessed August 12, 2015, http://chineseenglishmen.adelinekoh.org/. dLOC Home: Digital Library of the Caribbean website, accessed August 12, 2015, www.dloc.com/dloc1.
7. WordPress.com, accessed August 12, 2015, https://wordpress.com/. Omeka.org, accessed August 12, 2015, http://omeka.org/.

8. Matthew Jockers, *Text Analysis with R for Students of Literature* (New York: Springer, 2014). Folgert Karsdorp, *Python Programming for the Humanities*, GitHub, accessed August 12, 2015, https://fbkarsdorp.github.io/python-course/.

9. Columbia University Libraries, "Breaking the Code: The Developing Librarian Project," accessed August 12, 2015, www.developinglibrarian.org/.

10. Arianne Hartsell-Gundy, Laura Braunstein, and Liorah Golomb, eds., *Digital Humanities in the Library: Challenges and Opportunities for Subject Specialists* (Chicago: Association of College and Research Libraries, 2015).

11. Welcome to DH Training: Digital Humanities Training, Humanities Intensive Learning and Teaching, accessed August 12, 2015, www.dhtraining.org/. DHSI: Digital Humanities Summer Institute, Digital Humanities Summer Institute, accessed August 12, 2015, http://dhsi. org/.

12. THATCamp: The Humanities and Technology Camp, accessed August 12, 2015, http://thatcamp.org/.

13. Digital Library Federation, "DLF Forums," accessed August 12, 2015, www.diglib.org/forums/. "Code4Lib Conference," Code4Lib.org, accessed August 12, 2015, http://code4lib.org/conference.

14. Matthew Gold, ed., *Debates in the Digital Humanities* (Minneapolis: University of Minnesota Press, 2012). Melissa Terras, Julianne Nyhan, Edward Vanhoutte, eds., *Defining Digital Humanities: A Reader* (Farnham, UK: Ashgate, 2013).

15. *Humanist* Discussion Group, accessed August 12, 2015, http://dhhumanist.org. Association of College and Research Libraries, ACRL Digital Humanities Interest Group, accessed August 12, 2015, http://lists.ala.org/sympa/info/acrldigitalhumanitiesig.

16. dh+lib.

REFERENCES

Fuller, Matthew, ed. *Software Studies: A Lexicon*. Boston: MIT Press, 2013.

Gold, Matthew, ed. *Debates in the Digital Humanities*. Minneapolis: University of Minnesota Press, 2012.

Hartsell-Gundy, Arianne, Laura Braunstein, and Liorah Golomb, eds. *Digital Humanities in the Library: Challenges and Opportunities for Subject Specialists*. Chicago: Association of College and Research Libraries, 2015.

Jockers, Matthew. *Text Analysis with R for Students of Literature*. New York: Springer, 2014.

Karsdorp, Folgert. *Python Programming for the Humanities*. GitHub. Accessed August 12, 2015. https://fbkarsdorp.github.io/python-course/.

Kirschenbaum, Matthew. "Digital Humanities as/Is a Tactical Term." In *Debates in the Digital Humanities*, edited by Matthew Gold, 415–28. Minneapolis: University of Minnesota Press, 2012. http://dhdebates.gc.cuny.edu/debates/text/48.

———. "What Is 'Digital Humanities,' and Why Are They Saying Such Terrible Things about It?" *differences* 25, no. 1 (2014): 46–63.

———. "What Is Digital Humanities and What's It Doing in English Departments?" *ADE Bulletin* 150 (2010): 55–61.

Montfort, Nick, et al. *10 Print Chr$(205.5+Rnd(1)); : Goto 10*. Boston: MIT Press, 2013.

Terras, Melissa, Julianne Nyhan, and Edward Vanhoutte, eds. *Defining Digital Humanities: A Reader*. Farnham, UK: Ashgate, 2013.

Chapter Thirty

Future-Proof Your Career with Resilience and Proactivity

Heng Ge

In these past seven years, I have served as both a part-time and full-time librarian. I have worked in academic, public, special, and hybrid libraries. I've even moved from North America to East Asia, where I worked in a multilingual, multicultural international environment. In seven years, I have also gone through a whole gamut of professional experiences, ranging from the internal facets of library operations, such as cataloging, acquisitions, and collection development and policy creation, to external facets of library services, such as research consultations, library instruction, access services, and community outreach. Within the past eighteen months at a new library, I have also been professionally active, copublishing an article in *College and Research Libraries News*, presenting a poster at the 2015 American College and Research Libraries (ACRL) Conference, and coauthoring a scholarly article with a faculty member.

All of these experiences seemed like a whirlwind to me, yet none of them were specifically planned. I'd like to share my story of how a freshly minted library school graduate navigated through a plethora of rapid changes in a competitive employment terrain and managed to make the best of unpredictable circumstances. I will briefly describe how I got my start in the profession, how my initial steps snowballed into exposure to multiple facets of the library world, and what I have attained and learned from these experiences.

MY FIRST FORAY INTO THE LIBRARY PROFESSION

My career trajectory is largely a result of a combination of circumstances beyond my control and personal initiatives in response to those circumstances. My initial exposure to the library world started when I was offered a part-time job cataloging Chinese-language materials at the University of Toronto (U of T) Libraries soon after I started the library school at U of T in 2006.

As both a full-time graduate student and a student cataloger with long working hours, I had to juggle my responsibilities. The hands-on cataloging experience proved to be about as important as my library education. It helped me develop familiarity with library operations and build essential library skills. More important, this job provided me with an opportunity to network with librarians from the East Asian Library (EAL) at U of T, since the Chinese materials that I cataloged using the Research Libraries Information Network (RLIN) and OCLC were for EAL.

My experience as a student cataloger of Chinese materials and my interactions with EAL personnel and operations proved instrumental in my transition from a student cataloger to a student reference assistant at EAL in the winter of 2007. It was a small step, but it did provide me with my first experience working at a reference desk. Since traffic at the reference desk was usually light, I was able to further broaden my library experience by engaging in projects like weeding and digitization. I was able to build on my cumulative experience, moving from cataloging and reference to a growing number of other library-related responsibilities and functions. My initial successes emboldened me, but setbacks were on their way.

FROM A NOVICE TO A PROFESSIONAL

In June 2008, I graduated from my MLIS program and started job hunting. By then, the global recession had taken its toll on the library job market. The paucity of available jobs took me by surprise; jobs had seemed to be plentiful when I started library school. My once-buoyant optimism gave way to frustration and discouragement. As luck would have it, though, in 2008 U of T Libraries opened a brand-new Canada–Hong Kong Library (CHKL). The Chinese collections there needed to be cataloged. My previous experience helped me become a recipient of a contract job to complete the cataloging project at CHKL. Despite its small size in both its collection and staff, the new library was an ideal fit for me.

Since my previous cataloging experience had enabled me to readily handle my primary responsibilities, I was once again able to apply my extra energy and time to additional responsibilities. I trained student catalogers, created cataloging manuals, and covered the front desk. I provided both circulation and reference services. I even got involved with the new library's programming and outreach initiatives. Eventually, I organized a library event on my own, hosting an external guest speaker, locating a moderator, and coordinating with academic departments to promote the event.

In the second year of my work at CHKL, in 2009, I started pursuing my second master's degree at U of T's Department of East Asian Studies. I felt these studies would complement my undergraduate degree in Western civilization and provide me with a well-rounded knowledge base of the East and the West. Pursuing a graduate program while working full-time was an exhausting experience. Before long, however, my investment in my continuing education would prove both timely and wise.

By the time my two-year contract with CHKL expired, the job market was still very tight. I kept on looking for any library work that I could find. After a few months of painstaking search, I finally landed a temporary part-time position as a reference librarian at the downtown campus of George Brown College (GBC). I moved from a special library to a mainstream academic library, where, for the first time, my Chinese-language skills were not part of my job requirements. I also experienced high-volume traffic at the reference desk. Library patrons at GBC sometimes would wait in line to ask questions; this was a first for me.

At the same time, a seemingly insignificant job opportunity knocked on the door. A former colleague introduced me to a volunteer opportunity as a virtual reference librarian for askON, a live chat–based information help service offered by college libraries in Ontario, Canada. While I received zero income for my work, I felt I was paid very handsomely in experience. My part-time and volunteer work at GBC and askON helped me understand what intensive reference services and virtual reference were like. Paradoxically, while my employment status was discouraging and the pay unimpressive, my professional experience grew steadily.

By spring 2011, my part-time employment as a reference librarian at the GBC library ended, but the job market saw no significant progress. I decided to explore employment opportunities outside academia. Soon my new strategy paid off as I landed yet another part-time job as a Sunday information services associate at the Markham Public Library (MPL) near Toronto, Canada. It was my first and only public library experience. I came to know a different library clientele; the majority of the patrons I assisted were elders, children, teenagers, and immigrants. Even though public librarianship was not part of my career goals, I was surprised by how much I enjoyed my work at MPL. I discovered new aspects of society and librarianship. I appreciated the job so much that I kept it even after I had landed a full-time job at an academic library three months before my contract with MPL expired.

In September 2011, I embarked on my full-time job as the technical services coordinator at Caven Library, Knox College, a theological graduate school and also a federated college of U of T. It was a small library, where the lines between various departments and library functions were blurred.

This actually worked to my advantage; I was able to greatly expand the scope of my library experience. Despite my relatively limited professional experience and intermittent employment history up to that point, I was fortunate to be put in charge of cataloging, acquisitions, access services, student supervision, and the maintenance of the integrated library system (ILS). My committee service helped broaden my understanding of various pertinent issues surrounding library operations, services, and even future trends. Indeed, I made big gains in a small library as my professional experience grew exponentially during my tenure there. It was like a capstone project where the quantitative changes in my career path evolved into qualitative changes, resulting in a much-improved professional portfolio. By then, I had already transitioned from a special library and a virtual library to a public library and a mainstream academic library. My confidence grew with my experience and knowledge. I thought I was going to stay put for a while, but that was not the case.

FROM NORTH AMERICA TO EAST ASIA

In early 2013, a job opening at New York University (NYU) Shanghai Library caught my eye. The unusual hybrid nature of this library attracted me. It is a brand-new library of an international campus of a major research university with students hailing from all over the world. More important, I felt the reference and research services librarian position that was advertised was a place where societal needs and my skills and experience met. I would be able to use both my language skills and fluency with Chinese and Western cultures to the fullest. It was also a position that promised to help me further diversify my library experiences and gain some global perspectives. Last but not least, the Shanghai campus is about a stone's throw away from where I spent my formative years—it was too near and dear to my heart to resist.

As a consequence, despite my love for Knox College Library, I decided to give NYU Shanghai a try and succeeded. I started working in Shanghai in November 2013 following a training program at NYU's Bobst Library. My cumulative library experience and exposure to a variety of library operations proved invaluable in preparing me for the challenges at the new library. My major responsibilities include a wide array of brand-new library experiences for me, including information literacy instructions, vendor negotiations, LibGuides creation, and acting as an academic liaison. My new job also provides ample opportunity for me to interact with students from practically all over the world, network with colleagues from various disciplines, and engage in professional development in the United States, China, and elsewhere.

My new responsibilities were simultaneously exciting and challenging. As a technical services librarian for most of my career life, I encountered many difficulties when I embarked on my new job. Technical services at libraries often involve work behind the scene, but my new responsibilities, particularly library instruction and faculty liaison, have pushed me out of my familiar territory and comfort zone. Once again, resilience came to the rescue. Before each library workshop, I make detailed lesson plans and practice over and over. Consulting with and learning from my colleagues have also proved to be effective strategies. I have learned many useful tips through observing their teaching and by seeking advice from my colleagues in both Shanghai and New York. Aside from learning new skills, my previous work experiences, such as reference librarian and departmental liaison, also made a significant contribution to a smooth transition and helped me to take on my new job handily. Even though the Shanghai campus does not handle cataloging and acquisitions, my technical skills are helpful for a start-up library, as they enable me to help the library solve many technical services–related problems and make my expertise relevant to the new job.

Notwithstanding the significant challenges resulting from my decision to relocate from North America to East Asia, such as reverse culture shock, pollution, and the aforementioned transition from technical services to public services, the whole experience has turned out to be highly worthwhile. My career development has reached a new high at the end of my seven-year pursuit of career advancement.

CONCLUDING THOUGHTS

Looking back, I notice that many of my career moves were really the results of objective circumstances rather than proof of personal volition or evidence of a chosen plan. As a new immigrant to North America who had just completed four years of grueling undergraduate education in a field and language largely foreign to me, I pursued library education out of my passion for books, not knowing too much about what it actually entailed. As a student cataloger of Chinese materials, I started in the field of East Asian libraries, where I had some cultural and linguistic advantage. When my full-time employment at CHKL ended, I went with part-time or weekend jobs. When academic library jobs were unavailable, I worked at a public library. When paying jobs were unavailable to me, I worked as a volunteer. Indeed, I did whatever library work I could lay my hands on in order to keep myself financially afloat and professionally relevant.

But real life is complex, and environmental factors alone do not define and determine all of the outcomes. There is also the law of unintended consequences, which can affect one's life in unpredictable ways. This is certainly the case with my career trajectory. The sequence of events over the past seven years seems random and often necessity driven, but some inner connections slowly began to emerge. I acquired my student cataloger position just to get my feet wet, but it ended up opening the door to full-time cataloging at CHKL and exposure to many dimensions of library services. I earned my second master's degree as an investment in the future while part-time and volunteer work was necessitated by a fickle job market. However, the cumulative experiences from these odds-and-ends jobs contributed to my position, with several significant responsibilities, at Knox College. Finally, the combined effect of my experience as a cataloger at East Asian Library and a technical services librarian with extensive responsibilities at Knox College, coupled with my second master's degree, contributed to my securing the position at NYU Shanghai Library. All of these seemingly unrelated experiences led me to where I am today.

It is important to note that while odds-and-ends jobs are important factors in life, they seldom constitute the underpinnings of success. There were several other contributing factors to my relatively successful career transitions: patience, resilience, and proactivity. Part-time jobs early in my career did not provide full financial security and professional satisfaction, but I enjoyed them, recognizing that they might one day open the door to full-time jobs (and they did). Pursuing a second master's degree while fully employed was both expensive and exhausting, but it proved to be a worthy investment. Uprooting myself from Canada and moving all the way to China was both an emotionally difficult and physically challenging experience, but it led me to a workplace in an international setting where my career took off. My patience, resilience, and proactivity have allowed me the opportunity to help start two new libraries from scratch and build a strong career base in seven years. Without personal initiative, I may well have succumbed to life circumstances instead of making the best of them.

For anyone starting a library career, I would offer a few additional tips that I learned from my own experiences, including those from which I both benefited and learned.

A big mistake that I made was my failure to recognize the job market as an ever-changing place. It moves in ebbs and flows and is subject to numerous factors. My failure to recognize this caused me to be blindsided by the sudden decline of available jobs. Coping with the consequences of this oversight took both a financial and an emotional toll on me. It makes perfect sense, therefore, that one should start the job search early, know the market of today and tomorrow, and identify and address deficiencies while still in school or early in one's career. If you are involved with cataloging but realize that metadata librarianship is the way of the future, for instance, you should develop relevant skills in metadata librarianship now in order to be competitive.

Likewise, it is never too early to seek professional development opportunities in order to build your résumé and portfolio. No experience is too small or trivial. If you seek out such opportunities, you are bound to find them. If you are not ready to do it solo yet, try to find a partner. My collaborations with several colleagues prove that such experiences are often mutually beneficial and highly rewarding.

It also pays to engage strategically in continuing education while on the job to maximize your service to your organization and future-proof your career. Library schools can get you started, but they do not but necessarily prepare you for experiences such as supervision, management, and leadership. This is where continuing education can help significantly. Indeed, in this credentials-conscious world, a little bit of careful planning can go a long way.

Another trite but true piece of advice is that no library is too small, esoteric, or big to be beneath or above you. My experience at a public library helped me understand the library needs of the general public. I gained knowledge and understanding of popular literature, learned skills necessary to merchandise library items, and observed practices in community outreach. My work experience at Knox College with a relatively small academic library not only provided me with opportunities to develop significant hands-on experience in a number of key library operations, but it also gave me a sense of broad academic community through my work on several library committees at the University of Toronto Libraries.

Similarly, no experience is too trivial, tedious, or inconsequential for a nascent librarian and job seeker. Cumulative and diverse experiences often mean the world to a new librarian. Librarianship is a profession that interacts with so many facets of the society that you can almost always make a connection between what you are currently doing and the library world. If you cannot find a full-time job, volunteering often comes with benefits. My experience as a volunteer virtual reference librarian helped shape my library career and still benefits me today. The benefits and possibilities of preprofessional odds-and-ends experiences are limitless. They have helped me acquire so many valuable experiences and contributed greatly to my transition from a cataloger to a reference librarian and beyond. They should help anyone else as well. Grab any opportunity you have and turn it into a growth opportunity.

Last but not least, know that the library world is changing. Old job titles are phasing out and new ones are being created, such as digital initiatives librarian and first-year experience librarian. As twenty-first-century librarians, it is essential that we establish and then future-proof our careers by staying relevant to higher education and possessing the high level of agility and flexibility needed to continually succeed, regardless of the unpredictability of life circumstances. We should constantly sharpen our tools, exercise resilience, exhibit proactivity, and think ahead of the game. Change is inevitable, but failure to keep up with the changes and meet the challenges is not inevitable. As a recent library graduate or nascent librarian navigates through the career development process, there are bound to be obstacles and snags along the way. The challenges of human life often awaken us to sharpening our abilities and strengthen us so we can overcome these storms. Whatever the circumstances, we can always turn liabilities into assets, adversities into advantages, and reach shore safely and, sometimes, triumphantly.

FURTHER READING

Covey, Stephen. *The 8th Habit, from Effectiveness to Greatness*. New York: Free Press, 2005.
Miller, Rush G. "Call to Action: Creating Tomorrow's Libraries Today." *Choice*, April, 2015.
Peacock, Rebecca, and Jill Wurm. *The New Academic Librarian: Essays on Changing Roles and Responsibilities*. Jefferson: McFarland, 2013.
Shontz, Priscilla K. *The Librarian's Career Guidebook*. Lanham, MD: Scarecrow Press, 2004.

Chapter Thirty-One

From Lawyer to Librarian to Librarian Lawyer

Transitioning to Librarianship from the Legal Field

April M. Hathcock

"So, why librarianship?"

This is a question I have heard a lot in my library career, beginning with my first library job interview after leaving a budding litigation practice at a large global law firm. I had ditched my six-figure salary and myriad late nights poring over endless corporate documents in order to pursue a position as a telephone reference associate for the main branch of an urban library system. I could tell the interviewers were intrigued by the woman sitting across from them, bouncing with eagerness to begin answering calls on everything from overdue fees on DVD loans to downloading e-books on Kindles.

"Why librarianship?"

At the time, the decision seemed clear to me, the reason for transitioning apparent, and it has only become more so with time. My work as a litigation associate required that I take large amounts of complex information and organize them into cognizable parcels that could be easily accessed by my clients. Lawyers, like librarians, are information professionals, committed to meeting the needs of their patrons through customer service that's rooted in advocacy.[1] I was wholeheartedly committed to these ideals and was looking for a professional space in which to exercise them, though within a different context. I loved reading, writing, and researching. I loved working with information and educating others on working with information. Those were the aspects of my legal career that I cherished and wanted to continue while leaving behind the dreaded billable hours and corporate work environment. In my mind, librarianship was a natural fit.

As I have progressed in my library career, that fit has never seemed so apt. I obtained the job providing phone reference and eventually worked my way through an MLIS while spending time as a research associate at a community college library. After library school, I accepted a position as an academic law librarian, bringing my legal background to the forefront, before serving in my current role as the librarian for scholarly communications at a large research university, a position that is growing in popularity in the library world.[2] I have been a reference assistant, research support specialist, and fully minted librarian; I have worked in a public library, a law library, and a large research library. My career path has taken a meandering trajectory, and through it all, I have maintained the commitment to client service that I first developed in my early days as a fledgling lawyer. In particular, I have found that when faced with the question "Why librarianship?" I can easily respond by pointing out the parallels between legal and library work—both professions emphasize a commitment to patron service that arises from a position of advocacy.

ADVOCACY-BASED CUSTOMER SERVICE

Perhaps the greatest overlap between the legal and library professions lies in their common commitment to advocacy-based customer service. This type of customer service stems from a commitment to bridging the gap between client needs and current resources as effectively and meaningfully as possible. Like good librarians, good lawyers promote the best interests of their clients, protect their clients' privacy, and provide service equitably, without regard for personal beliefs or prejudices. Despite their differences in length—the American Bar Association's *Model Rules of Professional Conduct* is over 150 pages compared to the one-page *Code of Ethics* from the American Library Association—in many ways, the ethical code governing the librarian profession mirrors that of the legal profession in its commitment to protecting the interests of clients.[3] Regardless of whether I was teaching students how to use online resources or counseling a client on navigating the intricacies of securities regulations, I knew that my ability to advocate for and meaningfully address patron needs was among the strongest tool in my arsenal of transferable skills.

While interviewing for library positions, whether public or academic, I focused on providing advocacy-based service to all patrons. As a litigation associate, my internal client service entailed drafting detailed memos and case briefs for partners and senior associates on the important issues arising in a particular case. This "in-reach" also involved organizing and crafting case summaries and document-review work flows for teams of fellow young associates as we worked through the paper trail for any given piece of litigation. In the library world, providing service to internal clients involves a similar approach, focusing on the needs of my fellow librarians and of library administrators. Later, as an academic law librarian with an interest in digital pedagogy, I did a lot of work training my colleagues on the use of new technologies—some of which I had used in my legal work for presentations, such as Adobe Captivate and Screencast—to create flipped learning environments for our legal research courses. In my current role as a scholarly communications librarian, I provide service to subject specialists and library technologists in the form of training and workshops on the issues of copyright, fair use, and open access in the use of materials for teaching and research. Some of my work even involves stepping outside of my typical banker's hours to provide service to colleagues across the globe, such as a late-night copyright training session for fellow librarians in Shanghai. As a former associate at a global firm, I am accustomed to working with technology and time zones to provide service to internal clients. I also provide service to internal clients by serving as a go-between for the library and university counsel. Because I am fluent in both "languages," I can easily translate the legal issues taking place in the library for the counsel's advice and communicate that advice comprehensibly back to the library. This particular skill set has been invaluable.

My experience as a lawyer also prepared me for providing effective service to external clients. In the legal field, these were the actual clients of the firm, corporate executives, and agents, as well as pro bono clients, all seeking answers to their legal questions. In addition to drafting memos and briefs for other lawyers, I was also responsible for sending summaries and legal communications to clients, many of whom did not have a legal background. I developed the ability to communicate necessary information to clients in ways that would be easily understood. As a librarian, I continue to do the same kind of work. Whether it involves walking a student through citation software as a community college research support specialist or advising a faculty member on authorship rights for scholarly publishing, my work as a litigation associate has easily translated into effective advocacy-based service to external clients.

Regardless of where it is used, the key to truly effective advocacy-based service lies in the ability to tailor communication to meet the needs of clients in different situations and with individual educational backgrounds and knowledge gaps. As a law associate, my case memos to partners were markedly dissimilar to memos destined for client hands, even when they covered the same cases and involved the same legal issues and facts. One of the first lessons I had to learn as a new attorney was the technical knowledge gap that often exists between the client and the professional dedicated to serving them. This lesson continues to be pertinent in my library career. As a law librarian, I tailored my work in light of the information seeker sitting across from me. Conducting a research session for a law professor was markedly different than conducting the same session for a first-year law student. Moreover, that research session would be even more distinct if conducted for a member of the public with no legal background at all. In my position as a reference law librarian, I had to work with all of types of information seekers, and it was essential that I be adroit at adjusting my service accordingly. Likewise, in my current position providing copyright education to a large and heterogeneous campus, I call upon my skills of flexible communication, first honed as a law associate, to provide effective education for librarians, undergraduates, graduate students, and teaching and research faculty. From the law firm to the law library, from lawyer to librarian lawyer, my ability to engage flexible communication in the midst of advocacy-based service has been a significant contributor to my career success.

SO, WHY LIBRARIANSHIP?

For me, making the transition from law to librarianship was more than smooth and easy—it was worthwhile. From a reference associate answering phone queries to a law librarian managing legal database education and now as a librarian lawyer educating the campus community about ownership and rights in scholarship, my career transition has been a very fulfilling one. While the titles, surroundings, and even specific tasks have changed, the essential element of my work has not. My work as an attorney began in advocacy-based client service, and my work as a librarian lawyer continues in that same vein. What is more, I am increasingly finding fellow attorneys leaving the billable hour behind for the online catalog (figure 31.1).

April Hathcock
@AprilHathcock

@jrwlib Welcome to the side of goodness and light! Love meeting fellow "former" attorneys turned librarians.

1:10 PM - 9 Jul 2015

John R. Wallace @jrwlib · Jul 9
@AprilHathcock Haha thanks! I'm realizing there really are quite a few of us "converts." Found you from the #drll storify. Sounded great!

April Hathcock @AprilHathcock · Jul 9
@jrwlib Yep, we're a pretty sizeable crowd. #drll was great! I'm glad I stopped in.

Figure 31.1. Screenshot Twitter Exchange with John R. Wallace (@jrwlib)

As more and more lawyers enter librarianship, there will be less need for the question of "Why librarianship?" Hopefully, there will instead be more focus on integrating the transferable skills associated with advocacy-based service from a successful legal career to a successful librarianship career.

NOTES

1. Wendy Werner, "Customer Service for Lawyers," *Law Practice Today*, November 2006, http://apps.americanbar.org/lpm/lpt/articles/mgt11061.shtml.
2. Craig Finlay, Andrew Tsou, and Cassidy Sugimoto, "Scholarly Communication as a Core Competency: Prevalence, Activities, and Concepts of Scholarly Communication Librarianship as Shown through Job Advertisements," *Journal of Librarianship and Scholarly Communication* 3, no. 1 (2015): 12, http://dx.doi.org/10.7710/2162-3309.1236.
3. American Bar Association, *Model Rules of Professional Conduct* (Chicago: American Bar Association, 1995), rules 1.1–1.6; American Library Association, *Code of Ethics of the American Library Association* (Chicago: American Library Association, 2008), www.ala.org/advocacy/proethics/codeofethics/codeethics.

REFERENCES

American Bar Association. *Model Rules of Professional Conduct*. Chicago: American Bar Association, 1995.

American Library Association. *Code of Ethics of the American Library Association.* Chicago: American Library Association, 2008. www.ala.org/advocacy/proethics/codeofethics/codeethics.

Finlay, Craig, Andrew Tsou, and Cassidy Sugimoto. "Scholarly Communication as a Core Competency: Prevalence, Activities, and Concepts of Scholarly Communication Librarianship as Shown through Job Advertisements." *Journal of Librarianship and Scholarly Communication* 3, no. 1 (2015): eP1236. http://dx.doi.org/10.7710/2162-3309.1236.

Hathcock, April M., and John R. Wallace. Twitter posts. July 9, 2015. https://twitter.com/AprilHathcock/status/619237207975571456

Werner, Wendy. "Customer Service for Lawyers." *Law Practice Today*, November 2006. http://apps.americanbar.org/lpm/lpt/articles/mgt11061.shtml.

Chapter Thirty-Two

The Road from Medical to Science-Engineering Librarianship

Amani Magid

When I was a library student, I had a clear-cut plan. I thought I would stay in the biomedical field and make use of my background in science. With a specialization in medical libraries and special libraries, my goal was to stay in medical libraries for a couple of years and then make the big jump to either the World Health Organization or to "big pharma" libraries. I hoped to benefit from the high salaries obtained in for-profit medical companies as well. Those "couple of years" turned into six and a half at two different medical schools, and the leap was to academia instead, specifically a largely undergraduate university. In this chapter, I'll share my experiences at the medical school in Doha, Qatar, and my present position at an undergraduate university in Abu Dhabi, United Arab Emirates (UAE).

My official title at my present position in Abu Dhabi is reference and research librarian for the sciences and engineering. That's a mouthful! Most people on campus know me as the science and engineering librarian. I'm a liaison to the following undergraduate majors: biology, chemistry, physics, computer science, psychology, and all of the engineering majors—civil, mechanical, electrical, general, and computer. I'm also a liaison to the graduate students and postdoctoral researchers in the following research institutes: the Center for Genomics and System Biology (CGSB), the Center for Global Sea-Level Change Research (CSLC), the Center for Interdisciplinary Studies in Security and Privacy (CRISSP-AD), the Center for Prototype Climate Modeling (CPCM), the Center for Technology and Economic Development (CTED), Computational Modeling of Normal and Abnormal Cortical Processing, and the Public Health Research Center (PHRC).

In my previous role at the medical school in Doha, my official title was information services librarian, and I was one of five librarians with the same title. I was a liaison for the premedical program, the medical school, and the research program. It is an American medical school, with a two-year premedical program and a four-year medical program leading to the MD degree upon completion of the four years. The research program did not enroll students and instead consisted of lab groups headed by MDs and/or PhDs, with most labs employing research assistants and those who have earned master's degrees and PhDs.

The change from the medical school to a science and engineering librarian at an academic institution is definitely bringing me back to my science roots. The subject matter, needs of the faculty, instruction pedagogy, approach to outreach, and institutional culture make up just some of the many differences I encountered when adjusting from one type of library to another. Even with all the differences, the adjustment from a medical librarian to a science and engineering librarian has made for an enlightening and satisfying career transition.

AREAS OF STUDY

One of the core differences I encountered when I transitioned from a medical librarian to a science-engineering librarian was the areas of study for which I served as a liaison. At the medical school, I worked with the premedical program, which included classes in literature and the basic sciences; all four years of the medical program, which is largely clinical; and the growing research programs, most of which are biomedical. There was some overlap with regard to liaison assignments between my present position and my previous positions with the premedical program and the research program in the medical school.

Because there is no clinical medical curriculum in the Abu Dhabi school, my science and engineering role is at a primarily undergraduate campus with a growing research program that includes graduate students and postdoctoral associates. With my degree in integrative biology, and a minor in Arabic and research experience in pharmaceutical chemistry, I had never before encountered many of the subjects for which I am currently a liaison. The subjects most foreign to me are all of the engineering disciplines, computer science, psychology, and almost all of the institutes, with the exception of PHRC. Not surprisingly, I encountered a huge learning curve in (1) the subject matter and (2) the library resources for the subject matter.

As a librarian with over five years of experience, I know that most databases have similar features, so learning the new databases was one of the easier transition tasks to handle. Learning the subject matter, meanwhile, has been very enlightening for me. To bridge the gap in my knowledge, I attend as many of the seminars and lectures offered on campus by each of the departments and institutes as my schedule would allow. I encounter many unfamiliar subject terminologies, so I always bring my iPad to these lectures and look up the words on the spot or later in my office. Attending these lectures also gives me the chance to meet all of the faculty, graduate students, and postdoctoral fellows in that area. Another benefit of attending these seminars and lectures is that I learn about what research is conducted in this field. Then when it is time for me to select new resources for the library, I have a much more solid foundation on how to choose.

I also try to stay current in science and engineering news by subscribing to weekly e-mail newsletters. These newsletters give quick synopses of new developments in science and engineering. The news that is delivered is current research, and I still needed to satisfy my quest for basic knowledge in the sciences and engineering. Through these newsletters, I became aware of the Science Boot Camps for Librarians. These three- to five-day workshops are designed for librarians to learn about new subject areas. They are held in different regions of the United States and are hosted by different libraries and library associations. Each boot camp concentrates on a select number of science and engineering fields and provides instruction on basic knowledge of these fields. I recently discovered that some of these boot camps are available on YouTube. This is a great way for me to learn about different science topics without traveling or enrolling in classes.

I also subscribe to many science and engineering listservs for librarians and information professionals. This gives me a good idea of the types of reference and information literacy issues, as well as conferences and calls to papers in these fields.

OUTREACH SERVICES

Although the subject areas differ a lot in content, one of the similarities in my most recent two positions is the way I communicate with faculty. Scientists and engineers are very similar to medical faculty in that they do not need guidance on how to run their classes.

I was told of a situation at the medical library in Qatar concerning the group of librarians before me. They decided they wanted to have an impact on how medical students are taught. Their approach was literally to tell the medical faculty how they should run their classes. This, of course, completely dissuaded the faculty from wanting to interact with the librarians. As an unfortunate result, for a couple of years students did not benefit from the library as much because the librarians could not go into classes to teach students about library resources and services.

I keep this story in mind when I interact with the scientists and engineers at my current school. I know that they are more than capable of running their classes and do not need my input in that regard. Instead, I prefer to interact with the faculty by showing them what new resources can be used by the students and seeing if there is time in their class schedule for me to demonstrate to their students how these resources can be used. I realize that this is not different from what many librarians do already. I believe it's my science background, my personality, and my language skills that can at times make a difference in my communication with the scientists and engineers.

Although English is the language of all communication and instruction at the school in Abu Dhabi, there are some scientists and engineers who speak Arabic. Once they find out that I speak Arabic, it puts them more at ease. Sometimes these faculty members will relay their research questions to me in Arabic. This was also my experience working at the medical school in Qatar, though to a much lesser extent.

Although a small portion of the faculty spoke Arabic at the medical school, the culture was much more of an Arab culture. If I had an appointment with a faculty member to talk about instruction, I never started off talking about why I came. I always asked how they were, how their family was doing, how work was going, if they had any vacations planned, and so on. This was the case for all professors, not just the ones who spoke Arabic. It was an unofficial requirement to do this and was not anything I was told, but just something I picked up on. If a conversation automatically started with business, it was not viewed favorably at all. Small talk definitely helped in my outreach to faculty.

This isn't the case at the undergraduate school in Abu Dhabi. Although some of the faculty appreciate the small talk, I find that most would rather not waste time and prefer instead to start with the business at hand. Therefore, I've had to reengineer my outreach strategies. I still meet with the faculty to discuss different things, but I try to get a sense of the mood as I briefly start with small talk. If they are amiable, I find the faculty actively engaging in small talk. If they are not, they will start with "So we're discussing library resources for my class today, correct?" or something similar.

I also have created and publicized a "Sci-Eng Librarian Day," where I stay at the science building in a conference room all day for two days a month. I bring treats, and I'm there for any questions about library resources. These are well attended, and I receive many questions from faculty, graduate students, postdoctoral researchers, and staff, including lab technicians and executive assistants. However, sometimes people only want to stop by for a treat and a chat as part of their break from the workday. I completely welcome that and find that after a couple of times of coming by just to chat, they become comfortable with asking me library-related questions.

I send out a newsletter called *Science Bytes* once a month. It covers library resources and services of importance to the science and engineering community. Recently, I have formed a partnership with my colleague in the Center for Digital Scholarship and colleagues in the Office of Graduate and Postdoctoral Affairs to create programming that targets the science and engineering community. In addition, when new postdoctoral researchers or graduate students join the university, I provide a library orientation. This is also the case when faculty candidates come to the university for interviews and presentations.

My outreach efforts in the medical school were on a much smaller scale compared to what I'm presently engaged in. There were three main groups I reached out to: medical faculty, premedical faculty, and research scientists. Besides meeting with faculty, I contributed to a monthly newsletter produced by the library. The smaller size of the school and faculty did not require large-scale outreach efforts.

INSTRUCTION

Library instruction is a given for many librarians working in academic institutions. Teaching library resources to the science and engineering community is slightly different from teaching medical students. At the medical school I worked at, evidence-based medicine (EBM) was heavily integrated into the curriculum and, as a result, also translated into library instruction for searching for information for clinical scenarios that the medical students encounter.

Evidence-based medicine is defined as finding the best research evidence to solve clinical questions. The research evidence is ranked in a hierarchy to help form decision making. For example, systematic reviews and meta-analysis are at the top of the hierarchy, while background information is at the bottom. Because medical students still have a small knowledge base, they need to find the answers to background questions before they search for evidence. For example, what is type 2 diabetes?

The PICO technique, meanwhile, is used to translate a clinical situation into a research question. P is the patient, I is the intervention, C is the comparison, and O is the outcome. During this process, the medical student will need to determine what category this question falls under: therapy, diagnosis, prognosis, or etiology. Once the clinical question is formed, the students will take keywords in order to find evidence in the form of journal articles. Once the articles are found, there are CAT sheets, which are critical appraisal checklists that the medical student needs to look for in each article in order to determine if the article does indeed answer the clinical question.

In addition, the health-care provider must use his or her own background knowledge and take into consideration the patient's beliefs and wishes.

As a medical librarian, I was involved in teaching all aspects of this process. I underwent a lot of training and attended conferences in order to learn the process. I also was involved in evaluating the student responses to all of the above. As I'm now working at an undergraduate institution, I no longer use the EBM approach to teach students. However, there are some similarities between this approach and the method I use to teach how to search science and engineering resources. This is the style that most librarians will use to teach students how to search, regardless of discipline, and is what I used to teach researchers and premed students at the medical school. I still teach students to formulate a question based on keywords. I also teach them how to search the different databases. Although there is no clinical aspect, evaluating scientific and engineering evidence is similar in that there is a checklist of things to look for when evaluating the literature.

One key difference in instruction is that I teach engineering students how to search for patents using the United States Patent and Trade Office (USPTO) database. This is a seven-step process using a different type of database than most library databases. One searches for patents to determine if an invention has already been created. I attended a training course and went through tutorials to learn about this process. The correlation of searching for background questions in clinical questions is using different terms in order to search for a patent prior art in patent questions. Like clinical evidence and science journal articles, students must also learn how to evaluate a patent, and there is a checklist for doing this.

One aspect of teaching that I became quite attached to from my medical school days is teaching about medical mobile apps. Students in the medical school were provided with iPads and used them quite a lot while they were in their clinical years, carrying them in their white coats to look up information to help with their patients. I often taught the students how to access mobile apps and mobile websites that would provide them with reliable medical information. Teaching people how to use mobile apps is exciting and gives me quite a lot of enjoyment, and as a result, I still teach mobile apps at the undergraduate university. Obviously, I no longer teach medical apps. However, I offer out-of-class workshops on mobile apps for consumer health and apps for research, organizing, and everyday life.

UNDERGRADUATE LIBRARY AND UNIVERSITY

Working in a mostly undergraduate institution as opposed to a graduate school involves an adjustment from the library and student body perspective. From the library perspective, I switched from the National Library of Medical Classification system to the Library of Congress Classification system. Also, working in a university where the majority of students major in the social sciences or humanities causes a shift in the types of questions I receive when working at the reference desk and through chat. I enjoy this because I feel I have expanded my skills so that I now know where to search for these types of questions as well, while still being very grounded in science and engineering. Often when I tell the science and engineering students that I used to work at the only medical school in Qatar, I receive many questions from curious perspective students on what medical school is like. I attend events on campus with a focus on arts or social sciences, and this has opened my mind to the plethora of research being done on campus. There is also a big difference in the student body between my current university and the medical school. At the medical school, about 80 percent of the student body were Arab diaspora. In contrast, the undergraduate institution is not dominated by any diaspora and is quite diverse in that there are students who hail from almost every continent, and I hear many different languages spoken among the students, including English, Arabic, Chinese, Spanish, French, German, and many others. The diversity in student population has prompted me to continue the way I taught in the medical school in that I avoid Americanisms and American clichés.

Another interesting difference is that each of the librarians covers a different area of study, whereas at the medical school, we all were liaisons to the medical students and the premeds and a few of us to the research department. Because of this overlap in coverage, we frequently collaborated on journal articles and conference posters. There is some collaboration in my present position, but not to the extent I experienced in the medical school.

FINAL THOUGHTS

It has been quite an adjustment to transition from a medical librarian to a science and engineering librarian. Although the jobs are different, some of the core similarities of working in an academic institution remain. This includes answering questions in person and electronically, collection development, meeting with faculty, and conducting library workshops, among other duties. The challenges of learning new subject areas, developing a strong outreach program, and learning a different library classification system have strengthened my background and satisfy my personal career goals of continuing to learn and expand my knowledge as an information professional. I didn't seek the advice of any librarians who had made a similar transition, but I had faith, and still do, that it was the right transition to make. I don't feel I would have done things differently in my transition, as I believe I discover what I need to discover at the time that is right. It's great to be in a science environment again and to learn about all the new research that is being conducted. I find it satisfying to explore the different types of events on campus that are not science related as well, which makes working at an undergraduate institution a much richer experience culturally. Although this is not the path I had originally envisioned when I began my library degree, I'm satisfied and grateful for all the knowledge and experience I am gaining along the way.

FURTHER READING

Guyatt, Gordon, Drummond Rennie, Maureen O. Meade, and Deborah J. Cook. *Users' Guides to the Medical Literature: A Manual for Evidence-Based Clinical Practice.* 2nd ed. JAMA Evidence. New York: McGraw Hill, 2014.
New England Area Librarians. *Science Bootcamp for Librarians 2015.* YouTube. 2015. Accessed July 27, 2015. https://www.youtube.com/playlist?list=PLNtON4mU3aIdSsDOcOSGYcHjtlPJRLgDF.
CU Boulder Libraries. "Science Bootcamp West 2013: Ariel Paul and John Bonn." YouTube. 2013. Accessed July 27, 2015. https://www.youtube.com/watch?v=ggkkH20JX7k.

Chapter Thirty-Three

An Interview with Stacy R. Williams, Head of Architecture and Fine Arts Library, University of Southern California

Ray: Thanks for talking to us! We would love to hear about your move from New York University to the University of Southern California.

Stacy: Thank you! During the time that I was transitioning from New York University (NYU) to the University of Southern California (USC), I didn't fully consider everything that would and could happen before, during, and after the transition. I incorrectly assumed that because I was moving from one large private university to another large private university that it wouldn't be a big deal. But it was a big deal.

I went from being a staff member in the Business and Government Documents Reference Center at NYU to becoming a librarian with faculty status at USC. I was prepared for this in some sense, because I had worked within an academic library environment since I was in high school. So I felt like I could predict the type of patrons who would use USC Libraries and its services. I was confident that I could handle issues that would arise.

It also helped that I was a staff member who managed a collection of League of Nations, United Nations, and international document materials. My colleague at the time (Carol Arnold-Hamilton) and I were both responsible for managing two very different and large collections of noncirculating documents. Being responsible for those materials allowed me a certain freedom to learn and grow as a librarian. I learned how to copy catalog materials, answer reference questions, participate in instruction sessions, develop research guides, give tours, help researchers use the collection, promote the collection, and represent my department at campus events. Not only was I answering government-documents–related questions, I also participated in the general reference services, as well as our own departmental virtual reference services by answering business reference questions.

To prepare for USC and my new role, I did a lot of reading. As a librarian, I know that one way to keep up with the field is to read what is being published. I also read the library's and university's strategic plan. I looked at the university's demographics and thought about where the gaps were in library services and collections based on discipline. I also looked at the research guides written by my soon-to-be colleagues and researched what they published.

One of the first things that I did was talk to the people who had institutional knowledge. I spoke to both librarians and nonlibrarian staff to learn about the history of the different libraries at USC and library services. Talking was a way for me to get to know my new colleagues, listen to their thoughts on library services, and find out where they fit in within the library and how I could work with them in promoting services/collections/ideas.

Ray: What led to your decision to move across the country from NYC to California?

Stacy: There are many reasons why I decided to make this move. One thing that stood out to me at the time was that there were very few opportunities to advance into entry-level librarian positions. The USC position that I applied to was one of the few job descriptions that I read that gave new graduates a chance to get their foot in the door. USC has allowed me to fulfill my dream of being a librarian, developing my instruction skills, meeting a whole new community of library users, collaborating with great colleagues, and being a subject specialist in areas that I love. I feel very lucky to begin my career as a *librarian* at USC Libraries, and I feel very lucky to have developed as a future librarian at NYU.

Ray: What was USC's application process like?

Stacy: Having worked in an academic library setting for a really long time, I thought that the process for applying to USC was on par with what I observed as a staff member at NYU when they brought in librarians for interviews. I needed to submit a cover letter, curriculum vitae (CV), and a list of three references. A few weeks later, I received an offer to interview for the position via Adobe Connect, and then two weeks later, I received an offer to fly to Los Angeles and interview in person, as well as present on a topic. The interview process is typical of many academic libraries—it's an all-day process! My advice to anyone who receives an offer for an all-day interview is to practice, practice, and practice. Practice your presentation; get feedback from friends and colleagues. Practice interview questions; look at the job that you're applying to and develop questions from that. Do a "background" check on the school, library, committee members, and anything else that could help you familiarize yourself with the environment to which you're applying. Something that I learned a long time ago was that people do notice when applicants don't make the effort to research the place that they apply to.

Ray: What skills and experience did you use to show you were ready for this new type of position?

Stacy: I think what I was able to get across in the interview is that I worked in a similar academic library environment. Although both are unique in their own way, some things are similar. I felt comfortable talking about my experience with library patrons and their diverse set of needs, as well as discussing the library as a space and a place for students and community users.

Ray: Do you agree with the notion that librarians and archivists tend to get typecast based on their specific space within the field?

Stacy: Yes, absolutely. But librarians as a whole get typecast in popular/ mainstream culture, so it's not surprising that some of us typecast each other. From my observations as both a staff member and now a librarian, it usually begins with someone questioning why an applicant would apply for a job that is completely or slightly different than what they are already doing. Well, why not? If someone feels like they're qualified for a position, it's not my place to question why are they applying for the position. Forward-thinking applicants will address that within their cover letter or during an interview. I would encourage applicants, if you are transitioning from one area in a library to another, to address it in your cover letter or show via your CV why you are qualified to make the transition. Some search committees have a guiding matrix, and applicants have to be able to fit within this matrix in order to make it past the first-round applicant review.

Ray: What advice would you give for someone who is hoping to make a similar move?

Stacy: I would advise observing your colleagues within and outside of your department. Learn about the library from the inside out, and speak to as many people as you can about what they do. I can't promise that this will work for everyone and that people will want to talk to you, but you have to try to get to know your colleagues in the library. Find out the ins and outs of different services points, so that when a patron asks you a question, you'll be able to answer it or at least get them started on an answer before referring them to someone else. We should all work to avoid what some places call the "Campus Runaround." Say hi to the person who cleans your office, have coffee with someone in technical services and/or interlibrary loan, always be engaged and willing to learn. Nothing is worse than working with a know-it-all who doesn't know it all. There are obviously worse things, but in highly collaborative work environments like libraries, it really does take a village to keep the library going.

IX

Nontraditional Transitions, Internships, and General Advice

Chapter Thirty-Four

An Interview with Naomi House, Founder of INALJ

Ray: You've been recognized by *Library Journal* and, truthfully, most of our colleagues as the founder of the website I Need a Library Job. What led to your decision to find new types of roles?

Naomi: My decision to leave libraries was inspired by a shocking and unexpected layoff during the government shutdown of 2013. We had no warning at all. During the weeks I was unemployed, I began to evaluate whether or not I even wanted to be a librarian. I had worked for ten years in libraries and information centers in positions ranging from library assistant to supervisor to librarian, but I found my passion was in helping others, both at INALJ, a website that provides listings for positions in the field, and now with T160K, where I work on crowdfunding amazing African-led projects with partners from Mali, Ethiopia, Benin, and Burkina Faso. I don't have the desire for a traditional library job anymore because I believe I am better at being a library advocate outside the job.

I didn't actually start looking for a new employer. I became a founding partner and chief marketing officer (CMO) of T160K through a chance encounter. Since founding INALJ, I have been a speaker on the library conference circuit, and I had an opportunity at the beginning of 2014 to present in Cape Town, South Africa, where I met T160K founder and crowdfunding expert Stephanie Diakite.

Many may be familiar with the story of the rescue of the Timbuktu manuscripts; Stephanie was a key figure in crowdfunding this effort. We spent a great deal of time discussing community building. We eventually reconnected and began planning T160K as a social-purpose corporation (SPC) connecting individuals around the globe with opportunities to fund amazing projects like the cataloging efforts on the Timbuktu manuscripts and a new center for African historical photography in Benin.

I highly encourage LIS (library and information science) students and professionals who are able to do so to reach out to those in our field around the globe. You never know where opportunity will come from. I took on the CMO role because of my experience growing INALJ and marketing it.

Ray: You've managed to build a lot of flexibility into your work since your early INALJ days. What's it like to build your own position?

Naomi: INALJ (formerly I Need a Library Job) began as a way of sharing job ads as a daily listserv with my fellow Rutgers MLIS classmates that library and information science students, staff, and librarians might be interested in and qualified for.

I created it so that job hunters wouldn't have to duplicate efforts searching many different sites, and I have kept its simple list format and not created a database because I want job hunters to "shelf read" in a way, I want them to serendipitously find jobs they might have self-selected not to see. I created a product I wanted to use and in doing so, skipped a need to apply for a job and make that job match my skills. I took the skills I had and made something for myself and over six hundred volunteers who have worked with me in the last five years.

T160K's CMO position was also a case of taking skills I had and not matching them to a job ad but rather creating a position that works for the organization and for me. Once the original cofounders of T160K, myself included, decided to form the SPC, we had to decide what our operational goals and needs were and if those needs fit our skill sets or if we would need to hire outside help.

My work in libraries did include some marketing, but building INALJ as a grassroots volunteer movement made the CMO position a good fit for me. Although I didn't formally respond to a job ad, becoming T160K's CMO was a very similar process that shows how job hunting can be a translatable skill for business creation, especially within a team.

Ray: What lessons did you take from your time in libraries and with INALJ that applied to your work with T160K?

Naomi: In my case, I am not only the chief marketing officer, but—since we are a small team of five—I am the only person working on marketing. My skill sets that I employ in this job have quite the range! I brought social media skills, from grassroots campaign building on Facebook and Twitter to some experience managing a private LinkedIn group and Pinterest pages. Everything from "SWOT analysis" and big-picture thinking to doing the manual work was important. I began INALJ quite by accident, never envisioning the scope or breadth of the site, so I also bring my experience from the school of hard knocks and big mistakes. Learning from INALJ helped me make better choices as CMO for T160K.

There are many opportunities for LIS folk to volunteer or make social media and outreach part of their job. If being a CMO interests you, do some informational interviews and definitely get your feet wet on social media; this means not only lurking to learn but being active. The skills you need will vary even within a job title, but showing a willingness to engage and learn is priceless. If you don't show you understand specific platforms, it will be a tough sell that you *can* learn them.

Ray: Do you agree with the notion that librarians and archivists tend to get typecast based on their specific space within the field?

Naomi: Absolutely! And this is the fault of hiring managers and committees. I had argued and burned bridges serving on search committees about the "requirements," especially experience, because I think we unreasonably expect that "specific experience" is not translatable. Or for some reason do not feel that training is worthwhile. That is the only excuse for the narrowness of job ads, that the hiring committee cannot see the potential for translatable and transferable skills.

Why do we ask for two to three years' experience? Why don't we want to invest time in those new to the field? These are questions we need to ask before posting a job. This only allows for lateral movement or movement into supervisory positions within the job title and does not give, for example, catalogers or archivists room to expand or change job titles.

Ray: Do you have any advice for someone who may be seeking adventures in new fields, outside of librarianship?

Naomi: I would recommend really examining what makes you happy and what you are skilled at. Then make efforts if you can to meet people in tangential fields. I understand that it is time-consuming and costly to attend conferences and belong to outside organizations, so if you don't have monetary resources or much time, take advantage of networking and learning on social media, especially LinkedIn groups. E-mail people who hold jobs you consider a dream job and ask if you can do an informational interview. There is little you can do without some sort of investment of your time or money to learn more about another field, so always consider your own needs first, because ultimately, no matter if you are working as a librarian or a CMO, your career should fit your needs first.

Chapter Thirty-Five

Refining Your Career

Internships and Transitions

Sean A. Flores

My first full-time position as an information professional was as an associate librarian at Qualcomm. The Qualcomm Library is open twenty-four hours a day, seven days a week, and provides services to a population spanning the globe. As associate librarian, I was the first point of contact for colleagues at all levels of the company, from student interns to executives. I provided reference services in person, over the telephone, via instant message, through screen sharing, by e-mail, or any combination thereof. When I was interviewing for the job, the attributes that distinguished me from other candidates included my proven track record working in business environments as well as my time-management skills, customer service, ability to communicate effectively, and my understanding of the mission of the library department and how it fit within the overall mission of the organization.

Many of the skills that employers found valuable were gained from internships and part-time jobs I had earned as a student. When I was in the process of obtaining my master's degree in library and information science (MLIS) through San Jose State University, I immediately sought out real-world experience in libraries. At the time, it was 2009 and the U.S. economy was in the midst of a recession. While there were very few opportunities for full-time employment, I did find that internships and part-time positions for graduate students were abundant. Before even beginning my first semester in my MLIS program, I had already landed a part-time job at a military medical library. As it turned out, my status as a graduate student gave me priority to be placed in student-worker positions at the medical library. Since I was new to my library school pursuits, my new employers could keep me longer as a student employee; the time spent training me was fruitful for them for an extended period of time.

As a graduate student, I was trusted to provide a level of service that was on par with the medical librarians. This provided me with in-depth database research skills that I wouldn't have obtained otherwise. I also learned that I don't enjoy cataloging, though I have great respect for catalogers, as they provide incredible value with their meticulously detailed work. I did realize that I love using metadata and Boolean logic to search and refine information. This led me to take an online research course at school, which gave me a better understanding of databases and metadata.

Continuing to seek experience, I also found work as a digital asset management intern for the Balboa Park Online Collaborative (BPOC), an organization that helps arts and cultural institutions implement sustainable technology solutions, where I assisted digitization efforts for museums, repurposed digital media for exhibits and promotions, and edited metadata for thousands of records on collections management systems. There I learned that I enjoy repurposing media for promotions and events. I also realized the value of learning how to code. Just like my work at the medical library led me to metadata and cataloging courses, my experience at BPOC encouraged me to take more technology-based MLIS courses.

Given that I was pursuing my MLIS during the Great Recession, I was not in a rush to complete school and jump into a full-time job. Instead, I spent my summers at internships and part-time positions. One summer, I took a job as a library assistant with the knowledge management department for a for-profit pharmaceutical company. This job taught me the importance of documenting research, copyright clearance, and using business systems such as Salesforce to track article and research requests. I learned the value of a good work flow and the high level of service that can be provided with minimal staff. At the end of my internship, the pharmaceutical company offered me a full-time position, but I declined the offer in favor of continuing my exploration of the field; I wanted to find the right fit within the profession.

Toward the end of my MLIS program, I became an archives processing intern for the San Diego History Center. I created online pathfinders for historically significant paraphernalia and ephemera that are now available to researchers via the Online Archive of California. From this experience, I realized that I didn't enjoy working in archives as much as I enjoyed working with emerging technology, conducting literature searches, and working with the aggregation, dissemination, and repurposing of information.

Meanwhile, I took a job as the registrar and exhibits coordinator for the Japanese Friendship Garden. I worked directly with board members, managed volunteer work, and coordinated exhibits and programs with artists. I learned that I worked and communicated very well with all levels of organizations, and I enjoyed marketing and promoting events. Hosting art receptions was both daunting and a lot of fun.

From my first internship at the medical library through my time as a registrar and exhibits coordinator, I identified my strengths and preferences, and I used these experiences to guide my course selection at school. I realized that I didn't have what it took to fulfill my dream of being a children's librarian at a public library. My career goal had changed. My interests and skill set were better served with technology-based duties, and I was happy to know that. After graduating with my MLIS, I found myself with a great full-time job at Qualcomm, a company consistently voted as one of *Fortune* magazine's top 100 companies to work for in the United States.

I'm happy to report that sticking to my goal of exploring the field during my years in school paid off in the end. I have recently transitioned into Santa Barbara City College as their systems and technologies librarian from my previous position as the web librarian for San Diego Public Library. What attracted me to the librarian position at Santa Barbara City College was that it had touched on three points that I was excited about: service to a demographic pursuing higher education, a technology position that I could continue to grow in over the long term, and an opportunity to provide online and classroom instruction.

For those who are unable to pursue internships, I'd recommend gaining insight into library and information science environments by scheduling informational interviews or volunteering a small portion of your time in areas of the profession that interest you. I would also recommend including some areas of the profession you may not be interested in, because you simply never know what you will discover about yourself or the job responsibilities in the process. The early years in one's career are the perfect time to explore various working environments, and knowing your work preferences only helps you seize a great opportunity when it comes your way.

Chapter Thirty-Six

Gaining Experience without Forgoing Pay

Advice on Landing Paid Work as an LIS Student

Dinah Handel

The decision to attend a graduate program was a well-thought-out process for me. I had graduated college with a degree in women's history and spent the year following my graduation working two service-industry jobs and volunteering at a domestic violence shelter. I knew I wanted to attend library school, but I wasn't quite sure how to make it work financially.

At the time, I was living in the town where I went to college and making just enough money to support myself but nowhere near enough to relocate and start a graduate program. I decided the best option would be to move back in with my mother, in California, get a better-paying job, and save as much money as I could. I'll definitely acknowledge here, and probably throughout my piece, that this was a privilege. Not everyone has the ability to move home. For me, moving home and living rent free is what enabled me to attend graduate school.

Once I obtained a job in California, I started saving money each month and applying to graduate programs in earnest. Once I had decided to attend Pratt Institute and knew that I was going to live in Brooklyn, I began to think about what I might do when I got there. I only had library experience as an undergrad, and I knew that I needed to get my foot in the door somehow. This was where my savings came in. For my first semester, I did two unpaid internships and started volunteering at a radical community archive in Brooklyn. I told myself that after this first semester, I was only going to accept paid work going forward. Doing the two unpaid internships was an invaluable experience, but I started to feel uneasy and concerned about the larger implications of participating in an ultimately exploitive cycle. I also started to run out of savings, which played a role in my decision to seek out paid, almost full-time work.

I knew I wasn't going to be able to find one job that would fulfill my desire to obtain paid work experience in the field and have the flexibility I needed as a full-time graduate student, so I began to seek out multiple part-time paid positions. The first thing I explored was a position in my program's student association. At Pratt Institute, certain student leadership positions are paid, as they come with significant responsibility. I ran for secretary and won the election, which secured me enough money to pay my rent for the following semester. The commitment for this position was about ten hours per week, which left me room to find another part-time paid position. I applied to work as a graduate assistant in my program's libraries and began working a total of twenty hours per week at two different libraries. Finally, I secured a job as a personal assistant, working one afternoon a week for an academic. This was my best-paying job, paying almost twice as much as my graduate assistantship.

Between these three positions, I was employed nearly full-time and gaining experience in my field. Balancing three different working environments and being a full-time student was no easy task, but I knew I was obtaining valuable experience. I found the job search relatively easy and primarily relied on Pratt Institute's listserv. Graduate assistantships, while low wage, are a great way to gain valuable experience and try out new types of library work. Working in the library was also beneficial because I was able to do my own work when I wasn't assisting patrons. After spending a semester working as a graduate assistant in the library, I was offered a graduate assistant position with a professor for the summer.

The summer between my first and second year of library school, I decided not to take any courses and concentrate on continuing to gain work experience. While I loved the academic aspect of library school and wished I had more time to read and write, I knew that once I left school, a competitive job market awaited me, and I needed to be prepared. In addition to working as a research assistant with a professor in the program, I applied and accepted a position to work as a digital asset management freelancer. This was an amazing opportunity, and I felt really lucky to have been picked from the hundreds of applications submitted. According to my supervisor in this position, one of the reasons I was chosen was due to my name recognition—she was an alum of the same program as me and recognized my name from sending out student-government-related listserv e-mails. The other helpful aspect of this position was that the hours were relatively flexible, and coupled with the flexible position as a research assistant, I was able to balance both jobs with no difficulty.

When the school year started up again, I continued working as a research assistant and continued to serve as secretary. I also obtained a new position as a fellow in an academic library's archives and special collections. This position was an amazing opportunity and fundamental to my growth as an archivist. It was a ten-hour-per-week commitment, and I was given a monthly stipend based on entry-level wages for a processing archivist. As a fellow, I was treated and compensated like a legitimate archivist. I got to process collections and author-finding aids, develop and carry out projects involving the digital collections, sit in on job talks and bibliographic instruction sessions, learn about deed of gift and donor negotiations, and receive professional mentorship from my supervisors. The position was a year long, which meant I was really able to be immersed in the archive's daily operations.

In the spring of my final year at Pratt, I was elected to be president of the student association, which meant greater responsibility and also a larger stipend. Instead of using this as spending money, I put it into my savings to pay for my final course, which I would take during the summer. My spring semester was certainly a busy one. I balanced working two jobs with school-related tasks, but it was worth it. I had a résumé that I felt confident about, projects and deliverables to discuss in cover letters, and a network of library and archive professionals in New York City that I had met through each of my positions. Following the spring semester, I had one class to finish at Pratt and was asked to stay at my fellowship full-time for the summer to assist with a move off-site. Again, I was lucky that my employers were willing to be flexible and allow me to work while finishing my last class. During that time period, I also applied and accepted the position I am currently in now.

While I ultimately made the decision to transition from unpaid work to paid positions, I was also supported by employers, supervisors, and mentors within the field. I can see that there were many privileges in my personal life that made having three part-time jobs and being a full-time student possible. As a midtwenties, single, childless person, I could stand to work at odd hours and on weekends, spend a significant amount of time away from my home during the day, and live cheaply on peanut butter and jelly sandwiches when needed. I realize that many of my graduate school cohort do not have this same luxury. Taking into consideration my own situation and privileges, my advice to students in library school is as follows:

1. If you have to work full-time at a job unrelated to librarianship, make the most of your class projects. This way you can have a tangible deliverable to talk about in your cover letters.
2. Meet and grow your professional community. This can be done at local professional events, regional and national conferences, and using social networking like Twitter. You never know when someone will think of you for a position or offer to reformat your résumé.

3. If you can't get full-time employment in the field while in school, look for multiple part-time positions. This will grow your résumé and give you a chance to feel out different positions within the profession. I knew pretty quickly I wasn't interested in public services librarianship soon after I started working as a graduate assistant in an academic library.

4. If you feel like you absolutely have to get an unpaid internship in order to get your foot in the door, like I did, make sure you have good mentorship and project planning in the internship. The internship should have a tangible project and deliverable, and you should be supported in acquiring the skills to complete the project. Also, don't commit to working unpaid for more than eight to ten hours per week.

5. Try to cut costs in every other aspect of school. Go to a state school if possible and save money on tuition. Apply for every scholarship you possibly can, especially grants or stipends to attend professional events. Learn which stores have student discounts and which cultural institutions offer free or reduced admission with your student ID. Combine studying and socializing by making study plans with members of your cohort.

The decision to attend graduate school is not one to be taken lightly or without significant planning, particularly when it comes to personal finances. While taking an unpaid internship may feel necessary given the high number of opportunities for unpaid labor, it isn't. Even as a new professional, you deserve compensation for your work.

Chapter Thirty-Seven

An Interview with Dr. Janet H. Clarke, Associate Dean for Research and User Engagement, Stony Brook University Libraries

Ray: Like many of our colleagues, you explored a subject specialty quite deeply before becoming a librarian. What led you to become a librarian after a few years as a professor, especially since your primary subject expertise is so fascinating? What was it about librarianship that called to you?

Janet: I pursued and finished my doctorate in Asian American literature because I am a student of literature. My love is to study literature and engage with its discursive communities. Teaching what I studied was both gratifying and challenging on many levels: gratifying to see students discover and appreciate literature in ways that mattered to them; challenging because of the time commitment it took to be an effective teacher and scholar and also find a healthy balance with my personal life.

When I assessed my career trajectory midway through my tenure-track teaching position at a liberal arts college, librarianship appealed to me as a more reasonable choice. When I conducted my own unscientific, informal survey, I found librarians committed to their profession but also committed to a balanced personal life by pursuing personal interests as well as engaging in community life. This model called to me. I felt it would take me too long to achieve this balance with the demands of academic teaching. I considered teaching graduate LIS (library and information science) courses, but my advanced degree is in Asian American literature, not LIS. So I really wanted to get my feet wet in the practice of librarianship before I got in front of the classroom with LIS graduate students. I found an internship in an academic library and started working part time at a public library to broaden my experience in different types of libraries and to test my assumptions about my fit in academic libraries.

Ray: Once you had librarian experience under your belt, were you able to meet the requirements for academic positions? Was more training required of you?

Janet: When I first started applying for jobs and talking to librarians, I learned quickly that without the MLS, it would be difficult to get professional librarian positions because libraries were pretty strict about the MLS requirement then. Although this requirement is loosening; some academic libraries are looking for subject or functional expertise and thus accept a PhD rather than an MLS. But an MLS degree is still a standard requirement for most academic library positions.

So I knew that I needed to get the MLS degree, even though I was not thrilled about going back to school. Because librarianship is often a second career, many of the MLS students pursue this degree on a part-time basis while they hold down full-time jobs. I was able to go full-time, which helped shorten my period of unemployment. I was able to finish the degree in three semesters.

Ray: Which skills were you able to bring from your past experience that were helpful in your new position?

Janet: My experience as a teaching faculty was extremely valuable in helping me understand the principles, tenets, and infrastructure of higher education institutions, particularly public ones. I found I already know a lot about the research life cycle, tenure processes and expectations, professional participation at conferences and committees at national and regional levels, classroom environment, and the overall university/academic environment.

My decade of teaching as a graduate student and tenure-track faculty also gave me some relevant transferable skills, such as teaching, presentation, and research skills and publication experience. I could relate more easily with teaching faculty in terms of course time management, the logic of a syllabus, learning objectives, effective research-project design, student learning styles, and, in my own discipline of Asian American studies, the key resources and scholars.

This familiarity helped me in my new role as an instruction librarian. I understood the need for effective integration of information literacy skills into a course curriculum, the importance of learning what the teaching faculty's objective was for the library session so that it resonates with and reinforces the skill or learning objective, and the critical role that the teaching faculty can have before, during, and after the session. I also quickly saw some limitations of being on the other side of the fence: limits of one-shot sessions, dependence on teaching faculty for information before the sessions and effective follow-through and reinforcement of skills after the sessions, and difficulty of gauging student learning.

Ray: What were your biggest hurdles in making the move to academic librarianship from the professoriate?

Janet: There are four areas that I will discuss here.

First, the research requirement for library faculty. One of the main difficulties was finding time to do research in a twelve-month appointment, though there are academic libraries with nine- or ten-month appointments that mirror the teaching faculty obligations. The reality is that there is never enough time for research, for teaching faculty as well as for academic librarians whose portfolios include research productivity. But the delineation between teaching time and research time is more clearly made with teaching faculty, whose teaching time is determined by the institution's academic calendar. When their quarter or semester is over, their teaching obligation ends as well, unless they choose additional service during winter or summer sessions.

In theory and practice, the summer and winter breaks are used for concentrated research by teaching faculty, though it really occurs throughout the year. Many librarians, especially those who have twelve-month appointments, do not have clearly designated research time. And that can present challenges when research and publication are part of tenure or renewal processes.

I currently have a nine-to-five, Monday through Friday, twelve-month appointment. So that kind of structured workweek was a major transition for me. When my schedule was tied to the academic schedule, with summer to organize and conduct my own research, I had much more flexibility in arranging my workday. I was fortunate to have had the experience of research being a component of all of my work. So I didn't feel it was an extraneous part of my academic library work but often found myself relegating my research and writing to evenings and weekends throughout the year. Some of this had to do with my own work style, but some of it was due to the demands of my job, which required a lot of committee work, team coordination, and outreach with academic departments.

It was difficult to find large chunks of time to devote exclusively to research and writing. But I knew what I had to do in order to meet my tenure requirements, so I found projects that made use of my subject training in Asian American literature and the professional training in library science. It was important that these projects were intellectually challenging and relevant to my current responsibilities, contributed to the scholarly discourse in both of these fields, and was deliverable. Time management, concrete goals, and a very understanding and fully supportive family were key to those outcomes.

Second, the "separate but equal" status of academic librarians. This has been an interesting and ongoing challenge for academic librarians. Academic librarians have a wide-ranging variety of statuses, from faculty status down to staff status. Add tenure or permanent or term appointment to these, and we have another set of permutations. This lack of standardization contributes to the continuing ambiguity of the status of librarians in academic institutions and presents myriad challenges, including professional identity crisis; representation, or lack thereof, in faculty and university governance; union contracts; expectations in tenure requirements; credit for or expectation of teaching; and differential salaries from teaching faculty (see the articles by Bolin, Hosburgh, and Drobnicki in the references). Having been a former teaching faculty, I find there are specific differences in work flow, perception of status of librarians in higher education institutions, and differentiations of scholarly productivity. Regardless of the debate over faculty status, academic librarians who contribute to the scholarly discourse raise the visibility and stature of librarians as researchers, as do tenure-track/tenured teaching faculty.

Third, sabbatical leaves. Sabbatical or other kinds of paid research leaves for academic librarians are also not consistently available or equally granted among academic institutions, thus creating another instance of differentiation between teaching faculty and academic librarians that can impact research engagement by the latter. Sabbaticals or other leaves can be a double-edged sword if there is insufficient infrastructure for staffing during the leaves. I was fortunate to take advantage of a sabbatical leave.

Finally, managerial opportunities. I find that there are more expectations and opportunities for managerial experience in librarianship as compared with a teaching faculty position, where the most common "managerial unit" is the course and the students in the course. The academic library is a service unit of the institution. It is usually a complex organization within the larger institution, with functional and operational and reporting structures of its own. Librarians often manage or supervise these units within the library and have more structured opportunities to experience and expand their managerial or supervisory skills than teaching faculty, who might lead committees and task forces but don't have direct reporting oversight of the members, such as university/college administrators and department chairs would. As an academic librarian, I have had opportunities to grow as a manager and senior administrator at my institution, as well as in professional organizations.

Ray: Do you have any advice for folks who'd like to move to the academic library from a teaching position in higher education?

Janet: If you're thinking of getting a PhD before pursuing your career in librarianship, a subject PhD is appropriate for academic librarianship; a library/information science PhD is appropriate for teaching MLS. Here are some other specific and concrete suggestions for those considering transitioning from the professoriate to academic librarianship:

- Understand the expectations of academic librarians, including the research and professional participation components.
- Have clear and realistic research projects or areas of interest that you will continue to pursue.
- Exercise rigorous time management to fit in the research and publishing activity into a nine-to-five workweek and (most likely) twelve-month appointment.
- Update your skills and keep abreast of new technologies.
- Understand learning behaviors of college and university students.
- Network and find colleagues with similar research interests so that you have a community of practice.
- Join an active professional organization where you can participate and grow professionally. Especially in academic librarianship, it is important to have professional colleagues external to your organization who can comment on your scholarship and contribution to the profession.

For me, this career move was the right one. It allowed me to achieve a healthy balance between my personal and professional life. Academic librarianship has been very rewarding to me. I have found it to be an excellent place to grow professionally and intellectually. There is so much change happening in our profession, higher education, and technology landscape that we seem to have endless opportunities to explore and develop ways to make ourselves relevant and valuable to our constituents.

I often find myself feeling grateful to be in a profession so well poised to address and lead on policy and practice in information access, privacy, emerging technologies, preservation and stewardship of cultural productions, higher education, and diversity. There are so many ways to contribute to this changing profession and the life of the university. While I sometimes miss in-depth study of literature as a teaching faculty, I wholeheartedly embrace the sharing, generosity, and educational pillars of academic librarianship.

REFERENCES

Bolin, M. K. "Librarian Status at US Research Universities: Extending the Typology." *Journal of Academic Librarianship* 34, no. 5 (2008): 416–24.

Drobnicki, J. A. "CUNY Librarians and Faculty Status: Past, Present, and Future." *Urban Library Journal* 20, no. 1 (2014): 2–10.

Hosburgh, N. "Librarian Faculty Status: What Does It Mean in Academia?" *Library Philosophy & Practice*, 2011: 31–37.

Chapter Thirty-Eight

An Interview with Dr. Lian Ruan, Head Librarian, Illinois Fire Service Institute, University of Illinois at Urbana-Champaign

Ray: Thanks for chatting with us! Your transition is a bit different from many others in this book. Rather than finding a position in a different workplace, you stayed on at the Illinois Fire Service Institute. What did this experience mean to you?

Lian: My experience may look different because my transition was from a passive type of library to a more proactive type of library. In 1998, Director Richard Jaehne took over the Illinois Fire Service Institute (IFSI) at the University of Illinois at Urbana-Champaign. IFSI is the statutory state fire academy. He had an in-person, one-on-one interview with me. At that time, I was the research specialist and solo librarian in charge of the IFSI in-house technical library. The library joined only one consortium—the International Fire Information and Resource Exchange (inFIRE)—in 1991, and it did not have a budget. In the late 1990s, Google emerged as the most powerful search engine on the Internet, and many users believed that they could find any information that they wanted online. It seemed that the library was old-fashioned and soon to be obsolete. During the interview, Director Jaehne was not interested in my job description. Instead, he sincerely asked me the value and relevance of the library to the organization. It was a tough and shocking conversation, but it opened my eyes.

After developing a well-thought-out plan, I chose to stay. I believed that the library could thrive in the dynamic online information age by establishing

231

its niche position in delivering timely information services to every firefighter, no matter where he or she is located. I initiated the library's outreach program to provide no-cost information services to all firefighters in Illinois. In order to do this, I did a survey study of all fire departments (1,293) statewide in December 1998. With a 46 percent return rate, the survey findings indicated that the library's outreach program would benefit up to 42,675 firefighters; that 70 percent of those firefighters who were volunteer firefighters with little access to resources and information services locally would particularly benefit from the service. The IFSI Library joined the Lincoln Trails Library System in 1999, one of twelve library systems managed by the Illinois State Library. The library could provide international loans to over six hundred public libraries to serve their local firefighters and apply for grant programs offered by the state library.

Under IFSI Vision 2010, 2015, and 2020, IFSI's central objective is to help firefighters develop the core skills required to effectively meet the fire emergency service needs of their communities. IFSI's mission is to help firefighters do their job through training, education, information, and research. I accurately identified the IFSI Library's role in helping to fulfill this objective over the last ten years. Through this process, I was able to obtain support to change my job title from research specialist to head librarian, transforming a technical library to a public special library for all firefighters and managing a team of professional librarians and graduate students from the Graduate School of Library and Information Science.

Ray: That's an amazing accomplishment! Congratulations. What steps did you take when you transitioned your library to a new type of institution altogether?

Lian: I literally rewrote my job description with a list of requirements that I copied and learned from others. More important, I had to work hard on developing new skills to fulfill the changing responsibilities. I was not completely ready in terms of skills and experience at the beginning of this transformation; however, I was determined and motivated to take on the challenges. The learning curve was stiff, but it was exciting and rewarding. Along the way, I have acquired many new skills and gained valuable experience in areas such as budget planning, collaboration, conflict resolution, strategic planning, product design and delivery, project management, public speaking, and so on. I was touched by many colleagues and friends who lent their support whenever I needed it.

I have initiated and implemented six three-year strategic plans since 1999. The library's transformation was further aided by strong IFSI support and a series of Library Services and Technology Act (LSTA) grant awards totaling more than $248,481 from the Illinois State Library. My most notable grant awards include Internet Outreach to and Training of Illinois Fire Service Personnel, Public and Community College Librarians for Electronic Access to Fire Safety Information (FY2000, $75,000), Grow with Pro! (FY2002, $4,900) for a conceptual design of the new library building, and Illinois Firefighter Line of Duty Death (IFLODD) Digital Image Collection Database (FY2007, $20,500). With a professional team of two librarians, one archivist, part-time IT (information technology) staff, and four graduate student assistants from the Graduate School of Library and Information Science (GSLIS) at the University of Illinois at Urbana-Champaign, the IFSI Library answers more than four thousand reference requests annually and has received 467,991 web hits. Under Vision 2020, IFSI dedicated a $9 million Learning Resource and Research Center (LRRC) in 2011 to meet growing needs.

The four-thousand-square-foot library is an integral part of the LRRC, with increased space for collection materials, computer terminals, formal and informal study areas, and a temperature-controlled archival storage room, ensuring a permanent home for the library. As the only fire science dedicated library in Illinois, the IFSI Library holds the largest fire and emergency response multimedia collection in the state, consisting of over sixty thousand titles. It has become the second-largest fire service library in the United States, behind only the National Fire Academy Library of the U.S. Fire Administration. In 2015, the library was named a finalist of the National Medal for Museum and Library Service, the nation's highest honor given to museums and libraries for service to the community.

Ray: What skills did you pick up as a technical services librarian that proved useful to you once you earned your new title as head librarian?

Lian: Two sets of skills from my past experience were helpful: technical skills that I learned in library school and ten years of cataloging experience in two fire-related libraries at the Illinois Fire Service Institute and the Champaign Fire Department.

Ray: We've been asking many of our contributors this question, and we wonder what you have to say: Do you believe librarian and archivists tend to be typecast?

Lian: Yes. When I was in library school in the late 1980s, I was trained to some extent to focus on technical skills, such as cataloging, acquisition, reference, and computing. If we are going to address and change the stereotype, we must train future students to answer how libraries can add value to an institution. Is the library relevant to the organization? How can we demonstrate the library's value?

Ray: What advice would you give to someone who is hoping to make substantial changes to the environment in which they work?

Lian: Be open, flexible, and adaptable and think outside the box. Lifelong learning in multiple fields is critical. Through years of hard work, I have developed a user-centered management philosophy with a proactive, value-added, evidenced-based, and team-based approach. It has worked out well for the IFSI Library, its user community, and my own career development. I am thankful and grateful for the opportunity that I have had with the IFSI Library.

Chapter Thirty-Nine

Top Five Tips for Finding New Roles in Your Library

Davis Erin Anderson

As I reflect on my career thus far, it occurs to me that the two organizations that top my résumé both underwent major changes during my time there. I suppose transitions—the subject of this book—aren't just for individual employees!

I learned long ago that our only constant is change. Nothing gold can stay and all of that. In my first full-time role, I worked at the library of a major music publishing company. We were a blissfully independent company, and a major part of the classical music ecosystem, until our holding company realized it was time to reconfigure its portfolio and sell the business. The following couple of years were tumultuous; a buyer wanted to get into the music-publishing realm and therefore started a business by purchasing elements of a catalog from a global publishing company. Then they purchased another major music company in the United States. We were to merge our offices with theirs, which resulted in a survey of staff and the elimination of positions that were considered redundant. The saddest part of all of this, and a reality that's unfortunately not at all uncommon, was that a handful of very talented people were sent away.

Given our group's expertise in the catalog and our integral role managing a sizable work flow of performance requests, we were spared. Our primary adjustment to this new world order was a physical relocation from the heart of the Flatiron District in New York City all the way to a block adjacent to the Hudson River (so close to the water, in fact, that the library was inaccessible for weeks due to flooding from Superstorm Sandy in 2012). We also shared our space with a similar group from the other company. Talk about a cultural change!

Along with the transformation of the business itself, my role developed. I spent about four years working with our collection—ensuring we had enough material in stock to support performances going on all over the world, balancing our materials with available shelf space, and heading up a project to manage the relocation of about a third of our materials to off-site storage. Along the way, I pitched and then worked on a project to bring wiki software to the entire company. My newfound interest in organizing knowledge with end users in mind led me to enroll in the School of Information and Library Science, as it was known then, at Pratt Institute. I also became deeply involved with the New York chapter of the Special Libraries Association (SLA), where I chatted about organizing site content and taxonomy with fellow professionals.

Organizing the infrastructure of an intranet and creating content explaining the various facets and roles within the greater organization meant that I had to hone my writing skills. My direct manager witnessed, I think, my work in this regard, and so when an opening in a public-facing position within our department opened up, I was able to transition my work from focusing on materials to focusing on the individuals who worked at orchestras and needed access to said materials. I loved working with orchestral librarians, and I loved getting to know the inner workings of copyright. Alas, as many professionals who move from publishing into librarianship can attest, I found that there was a certain attachment to the status quo, at least where staffing is concerned. In spite of my slight shift in my work for the library, I began to feel that I had hit a ceiling.

I also realized that I didn't have line items in my résumé that pointed to traditional library work. I could lay no claim to expertise in any of our databases, nor could I relate experience at the reference desk or at an instruction session. So I took a blind leap by quitting my job without having a paid position otherwise lined up. I did, however, have one semester left in my LIS program to use as cover while I went out and explored the field. With thanks especially to my partner for his support while I meandered about in search of a future (a privilege if there ever was one), I began to fill my days with internships. I interned in the reference department, with an emphasis on government documents, at Brooklyn College. One day, a group of four of us attended a special interest group at Metropolitan New York Library Council (METRO), where I ran into an SLA buddy of mine. With lots of gratitude for seeing a familiar face, I shared my adventure story and asked if they had any projects in the works for which they required assistance. Fortunately, they did, and my colleague was able to share my résumé with METRO's executive director. After an interview, I was tasked with helping to plan their first annual conference, a task I took too easily, thanks to the time and energy I had put into planning events as an officer with SLA@Pratt and ASIS&T@Pratt.

The conference was a success, as were my outreach strategies, and so I was asked to work for METRO on their digital presence in a part-time capacity. I wrote content for METRO's website and assisted with a complete redesign. When I was officially hired, I was tasked—in a lovely twist—with overseeing the special interest group program.

Right from the start of earning my full-time position, METRO, too, began to evolve. Our staff nearly doubled in size, we began focusing on nationally recognized digital initiatives, and we won a couple of major grants. Our executive director moved on, and we hired someone new. My interests began to change from focusing on entertaining METRO members with web content and social media to planning face-to-face engagements like trainings and social events. And, yes, our annual conference, which is in its fourth year as of this writing.

Moving from content strategy to planning in-person professional development events is proving to be a much bigger shift than I'd envisioned. For one thing, there's a tremendous amount of organizing underway: working with our community to find interesting topics, finding great facilitators, and enticing registrants. For another, I've learned that all of my great ideas came from being super plugged-in to our community via our social media channels. While this option is still available to me, I find I'm offline more than online while I work to bring events to fruition. Bringing back some semblance of balance has become a major goal of mine!

No matter how bumpy the transition, changing roles within one organization is certainly an option for expanding one's skill base. And with this in mind, it's time for a top-five list of my own (I love them so) for managing transitions at the company level and within:

5. *Make connections (a.k.a. "network") with your colleagues.* I'm a curious person by nature, and I love to know what the people around me do all day long. This came in handy when I started my intranet project and then again when it became evident that staffing changes were afoot at both organizations. Creating a community of trust within each organization meant that colleagues understood that I could roll with changes in my day-to-day work.

4. *Stay involved with professional organizations.* You've heard it about a million times (probably thirty times in this volume alone), and that's because it is super important. So many good things have come to me as a result of staying involved with SLA NY, especially: my friendship with my coeditor, Ray Pun; advice on establishing an intranet from the ground up; a connection that ultimately helped me get my job at METRO. And be sure to volunteer: my belief that it's key to try to give more than you take has definitely been a boon to my career.

3. *Share your strengths.* Let other people know what makes you tick. It's always helpful for others to know how you see yourself; that way, they'll think of you when opportunity emerges.

2. *Explore new things.* Since change is all we've got, really, it's pretty important to be willing to explore new things. And to stay flexible when it comes to the unknown. It's not possible to know everything all the time, so there's really no need to shrink back from opening up to new experiences. This applies to life in general as well as to the workplace, I think. *Side note:* if it's not really possible to expand your work each day, there are plenty of venues that would love to take advantage of your pioneer spirit (see number 4 above).

1. *If you see a gap, work to fill it.* New projects and new opportunities to try new things are often hiding in plain sight. If you notice an area where additional energy or resources could help your library improve, do what you can do to address it. While you may not be able to work on all of the opportunities you see, developing a habit of locating these gaps is a great mind-set to carry with you as you move forward.

Index

239

About the Editors and Contributors

Davis Erin Anderson is community engagement manager at the Metropolitan New York Library Council (METRO). She received her master of science in information and library science from Pratt Institute in 2013. Davis is proud to have received the Special Libraries Association's Rising Star Award and to have been included in *Library Journal*'s Movers and Shakers Class of 2012.

Gerald "Jerry" Anderson is retired faculty librarian emeritus at Joliet Junior College. He currently lives in the Chicago, Illinois, area with his wife, Roberta Gocring. Jerry graduated from Buffalo State, the State University of New York, with a bachelor of arts in history and the Syracuse University School of Information Studies with a master of library science. His career encompassed positions in museum, public, and academic institutions. Jerry is the proud father of Davis Erin Anderson and Katherine Goering-Anderson.

Jan Chindlund was named library dean at Columbia College Chicago in fall 2012. Prior to joining Columbia College Chicago in September 2007 as library director, Jan led two libraries in the Chicago metro area: the Research Library of Duff & Phelps (investment advisory firm) and the McDonald's Corporation Global Business & Consumer Insight Information Center (where she was honored with the President's Award). Jan holds a master of library and information science from Dominican University and a master of business administration from Benedictine University. Very active in Special Libraries Association (SLA) work at the chapter, division, and association levels since 1987, Jan was honored with the SLA Dow Jones Leadership Award in 2000; she was named an SLA fellow in 2006 and in 2010, received the SLA Rose L. Vormelker Award for mentoring. She coauthored a book on library management and a book chapter about knowledge management in health care. At Columbia, she has served on several college cross-functional committees.

Lisa Chow cofounded People Interact, a consultancy that works with libraries and nonprofits to implement creative solutions to effectively improve individual and organizational performance by focusing on the human element. Lisa is a people-centered design advocate and information professional with a few "library ribbons," including Special Libraries Association (SLA) Rising Star, *Library Journal* (LJ) Mover and Shaker, American Library Association (ALA) Emerging Leader, and Association of Research Libraries (ARL) Diversity Scholar. Her professional interests include consumer health, emerging technologies, health literacy, project management, unconferences, and usability.

Janet H. Clarke is associate dean for research and user engagement at Stony Brook University Libraries. She has a PhD in English from Stony Brook University and an MLS from Queens College. Her research areas include diversity in librarianship, information literacy, and Asian American studies.

Sachiko Clayton has worked as an educator and librarian for over ten years in public schools, academic libraries, and public libraries. While reference work initially drew her to librarianship, she has had the privilege of a range of experiences in the field, which include instructional librarianship, cataloging and metadata, acquisitions, social media, and collection development. Her most recent career transition was from the New York Public Library to City Seminary of New York. She lives with her husband and son in Queens, New York.

Allison M. Cloyd graduated from Pratt Institute with a master in library and information science with a certificate in archives, and since then has worked in a variety of positions and libraries before landing at her current position as customer success manager for Imagine Easy Solutions in New York City. She manages all technical support and customer success matters for six products while growing a small but mighty team.

Zach Coble is digital scholarship specialist at New York University Libraries, where he provides consultation and project management for students and faculty incorporating digital humanities tools and methods into their research and teaching. He has published and spoken widely on the intersections of digital humanities, scholarly communication, and digital publishing. He is a coeditor of dh+lib, a site "where the digital humanities and librarianship meet"; the founding editor of the *dh+lib Review*; and has served as the convener of the American College & Research Libraries' Digital Humanities

Interest Group. He received a BA in history from Hendrix College, an MLIS from the University of Missouri, and is currently an MA student in the Interactive Telecommunications Program at New York University.

Nicole A. Cooke is assistant professor at the Graduate School of Library and Information Science at the University of Illinois at Urbana-Champaign, having graduated from Rutgers University with a PhD in communication, information, and library studies in 2012 (where she was an American Library Association Spectrum Doctoral Fellow). Previously, she was an instruction librarian and tenured assistant professor at Montclair State University's Sprague Library (New Jersey). Her research interests include human information behavior, particularly in an online context; critical information literacy; e-learning; and diversity and social justice in librarianship. Named a Mover and Shaker in 2007 by *Library Journal*, Nicole is professionally active in the American Library Association, the Association for Library and Information Science Education, and several other professional library organizations. In addition to her PhD, she holds the MLIS degree from Rutgers University and an MEd in adult education from Pennsylvania State University.

Veronica D'Aquino is reference and instructional librarian at California State University, Dominguez Hills (CSUDH). Appointed to the position in 2013, she is the University Library liaison for the College of Humanities and community outreach and the recipient of the 2014 and 2015 Research, Scholarship, and Creative Activity (RSCA) grant at CSUDH. Additionally, she has served on several standing committees and task forces, including University Student Learning Outcomes Assessment Committee and the WSCUC Task Force, among others. She is also a member of the Association of College and Research Libraries, the American Library Association, and the Free Software Foundation.

Sean A. Flores is systems and technologies librarian for Santa Barbara City College. He was previously the web librarian for the San Diego Public Library and an associate librarian for Qualcomm Inc. Before obtaining his MLIS, he held various part-time and internship positions: junior library technician at Naval Medical Center San Diego, library assistant for Amylin Pharmaceuticals, digital asset management intern for the Balboa Park Online Collaborative, registrar and exhibits coordinator for the Japanese Friendship Garden of San Diego, and archives intern for the San Diego History Center.

Heng "Helen" Ge has worked as reference and research services librarian at New York University (NYU) Shanghai since September 2013. Her work includes reference services, faculty liaison, library instruction, collection development, and a variety of other duties. Prior to her appointment at NYU, Helen was the technical services coordinator at Knox College, University of Toronto, where she was responsible for cataloging, acquisitions, reference services, and supervision of library projects. Helen holds a master of information studies in library and information science and a master of arts in Chinese history from the University of Toronto.

Zena George is currently library director for Berkeley College Library in downtown Brooklyn, New York. She began her employment at Berkeley College in mid-January 2015 after ending thirteen years of public library service with the New York Public Library the same year. She is of Caribbean American descent with an ethnicity of Trinidadian. Zena is the first and only librarian in her family and the only girl of five siblings. Zena takes pride in having nontraditional librarian attributes. She does not own a cat, and she refuses to have a bookcase of books in her home. She does, however, own an extensive collection of colorful cardigans/sweaters.

Dinah Handel is presently National Digital Stewardship Resident at CUNY Television. She holds an MLIS from Pratt Institute and a BA in women's history from Hampshire College.

Brian Hasbrouck recently completed his MLS and started as outreach librarian for the Brooklyn Public Library's Red Hook branch. Follow Brian on Twitter at @BrianDLibrarian.

April M. Hathcock is librarian for scholarly communications at New York University. She received her JD and LLM in international and comparative law from Duke University School of Law and her MLIS from the University of South Florida. After a career in private practice specializing in intellectual property and antitrust law, she currently works to educate members of the research community on issues relating to access, ownership, and control.

Sandra Hirsh, PhD, is professor and director of the School of Information at San Jose State University. She worked in Silicon Valley for more than a decade at major technology companies, including Hewlett Packard, Microsoft, and LinkedIn, resulting in one U.S. patent. Before arriving at San Jose State, she was an assistant professor at the University of Arizona. She earned her BA and PhD from the University of California, Los Angeles, and her MILS from the University of Michigan. She served as the 2015 president of the Association for Information Science & Technology, cofounder and cochair of the Library 2.0 global virtual conference series, and editor of *Information Services Today: An Introduction*.

Yujing Hong is currently electronic resources librarian at the Kyung Hee University, Seoul, Korea, where she manages all e-resources and systems for patrons' research. She received her bachelor's degrees in library and information science and education from the Ewha Womans University, Seoul, Korea. She has worked as a school librarian at a high school and as a reference librarian at the Sogang University, Seoul, Korea. Her research interests are engaging international students in information literacy, institutional repositories, and learning commons.

Naomi House, MLIS, is the founder and publisher of the popular webzine and jobs list INALJ (formerly I Need a Library Job) and chief marketing officer of T160K, a new crowdfunding platform focused on African patrimony, heritage, and cultural projects. Naomi was a reference, marketing, and acquisitions librarian for a contractor at a federal library outside Washington, DC, and has relocated to New Orleans, Louisiana. She runs her husband's moving labor website, Khan Moving; fixes and sells old houses; and assists her husband in cooking delicious Pakistani food. She is starting a new social-purpose company and looks forward to making a difference. She has heard of spare time but hasn't encountered it lately. She pronounces INALJ as "eye-na-elle-jay."

Catharina Isberg is currently library director at Helsingborg Public Library. She was the former deputy library director and manager of scientific information management at the Swedish University of Agricultural Sciences (SLU). In special libraries, Catharina is the former vice president for corporate communication and information and the library director for Ferring Pharmaceuticals. In 2015, Catharina became a member of the regional library committee in Scania, Sweden. She is an active member of the International Federation of Library Associations (IFLA), where in 2011 she became a standing committee member for the Continuing Professional Development and Workplace Learning Section, the cochair of the section in 2013, and information coordinator from 2011 to 2013. She was also chair of the Expert Committee on Skills Management for the Royal Library of Sweden and a board member of the Swedish Association for Information Specialists (SFIS).

Sarah T. Jewell is reference librarian at the George F. Smith Library of the Health Sciences, Rutgers University, where she serves as a clinical medical librarian to internal medicine; teaches library workshops on PubMed, EndNote, and other resources; and conducts systematic reviews. Previously, she worked for about seven years at the Memorial Sloan Kettering Cancer Center Library as a reference librarian, serving as a clinical medical librarian for the critical care department. Her first full-time position was held for three years

before that, at the Science, Industry, and Business Library, one of the research locations of the New York Public Library. In addition to teaching
librarians about how to participate in systematic reviews, she enjoys keeping
up with the latest mobile technologies and incorporating them into her work.

Deborah Keller is principal of Keller & Associates, a consultancy that provides bespoke research training and knowledge management services. Since
2010, she has served as research librarian at the Department of Homeland
Security. She joined her first government library in 2003, working for the
Department of the Army. Prior to that, she held positions in both reference
and technical services in several college and university libraries in Pennsylvania. She earned an MA in history from the Pennsylvania State University,
an MLIS from Rosary College, and an AB in chemistry and history from
Mount Holyoke College.

Lorene Kennard is director of the Morris Area Public Library in northern
Illinois. She previously owned the freelance research business Walnut Avenue Research. She also worked the adult services desk at White Oak Library
district in Romeoville, Illinois, while working as the co-interim director of
the Pontiac Public Library, Illinois. She worked as the corporate librarian at
Morningstar in Chicago and served as president of the Illinois chapter of the
Special Libraries Association. She has presented at the American Library
Association annual conference and the Association of Independent Information Professionals annual conference. She earned her library degree at the
University of South Carolina and her undergraduate degree in communica-
tions and English at Illinois State University.

Mary Lee Kennedy, a nationally respected leader in the library community,
was named chief library officer of the New York Public Library (NYPL) in
2013. She is tasked with accelerating the library's digital initiatives and
further strengthening both the research and circulating divisions of the library. Prior to her appointment at NYPL, Kennedy was senior associate
provost at Harvard University, where she was the central administrative leader of one of the world's greatest research library networks. In the position,
Kennedy led projects and initiatives connected to Harvard priorities, such as
open access and scholarly communications, digital scholarship, online learning, and collections development and management. Previously, she was executive director of knowledge and library services at Harvard Business
School, where she was also on the Presidential Task Force to establish a
twenty-first-century strategy and structure for Harvard's seventy-three libraries. She has ten years of experience in the information technology field,
including seven leading Microsoft's knowledge network group. She earned

her BA at the University of Alberta and her MLS at Louisiana State University.

Holland Kessinger received her MLIS from San Jose State University and her BA in art history from the University of California, San Diego. A dedicated and innovative information professional, she is currently working as a part-time teen services librarian for the San Diego Public Library in the Pauline Foster Teen Center. In order to encourage information literacy skills in the next generation and to satisfy her need to be around chaos and books as much as possible, she has also recently accepted a part-time position as an elementary school librarian. Her life goals include owning a llama and completing an entire week of the *New York Times* crossword puzzle.

Amani Magid, MLIS, AHIP, is presently reference and research librarian for the sciences and engineering at New York University in Abu Dhabi. She earned her undergraduate degree in integrative biology with a minor in Arabic from the University of California, Berkeley. She worked as a researcher in pharmaceutical chemistry and a manager of biology lab classes before she realized that her true passion was finding scientific information. After earning her MLIS at the University of Pittsburgh, she worked at one medical library and then at Weill Cornell Medical College in Qatar as an information services librarian before her library career transition.

Jia Mi has been electronic resources/serials librarian at the College of New Jersey since September 2003. Prior to working at the College of New Jersey, she worked as a system support analyst/research specialist at Factiva, a Dow Jones & Reuters Company, from 1999 to 2003. Her past experience includes working as an electronic resources librarian at Rutgers University Kilmer Library and Saint Peter's College Library. Jia Mi received her MLS from Rutgers University in 1994 and her MBA/MIS from Saint Peter's College in 1998.

Linda Miles is librarian for public services and user experience at Yeshiva University, where she directs initiatives related to the quality of user experience, leads information literacy efforts, and oversees electronic reserves. Linda currently serves as president of the Greater Metropolitan New York Chapter of the Association of College and Research Libraries (ACRL/NY) and cochairs the ACRL/NY New Librarians Discussion Group. She is coconvener of the Metropolitan New York Library Council's bibliographic instruction special interest group and is a member of the Theatre Library Association's Book Awards Committee. Linda holds an MLS from St. Johns University, a humanities PhD from the University of Texas at Austin, and a BA from Hope College.

Carrie Netzer Wajda is new business research specialist at Y&R Advertising, providing integrated custom internal and external research support to Y&R's 189 global offices in business development. She is a past president of the Association of College and Research Libraries, Greater Metropolitan New York Chapter, and the chair of the 2012 ACRL/NY symposium, Cultivating Entrepreneurship in Academic Libraries. Her work has appeared in *Library Journal* and other publications. She answers career questions with Susanne Markgren at Library Career People (http://librarycareerpeople.com/)—if you have a question, submit it to the site for a personalized response.

Lisa Liang Philpotts is knowledge specialist for research and instruction at the eTreadwell Virtual Library at Massachusetts General Hospital. She worked as a nurse, a college instructor, and a public library page before finding her niche in the wonderful world of health sciences librarianship. She loves being able to improve the quality of health care by supporting evidence-based practice and empowering people by connecting them with the information they need to make informed decisions about their health. In her free time, Lisa enjoys taiko drumming as a performing member of the Genki Spark, a pan-Asian women's arts and advocacy organization. She tweets on medical librarianship @LisaPhilpotts.

Christina Podenski is archive librarian and associate producer at CNN's World Headquarters in Atlanta, Georgia. She has a master's degree in library and information science from the City University of New York, Queens College, and a bachelor of arts in political science from the George Washington University. She currently lives in Mableton, Georgia, with her husband, Zach, and their two dogs, Maggie and Olive.

Raymond Pun is first-year student success librarian at California State University, Fresno (Fresno State). He has held positions at New York University Shanghai and the New York Public Library. He has published widely and presented extensively on various topics of academic and public librarianship in national and international conferences such as at the American Library Association (ALA), Special Libraries Association (SLA), and the International Federation of Library Associations and Institutes (IFLA). Raymond is also the coeditor of *Bridging Worlds: Emerging Models and Practices of U.S. Academic Libraries around the Globe* (2016). He was nominated as an ALA Emerging Leader (2014) and a *Library Journal* Mover and Shaker (2012) and was selected for the SLA's Achievement in Academic Business Librarianship Award (2015).

Before coming to work at the Mid-Manhattan branch of the New York Public Library in August of 2015, **Arieh D. Ress**, MLS, was an adjunct business reference librarian at New York University. He earned a bachelor of arts in philosophy from Purchase College, State University of New York (SUNY), and a master's in library science from the University of Buffalo, SUNY. He approaches life and work as the search for not only answers but the right questions as well.

Celia Ross has gained over a decade of practical business reference experience in a variety of settings, including a venture capital firm, a large public library, a global consulting firm, and academic libraries. She is active in the American Library Association (ALA) and was the 2009–2010 chair of the ALA Business Reference & Services Section (BRASS). Her book, *Making Sense of Business Reference*, was named an Outstanding Business Reference Source of 2013, and she is the recipient of the 2014 BRASS/Gale Cengage Learning Award for Excellence in Business Librarianship. She is currently an associate librarian at the University of Michigan's Ross School of Business.

Lian Ruan has been head librarian (1999–present) and director of IFSI International Programs (2006–present) for the Illinois Fire Service Institute (IFSI) at the University of Illinois at Urbana-Champaign (UIUC). Previously, she was an adjunct faculty at UIUC's Graduate School of Library and Information (2002–2014). She has served on Chinese American Librarians Association (CALA) committees and is currently CALA president (2015/2016). She has also served on state and international committees, including the Illinois State Library Advisory Committee, the inFIRE (an international fire library consortium) Executive Committee, the Special Libraries Association (SLA) Emergency Preparedness and Recovery Council, and the Association of College and Research Libraries Seventy-Fifth Anniversary Celebration Task Force. She is the winner of the UIUC Chancellor's Academic Professional Excellence Award and the SLA Diversity Leadership Development Program award. She has organized the Chinese Librarians Scholarly Exchange Program in Illinois, which has trained 274 librarians from ninety-one organizations in China since 2005.

Laura Ruttum Senturia is library director at the Stephen H. Hart Library & Research Center at the History Colorado Museum in Denver. She holds a BA in international affairs from the University of Colorado Boulder; an MA in Russian, Eurasian, and Eastern European regional studies from Columbia University; an MLIS from Rutgers University; and is currently pursuing an MFS certificate in museum studies at the University of Colorado Boulder. Her career has included a variety of responsibilities, including roles as a processing and reference archivist in a public research library, a genealogy librarian, an archives consultant, a paraprofessional in a medical library, a collection development librarian in an academic library, and, finally, as library director in a museum.

Sandra Sajonas cofounded People Interact, a consultancy that works with libraries and nonprofits to implement creative solutions to effectively improve individual and organizational performance by focusing on the human element. In her past life as a public young adult librarian, she gained professional recognition as an American Library Association (ALA) Emerging Leader and *Library Journal* Mover and Shaker. Her professional experience includes education and career services, small business and basic financial literacy, "disconnected youth," and project management.

Gretel Stock-Kupperman is director of the library, instructional design, and academic affairs initiatives at Viterbo University. She received her master's in library science from the University of Illinois at Urbana-Champaign, and her master's in management and organizational behavior from Benedictine University. Prior to Viterbo, she was the director of member services at the Metropolitan Library System in Illinois, providing consulting, continuing education, and training services for corporate, academic, special, and school libraries. She has also worked as an information professional in other academic and corporate settings. Outside of work, she is an avid knitter, costumer, gamer, and mother of two.

Kara West is arts and culture exhibition manager at the San Diego Public Library. A San Diego native, she earned her MLIS from San Jose State University and a BA in art history from the University of California, Santa Cruz. As an information professional, she has provided collection management support at academic libraries, museum libraries, local historical societies, art museums, art galleries, and corporate archives. Equally happy in a library or museum, she has a fear of being more than ten feet from a cardigan and frequently finds herself giddy over hanging hardware and good didactic labels.

Stacy R. Williams is head of the Helen Topping Architecture and Fine Arts Library at the University of Southern California. She received her MLS degree from Queens College, City University of New York, and her BA in social sciences from New York University. Her research interests include studying the information-seeking behaviors of visual art students, visual/media literacies, and the global influence of celebrity culture. When she isn't missing her hometown of New York City, she can be found exploring the urban sprawl that is Los Angeles.

Joseph M. Yap finished his master of library and information science at the University of the Philippines' School of Library and Information Studies in 2010. He received his bachelor of library and information science from the same university with a distinction (cum laude) in 2006. He is the recipient of the 2014 Service Award from the Association of Special Libraries of the Philippines, the 2013 Young Achiever Award given by the University of the Philippines Library Science Alumni Association, and the 2012 Asian Early Career Award bestowed by the Special Libraries Association. When he was still a graduate student, he placed third during the First International Collegiate Information Literacy Contest in the School of Information Management, Wuhan University, China, in July 2010. He has published journal articles and book chapter contributions on collaboration, consortia, information literacy, social media, corporate social responsibility, and library management.

LONGWOOD PUBLIC LIBRARY
800 Middle Country Road
Middle Island, NY 11953
(631) 924-6400
longwoodlibrary.org

LIBRARY HOURS

Monday-Friday	9:30 a.m. - 9:00 p.m.
Saturday	9:30 a.m. - 5:00 p.m.
Sunday (Sept-June)	1:00 p.m. - 5:00 p.m.